ADVANCE PRAISE FOR *Between the Lines*

This unusual combination of memoir and diary offers insight into the life of one woman navigating the Holocaust and the aftermath of the war in the streets of Budapest as she attempts to rebuild life among the rubble. Written for her husband who was in Hungary's forced labour service, Margit Kassai's memoir reads almost like an adventure story, detailing the twists and turns of daily life in wartime Budapest. This translation brings Kassai's remarkable memoir-diary into the hands of English-language readers for the first time.

Tim Cole, University of Bristol

Margit Kassai's diary is a compelling read, as her self-reflexive narrative not only uses humour, mitigating language and ironic rhetoric as coping mechanisms but also illuminates her struggle to survive the war in Budapest. Additionally, it demonstrates how Kassai used writing as a powerful tool to reclaim control over her experiences and present them as a success story.

Andrea Pető, Central European University

Margit Kassai's memoir-diary is unusual in many ways. Her text reverses the expected genre chronology: her memoir covers the months of the persecution of Jews in Hungary and the siege of Budapest, while her diary describes the end of the siege through liberation. The memoir-diary is also stylistically significant, not least for the self-irony predominant throughout the text, which can of course be read as a kind of trauma-processing. Its very special style, preserved in the brilliant translation, brings back something of that bygone rich urban Jewish culture and humour, which survived only in fragments after 1945.

Éva Kovács, Vienna Wiesenthal Institute for Holocaust Studies

Margit Kassai's book is an outstanding addition to the body of diaries and memoirs depicting the fate of Hungarian Jews during and after the Shoah. Kassai and most of her extended family survived the last year of the war in Budapest in hiding. We have very few examples of this sub-genre: the best-known Hungarian accounts of the Holocaust are by survivors of the ghettos and camps, even fewer are written by women and only a handful possess such a high literary merit. Kassai, with remarkable verve and humour, underplays her own hardships and heroic efforts during the months of German occupation, deportations, Arrow Cross terror and the mixed blessings of liberation by the Soviet army. Her unvarnished, sharp commentaries on the interactions between Jews thrown together by murderous measures and between Jewish and non-Jewish Hungarians make the book especially valuable to students of history. And her snapshots of apocalyptic scenes, broken-down social fabric and constant hunt for food in post-siege Budapest arc unforgettable. Kassai's keen eye for sociological detail and her awareness of the broader political context place her book in the company of celebrated wartime diaries such as those written by Jenő Heltai and Miksa Fenyő.

Judith Szapor, McGill University

Margit Kassai's *Between the Lines* is remarkable. Kassai's ability to invoke various states of intimacy without becoming maudlin drives the narrative with a kind of sanguinity. Her gifted use of irony and sense of humour — sometimes muted and sometimes sardonic — soften the blows of Hitler's violent last-minute attacks on Budapest and the homegrown terror perpetrated by the Hungarian Arrow Cross Party. Our narrator's self-presentation is confident and wry, always on the ready for whatever befalls her in a terrible time.

Among the marvels of this book are the evocative black-and-white photographs that Kassai had the wherewithal to take during and just after the war. Kassai's aesthetic sensibility and uniquely creative intelligence cradles the narrative. Kassai is multilingual; she is a talented photographer and is interested in music; she is quick-witted and worldly.

As noted in the Afterword, Kassai's triumph was "life wisdom" — the wisdom to walk into the day no matter how bleak, the wisdom to laugh, the wisdom to apply her quick wit to all manner of obstacles so she could survive.

Marlene Kadar, York University

Between the Lines

THE AZRIELI SERIES OF HOLOCAUST SURVIVOR MEMOIRS: PUBLISHED TITLES

ENGLISH TITLES

Judy Abrams, *Tenuous Threads*/ Eva Felsenburg Marx, *One of the Lucky Ones*
Amek Adler, *Six Lost Years*
Ferenc Andai, *In the Hour of Fate and Danger*
Molly Applebaum, *Buried Words: The Diary of Molly Applebaum*
Claire Baum, *The Hidden Package*
Bronia and Joseph Beker, *Joy Runs Deeper*
Tibor Benyovits, *Unsung Heroes*
Pinchas Eliyahu Blitt, *A Promise of Sweet Tea*
Max Bornstein, *If Home Is Not Here*
Sonia Caplan, *Passport to Reprieve*
Felicia Carmelly, *Across the Rivers of Memory*
Ben Carniol, *Hide and Seek: In Pursuit of Justice*
Stefan A. Carter, *A Symphony of Remembrance*
Judy Cohen, *A Cry in Unison*
Tommy Dick, *Getting Out Alive*
Marie Doduck, *A Childhood Unspoken*
Marian Domanski, *Fleeing from the Hunter*
Anita Ekstein, *Always Remember Who You Are*
Margalith Esterhuizen, *A Light in the Clouds*
Leslie Fazekas, *In Dreams Together: The Diary of Leslie Fazekas*
John Freund, *Spring's End*
Susan Garfield, *Too Many Goodbyes: The Diaries of Susan Garfield*
Myrna Goldenberg (Editor), *Before All Memory Is Lost: Women's Voices from the Holocaust*
René Goldman, *A Childhood Adrift*
Elly Gotz, *Flights of Spirit*
Ibolya Grossman and Andy Réti, *Stronger Together*
Pinchas Gutter, *Memories in Focus*
Anna Molnár Hegedűs, *As the Lilacs Bloomed*
Rabbi Pinchas Hirschprung, *The Vale of Tears*
Bronia Jablon, *A Part of Me*
Helena Jockel, *We Sang in Hushed Voices*
Jack Klajman, *The Smallest Hope*
Eddie Klein, *Inside the Walls*
Michael Kutz, *If, By Miracle*
Ferenc Laczó (Editor), *Confronting Devastation: Memoirs of Holocaust Survivors from Hungary*
Eva Lang, David Korn and Fishel Philip Goldig, *At Great Risk: Memoirs of Rescue during the Holocaust*
Nate Leipciger, *The Weight of Freedom*
Alex Levin, *Under the Yellow & Red Stars*
Rachel Lisogurski and Chana Broder, *Daring to Hope*
Fred Mann, *A Drastic Turn of Destiny*
Michael Mason, *A Name Unbroken*
Leslie Meisels with Eva Meisels, *Suddenly the Shadow Fell*
Leslie Mezei, *A Tapestry of Survival*
Muguette Myers, *Where Courage Lives*
David Newman, *Hope's Reprise*
Arthur Ney, *W Hour*
Felix Opatowski, *Gatehouse to Hell*
Malka Pischanitskaya, *A Mother to My Mother*
Marguerite Élias Quddus, *In Hiding*
Maya Rakitova, *Behind the Red Curtain*
Henia Reinhartz, *Bits and Pieces*
Betty Rich, *Little Girl Lost*
Paul-Henri Rips, *E/96: Fate Undecided*

Margrit Rosenberg Stenge, *Silent Refuge*
Steve Rotschild, *Traces of What Was*
Judith Rubinstein, *Dignity Endures*
Martha Salcudean, *In Search of Light*
Kitty Salsberg and Ellen Foster, *Never Far Apart*
Morris Schnitzer, *Escape from the Edge*
Joseph Schwarzberg, *Dangerous Measures*
Zuzana Sermer, *Survival Kit*
Rachel Shtibel, *The Violin*/ Adam Shtibel, *A Child's Testimony*
Maxwell Smart, *Chaos to Canvas*
Gerta Solan, *My Heart Is At Ease*
Zsuzsanna Fischer Spiro, *In Fragile Moments*/ Eva Shainblum, *The Last Time*
George Stern, *Vanished Boyhood*
Willie Sterner, *The Shadows Behind Me*
Ann Szedlecki, *Album of My Life*
William Tannenzapf, *Memories from the Abyss*/ Renate Krakauer, *But I Had a Happy Childhood*
Elsa Thon, *If Only It Were Fiction*
Agnes Tomasov, *From Generation to Generation*
Joseph Tomasov, *From Loss to Liberation*
Leslie Vertes, *Alone in the Storm*
Anka Voticky, *Knocking on Every Door*
Sam Weisberg, *Carry the Torch*/ Johnny Jablon, *A Lasting Legacy*

TITRES FRANÇAIS

Judy Abrams, *Retenue par un fil*/ Eva Felsenburg Marx, *Une question de chance*
Amek Adler, *Six années volées*
Molly Applebaum, *Les Mots enfouis: Le Journal de Molly Applebaum*
Claire Baum, *Le Colis caché*
Bronia et Joseph Beker, *Plus forts que le malheur*
Max Bornstein, *Citoyen de nulle part*
Tommy Dick, *Objectif: survivre*
Marian Domanski, *Traqué*
John Freund, *La Fin du printemps*
Myrna Goldenberg (Éditrice), *Un combat singulier: Femmes dans la tourmente de l'Holocauste*
René Goldman, *Une enfance à la dérive*
Pinchas Gutter, *Dans la chambre noire*
Anna Molnár Hegedűs, *Pendant la saison des lilas*
Helena Jockel, *Nous chantions en sourdine*
Michael Kutz, *Si, par miracle*
Eva Lang, Fishel Philip Goldig, David Korn, *Un si grand péril : mémoires de sauvetage durant l'Holocauste*
Nate Leipciger, *Le Poids de la liberté*
Alex Levin, *Étoile jaune, étoile rouge*
Fred Mann, *Un terrible revers de fortune*
Michael Mason, *Au fil d'un nom*
Leslie Meisels, *Soudain, les ténèbres*
Muguette Myers, *Les Lieux du courage*
Arthur Ney, *L'Heure W*
Felix Opatowski, *L'Antichambre de l'enfer*
Marguerite Élias Quddus, *Cachée*
Henia Reinhartz, *Fragments de ma vie*
Betty Rich, *Seule au monde*
Paul-Henri Rips, *Matricule E/96*
Margrit Rosenberg Stenge, *Le Refuge du silence*
Steve Rotschild, *Sur les traces du passé*
Kitty Salsberg et Ellen Foster, *Unies dans l'épreuve*
Morris Schnitzer, *Sur la corde raide*
Joseph Schwarzberg, *Sur les sentiers de la guerre*
Zuzana Sermer, *Trousse de survie*
Rachel Shtibel, *Le Violon*/ Adam Shtibel, *Témoignage d'un enfant*
George Stern, *Une jeunesse perdue*
Willie Sterner, *Les Ombres du passé*
Ann Szedlecki, *L'Album de ma vie*
William Tannenzapf, *Souvenirs de l'abîme*/ Renate Krakauer, *Le Bonheur de l'innocence*
Elsa Thon, *Que renaisse demain*
Agnes Tomasov, *De génération en génération*
Leslie Vertes, *Seul dans la tourmente*
Anka Voticky, *Frapper à toutes les portes*
Sam Weisberg, *Passeur de mémoire*/ Johnny Jablon, *Souvenez-vous*

Between the Lines:
The Diary of Margit Kassai

Margit Kassai

TRANSLATED FROM HUNGARIAN

by Ladislaus Löb, Marietta Morry and Lynda Muir

FIRST EDITION

First published in Hungarian as Óvoda az óvóhelyen by Magvető in 2020. Translated by Ladislaus Löb, Marietta Morry and Lynda Muir, 2024.

THE AZRIELI FOUNDATION · www.azrielifoundation.org
THE HOLOCAUST SURVIVOR MEMOIRS PROGRAM · Publisher, Naomi Azrieli · Director, Jody Spiegel · Managing Editor, Arielle Berger

Edited by Matt Carrington, Arielle Berger and Emily Standfield · Book design by Mark Goldstein · Cover image by David Drummond · Endpaper maps by Martin Gilbert · Interior map by Merritt Cartographic · Documents on pages 292–294 courtesy of Katharine Gerbner · Photo on page 307 of Margit Kassai by Kaz Novac from October 16, 1989, published with permission from the *Hamilton Spectator*

LIBRARY AND ARCHIVES CANADA CATALOGUING IN PUBLICATION

Tolnainé Kassai, Margit, 1909–2000, author.
Between the lines: the diary of Margit Kassai / Margit Kassai; translated from Hungarian by Ladislaus Löb, Marietta Morry and Lynda Muir. Translation of Óvoda az óvóhelyen: feljegyzések a Sztehlo-gyermekmentésről.

(Azrieli series of Holocaust survivor memoirs. Series XVI)
Includes bliographical references and index.
Canadiana (print) 20240464966 · Canadiana (ebook) 20240465008 · ISBN 9781998880164 (softcover) · ISBN 9781998880171 (EPUB) · ISBN 9781998880188 (PDF)

LCSH: Tolnainé Kassai, Margit, 1909–2000 — Diaries. LCSH: Jewish women — Hungary — Budapest — Diaries. LCSH: Jews — Hungary — Budapest — Diaries. LCSH: Holocaust, Jewish (1939–1945) — Hungary — Budapest — Personal narratives. LCGFT: Diaries.

LCC DS135.H93 T65 2025 DDC 943.9/0049240092—dc23

PRINTED IN CANADA

Contents

Series Preface: In their own words...

In telling these stories, the writers have liberated themselves. For so many years we did not speak about it, even when we became free people living in a free society. Now, when at last we are writing about what happened to us in this dark period of history, knowing that our stories will be read and live on, it is possible for us to feel truly free. These unique historical documents put a face on what was lost, and allow readers to grasp the enormity of what happened to six million Jews — one story at a time.

David J. Azrieli, C.M., C.Q., M.Arch
Holocaust survivor and founder, The Azrieli Foundation

Since the end of World War II, approximately 40,000 Jewish Holocaust survivors have immigrated to Canada. Who they are, where they came from, what they experienced and how they built new lives for themselves and their families are important parts of our Canadian heritage. The Azrieli Foundation's Holocaust Survivor Memoirs Program was established in 2005 to preserve and share the memoirs written by those who survived the twentieth-century Nazi genocide of the Jews of Europe and later made their way to Canada. The memoirs encourage readers to engage thoughtfully and critically with the complexities of the Holocaust and to create meaningful connections with the lives of survivors.

Millions of individual stories are lost to us forever. By preserving the stories written by survivors and making them widely available to a broad audience, the Azrieli Foundation's Holocaust Survivor Memoirs Program seeks to sustain the memory of all those who perished at the hands of hatred, abetted by indifference and apathy. The personal accounts of those who survived against all odds are as different as the people who wrote them, but all demonstrate the courage, strength, wit and luck that it took to prevail and survive in such terrible adversity. The memoirs are also moving tributes to people — strangers and friends — who risked their lives to help others, and who, through acts of kindness and decency in the darkest of moments, frequently helped the persecuted maintain faith in humanity and courage to endure. These accounts offer inspiration to all, as does the survivors' desire to share their experiences so that new generations can learn from them.

The Holocaust Survivor Memoirs Program collects, archives and publishes select survivor memoirs and makes the print editions available free of charge to educational institutions and Holocaust-education programs across Canada. They are also available for sale online to the general public. All revenues to the Azrieli Foundation from the sales of the Azrieli Series of Holocaust Survivor Memoirs go toward the publishing and educational work of the memoirs program.

~

The Azrieli Foundation would like to express appreciation to the following people for their invaluable efforts in producing this book: Stephanie Corazza, Anna Elődi, Vivian Felsen, Elena Gwynne, Aliza Krefetz, Ferenc Laczó, Alison Strobel and Judith Szapor.

Editorial Note

The editors of this English edition of Margit Kassai's memoir-diary worked to follow the editors of the Hungarian edition to faithfully reproduce a translation of the typescript Margit created in 1945. Our decision to conform as much as possible to Margit's typescript includes maintaining her unconventional typography, such as all-caps for emphasis, multiple exclamation marks and lists within her narrative. Some terminology that the editors generally avoid, such as the casual use of "Aryan" or "extermination" to refer to the mass murder of Jews, has been kept in accordance with Margit's usage. Chapter headings have also been added, which correspond to Margit's own chapter outline included in her memoir. Although our standard editorial practice is to include the present-day names of places and to correct any factual errors, we have instead left names of places as Margit wrote them and included explanatory footnotes for clarification or to provide key information for understanding the text and to provide translations of the many non-Hungarian terms used by Margit. Other general information on major organizations, significant historical events and people, geographical locations, and religious and cultural terms that will help give context to the events described in the text can be found in the glossary beginning on page 311.

Introduction

Between the Lines: The Diary of Margit Kassai is the diary-memoir of a Hungarian woman who was born Jewish and survived the anti-Jewish persecution in Budapest, Hungary, as well as the siege of the city during the Holocaust.[1] Writing a few months after liberation by the Soviets, Margit documents the Nazi occupation of Hungary, roughly from March 1944 to February 1945. Her many traumatic memories detail the sewing on of the yellow star; moving to a "yellow star" house; the complete and rapid loss of livelihood; everyday life at a yellow-star house; the Arrow Cross terror; becoming a child care worker during the siege of Budapest; and the first month or two after liberation.

Margit Kassai was born in 1909 in Budapest, a modern city that was becoming highly urbanized and had the most advanced infrastructure of the era. Her birthplace played a key role in her later survival. She grew up in a typical assimilated Jewish family, which had abandoned most Jewish traditions and customs but had not converted, so they were considered Jewish and kept the most important Jewish holidays. Her mother, Janka Beck, was a kindergarten teacher, and her father, József Kassai, was a clerk. Her father's family

---

1 In 2020, this book was published as *Óvoda az óvóhelyen* (Kindergarten in the Bomb Shelter); this is the first edition of Margit Kassai's diary in English.

Hungarianized its original German surname (Spielberger) to Kassai.[2] Margit had a younger brother, Dénes, born in 1911. The family lived in Óbuda, which was a less built-up, forested, hilly area of Budapest. Here, at 30 Kecske Street, they rented a three-room apartment in a newly built and modern apartment building, which they moved into in 1928. Margit lived here during much of the war with her parents, who were elderly and retired by then.

In May 1941, she married Dr. György Tolnai, a lawyer, who, like Margit, came from a Hungarian Jewish family that was also assimilated. The Tolnai family had converted to Lutheranism at the beginning of the twentieth century, since — unlike the Kassais — the parental generation had already converted. György Tolnai was born Lutheran and received his primary and secondary education in Lutheran institutions. Margit Kassai and her brother both converted as adults. She followed her husband's religion and was baptized as Lutheran on August 31, 1941. Dénes Kassai was listed as a Roman Catholic in the 1941 census.

Margit had two hobbies: photography and hiking. To develop her pictures, she set up a darkroom in one of the rooms of her apartment in Buda. As an enthusiastic amateur photographer, she entered several competitions. She was also drawn to hiking by photography and on several occasions she organized excursions combined with photography. Besides photography and hiking, she was also interested in psychology. She knew personally or through their work the main Hungarian and foreign psychoanalysts in the interwar period.

After graduating from high school, Margit worked as a secretary and correspondent for various companies. The *numerus clausus,* the Hungarian law that severely restricted the number of Jewish students admitted to universities from 1920 onwards, probably played a key role in her failure to apply to university. In October 1934, Margit

2 Kassa (present-day Košice, Slovakia), was part of the Austro-Hungarian Empire and then the Kingdom of Hungary, and part of the family came from there.

was recruited as a clerk at the Hitelbank (Hungarian General Credit Bank), where she worked until the summer of 1944 and where she met György. Her main duties included handling the bank's correspondence, and she was a stenographer and typist for the company. Due to her excellent knowledge of French, English and German, she was also involved in correspondence in foreign languages.

By the late 1930s, several anti-Jewish laws were introduced in Hungary, discriminating against Jews both economically and socially.[3] The two most significant of these were passed by the Hungarian parliament in 1938 and 1939, resulting in hundreds of thousands of lower- and middle-class families losing their livelihoods.[4] Margit's case is unique in that this is not what happened to her — even though the discriminatory rules applied to her, Margit was one of the bank's employees who was not dismissed. She was deeply embedded in the community of bank officials and had an extremely good relationship not only with her colleagues but, significantly, also with her bosses. She had a particularly good working relationship with Lajos Szentkirályi, the bank's general manager.

Margit and her elderly parents were unaffected by the outbreak of war, but the men were affected, with both her husband and her brother — although converts — conscripted as Jews into the labour service.[5] Her husband survived, but like so many others, Margit's only

3 Yehuda Don, "The Economic Effect of Antisemitic Discrimination: Hungarian Anti-Jewish Legislation, 1938–1944," *Jewish Social Studies* 48, no. 1 (1986): 63–82.

4 István Pál Ádám, *Budapest Building Managers and the Holocaust in Hungary* (Switzerland: Palgrave Macmillan, 2016).

5 The labour service was introduced in 1939 to involve in the war effort male members of groups who were considered untrustworthy by the political authorities and consisted of the unarmed forced labour of Jewish men on the front line and in the hinterland, under extremely cruel and inhumane conditions. The legal basis for the labour service was provided by the Defence of the Fatherland Act, which came into force in March 1939, parts of which provided a legal framework for subsequent anti-Jewish actions. With Hungary's entry into World War II, labour service became a permanent institution that deliberately targeted Jews.

brother, Dénes Kassai, died. Margit did not know this at the time of writing this memoir. More information about the circumstances of his death has not been uncovered.

Margit was left alone with her parents during the war, struggling financially but maintaining their standard of living and apartment in Budapest. This changed radically in March 1944 when German troops invaded Hungary. With the help of the Hungarian authorities, and with the passive and active support of the majority of society, the implementation of the final solution began under the leadership of Adolf Eichmann, a German SS officer. The German occupation rightly caused mortal fear among Hungarian Jews. The Germans typically began their genocide in occupied countries by setting up a Jewish Council (Judenrat). In Budapest this happened on the orders of Eichmann two days after the invasion, on March 21, 1944. The leader of the Jewish Council was Samu Stern. His task was to convey the demands of the Germans to the Hungarian Jewish population. Whether the Council's cooperation with the Germans was forced on them or whether the collaboration was traitorous is still the subject of violent disagreement.

From that time onwards, the anti-Jewish measures and decrees all affected the Kassai family. At the beginning of April 1944, the yellow star was introduced, as it had been in other states under German occupation, and made compulsory for Jews to wear.[6] Then, from mid-April, ghettoization began in the countryside, followed a month later by deportation. Instead of a ghetto in Budapest, "yellow-star" houses were designated at the end of June 1944.[7] These were apartment

---

6 Louise O. Vasvári, "The Yellow Star and Everyday Life under Exceptional Circumstances: Diaries of 1944–1945 Budapest," *Hungarian Cultural Studies: Journal of the American Hungarian Educators Association* no. 9 (2016), DOI: 10.5195/ahea.2016.260.

7 Tim Cole, *Holocaust City: The Making of a Jewish Ghetto* (New York: Routledge, 2003).

buildings scattered around the city, their gates marked with a yellow Star of David on a black background. All citizens of Budapest who were Jews had to move to such housing, which was terribly crowded, with several families assigned to one flat. Alongside this, the Kassais were experiencing other restrictions that made freedom of movement and transport and access to food nearly impossible. On May 1, 1944, the Minister of Public Supply issued a decree restricting the supply of foodstuffs such as sugar, cooking oil, meat and milk to Jews; Jews were not allowed to receive items that were subject to food stamps, such as butter, eggs, rice and pepper.

When the forced move to the yellow-star houses, which Margit refers to as "the Great Relocation," affected the Kassai family, they were required to exchange their Óbuda apartment for one in the middle of the Jewish quarter of Pest, at 55 Dohány Street, to be shared with a family who kept Jewish traditions, including a kosher kitchen. This apartment was only a few minutes' walk from the Dohány Street Synagogue, the largest synagogue in Europe, built for modern (Neolog) Jews. During the move they lost all their belongings and furniture. In addition, the German occupation meant that her bosses could no longer protect her position in the bank, and at the end of July 1944 she was dismissed.

Margit and her family were classified as Jews under Hungarian law, but Margit did not have a Jewish identity, although she was aware of her origins. Her Jewish ancestry lived in legends and stories in the family memory. This meant that her Jewishness was not important to her; she did not participate in Jewish community life and she did not follow religious traditions and expectations. As an enlightened, independent woman, she based her identity on many other things, including her work, leisure activities and circle of friends. These characteristics were very typical of assimilated Hungarian Jewry. Her case illustrates the contrast between the Nazis' idea of the Jews as a race and the diversity of Jewish identities.

For Kassai, unassimilated Jews were a distinctly foreign group with whom she had no cultural ties. It was strange and alien for her when she was forced to move to the heart of the Jewish quarter of Pest. Margit had a controversial attitude toward Jews as a group, which is evident from her description of Jews in the yellow-star house on Dohány Street:

> I DO NOT ACCEPT THEM, cannot bear them, do not want them, have nothing in common with them and want to have nothing in common with them. I want to go to the other end of the world and deny my Jewish origin. Not that I was surprised that they are greedy, violent, loud, ill-mannered and stupid, although this was the first time I experienced it from so close up, through my own skin. But it upset me that they don't pull together even when they are in great trouble. They treat each other meanly and cause as much harm to each other as they can. (28)

In her text, the Jews of Pest are presented as a clearly identifiable and repugnant group, acting collectively, and she associated with this group a number of negative images, from insolence to corruption to hysteria. She also defined herself against them. This distinction resulted from the fact that she saw herself as a resident of Buda and classified herself as belonging to a different cultural milieu from Pest, which was symbolized to her by the inhabitants of the yellow-star house on Dohány Street. Kassai felt alienated among all those Jews whom she identified as primitive proles or wealthy. But she had complete empathy for Jews who were poor.

In the summer of 1944, Margit started to organize a kindergarten for the children living in the yellow-star house, to replace the school and kindergarten no longer available to these Jewish children. Her elderly mother, who had worked as a kindergarten teacher before retiring, helped her in this work. Margit lived with her elderly parents in this yellow-star house, an uncomfortable, strange, tense but safe place until October 1944, when the head of state, Regent Miklós Horthy, made an ill-prepared and unsuccessful attempt to withdraw Hungary from the war. The Germans intervened and helped the far-right Arrow Cross Party to power, with the aim of fighting the Soviets and holding out to the last drop of blood. The Arrow Cross Party soldiers used their rise to power to murder the Jewish community in Budapest, which was the last in the country. As part of this, they engaged in open terror against Jews and all those they perceived to be Jewish, and the yellow-star houses became easy targets. The Arrow Cross attacked many of these houses and killed all the inhabitants, regardless of age or gender. In other cases they killed in the open streets. The number of Jews taken by Arrow Cross soldiers and executed on the banks of the Danube River in Budapest reached around eight thousand. The number of victims was further increased by the fact that the Arrow Cross government handed over Jewish labourers to the Third Reich for forced labour, sent on foot on the so-called death marches. By this point, the supervisors of the unarmed labourers were members of the armed officers and non-commissioned officers, who were colloquially known as "keretlegények" (in literal translation: lads of the frame), or frame men. In many cases, they were cruel to the men in their charge. For example, on the Eastern Front, the labourers were used for mine clearance. Thousands of them died or were taken prisoner of war; the total number of victims is estimated at between fifty thousand and seventy thousand.

When Margit's situation in the yellow-star house became dangerous, she realized that she had to leave the building on at Dohány Street, which had become a target of the Arrow Cross. In the autumn of 1944, Margit applied for a job as a caregiver at the children's home run by the Lutheran pastor Gábor Sztehlo, under the protection of the International Red Cross.[8] The official aim of this child rescue operation was to save children of Jewish origin who had been baptized

---

8 For more, see Arieh Ben-Tov, *Facing the Holocaust in Budapest: The International Committee of the Red Cross and the Jews in Hungary, 1943–1945* (Dordrecht: M. Nijhoff, 1988).

and converted to the Lutheran faith. In addition to her experience, her Lutheran religion played a role in her being hired. Working in a protected children's home, she had a much better chance of survival than if she had tried to survive the Arrow Cross terror and the siege of Budapest on her own. It was one of the most devastating sieges of the city in World War II, lasting from Christmas 1944 to mid-February 1945. Budapest was liberated in February 1945, at which time the children's home became occupied by Soviet troops.

Although this wasn't Margit's own experience and is not evident in Margit's story, it's important to keep in mind the context of the experience of the Holocaust for most Hungarian Jews. Two things make the story of the systematic mass murder of the Jews in Hungary unique in the transnational history of the Holocaust: its intensity and its speed. The deportations, which happened largely outside the city of Budapest during the first months of the Nazi occupation, took place in the final year of World War II. The first cattle cars to Auschwitz-Birkenau were launched in mid-May 1944, and three weeks later the Allies landed at Normandy. On D-Day, more than twelve thousand people were deported to the death camp from Hungary, as was the average every day.[9] On July 7, 1944, Hungary's regent, Miklós Horthy, temporarily suspended the deportation. During that short period of time, the Hungarian authorities had deported approximately 435,000 Hungarian Jewish citizens to Auschwitz-Birkenau, where the Germans immediately sent most of them to the gas chambers. The suspension of the deportations meant that some two hundred thousand Jews from Budapest, like Margit and those who had fled there, survived. However, almost the entire Jewish population of the Hungarian countryside was murdered.

---

9 Randolph Lewis Braham, *The Politics of Genocide: The Holocaust in Hungary*, Condensed Edition (Detroit: Wayne State University Press, 2000), 137.

The History of the Child Rescue Mission in Budapest — The Good Shepherd Committee and the International Red Cross

The Good Shepherd Committee was set up by the Reformed Church in Hungary in October 1942.[10] The Committee aimed to provide aid during World War II for Jews who had converted to Protestantism. It became the most important organ for the rescue work organized by the Protestant churches. The Lutheran Church delegated Pastor Gábor Sztehlo to this committee in May 1944. The International Red Cross also played a key role in the Good Shepherd Committee's change from its earlier charitable work to rescue people.

In the Good Shepherd Committee, Sztehlo's task from the early summer of 1944 was to rescue Christian children who had been identified as Jews, with the aim of setting up homes for them. This, however, ran into many difficulties, because it was impossible to buy or rent large properties for the growing number of children without being noticed by the authorities. In August 1944, thanks to the efforts of the chief delegate Friedrich Born, the children's rescue operation came under the auspices of the International Red Cross. From that time onwards, property owners also found it advantageous to offer their flats, villas and mansions free of charge for the purpose of setting up a children's home, because they could continue to live there as residents with the property under the protection of the Red Cross. It is questionable what proportion of the owners were moved by humanitarian commitments and altruistic motives.[11] The owners were

---

10 For more, see Gergely Kunt, *The Children's Republic of Gaudiopolis: The History and Memory of a Children's Home for Holocaust and War Orphans* (New York: Central European University Press, 2022).

11 For new historical research that critically examines the motivations behind Gábor Sztehlo's rescue activities and shows how the financial interests of the Christian upper middle class contributed to the saving of human lives, see Tamás Kende, *Embermentés, vagyonmentés, státuszmentés 1944–1945-ben Sztehlo Gábor emlékezetében* [Saving People, Saving Property, Saving Status in 1944–1945 In The Memory of Gábor Sztehlo] (Budapest: Kronosz könyvkiadó kft, 2023).]

primarily concerned with saving their own property and trusted that property under the protection of the International Red Cross would enjoy the same territorial sovereignty as diplomatic residences. The owners hoped that the properties under the protection of the International Red Cross would not be looted by the Germans, the Arrow Cross or, later, the Soviets. So saving the children was only secondary from the point of view of the property owners. They were guided primarily by rational and only partly humanistic interests when they offered their property. The first home was opened on October 5, 1944, a week before the Arrow Cross terror began.

From the end of October 1944, on behalf of the Good Shepherd Commission, Sztehlo headed the so-called "B" section of the Red Cross, which was officially dedicated exclusively to the rescue of converted children, and whose activities were financed by private donations and Red Cross subsidies. By mid-November 1944, the economic office set up by the Red Cross to support Section B was already providing for eighteen homes. A separate network of warehouses was set up to supply each home with food and fuel and also to arrange transport between the warehouses and the homes. When Margit Kassai joined the Red Cross in mid-November, the homes were being set up at a fast pace, and there was a shortage of staff and specialists.

In mid-November 1944, only eighteen homes were still in operation, but by the end of the month twenty-six new homes had been established, eight in less than two weeks. They also increased the number of refugees by hiring caregivers for the children, most of whom were also Jews. According to Sztehlo, around Christmas 1944 there were about 1,290 people under Red Cross protection.[12] By February 1, 1945, this number had increased further, with some two thousand

---

12 Gábor Sztehlo, *Háromszázhatvanöt nap — Emlékek a magyarországi zsidómentésről 1944-ben.* [Three Hundred and Sixty-Five Days — Memories of the Jewish Rescue in Hungary in 1944] (Budapest: Magvető kft, 2022), 495.

survivors organized at twenty-eight sites during one of the most brutal sieges of World War II.

The Arrow Cross government — especially the Ministry of Foreign Affairs — knew about the Red Cross action. Ferenc Szálasi, the leader of the Arrow Cross government, had long hoped that states neutral in the war would recognise his regime as legitimate, and was therefore willing to treat the homes as shelters. The homes under the protection of the International Red Cross were officially Christian homes. The names of the caregivers and the children had to be handed in to the Ministry of Foreign Affairs. All the children were given new identities and Christian documents, and these forged details were then submitted to the Foreign Office registry. The whole group could be put at risk if either the children or the caregivers had inadequate fake IDs. The Arrow Cross Party officers, who knew and suspected what the homes actually did, carried out numerous attacks on homes under the protection of the International Red Cross. During the Arrow Cross raids, they sometimes did not ask for the children's papers but checked at random to see if the boys were circumcised, and this decided the fate of the whole home.

Very little is known about the majority of adults involved in the child rescue work led by Lutheran pastor Gábor Sztehlo. Women are particularly forgotten, even though they were key players in the rescue. For adult men, this would have been a much more dangerous, almost impossible task during the siege of Budapest, as they would have been immediately considered deserters or escaped forced labourers by the authorities. Most of these Jewish women volunteered to become caregivers and nannies to survive. They helped run the International Red Cross children's homes and to ensure the survival and care of children during the Arrow Cross regime and the siege of the city.

From Bank Clerk to Amateur Kindergarten Teacher

There were also many children in the huge yellow-star house on Dohány Street, where Kassai was forced to move with her parents in summer of 1944. The situation for mothers who moved with their children into a yellow-star house was particularly difficult, since they could no longer use the nursery, kindergarten and school services that had previously been available. Because fathers were usually on forced labour, mothers had to manage child care on their own. This was made more difficult by the fact that, in the limited time during the day that Jews were allowed free movement they had to buy their own food and manage everything else.

The children were generally less traumatized by the move to the yellow-star house, since they had less room for play after the German occupation, when the school year ended abruptly. After the German occupation, parents tried to keep their children at home, in a well-controlled and safe place, and only rarely let them out on the streets. The yellow-star house brought some positive changes for the children after their confinement at home, as many memoirs report. Even if cramped in a small space and severely restricted, the yellow-star houses were primarily places for children to socialize, to talk and play with a large number of peers. The house on Dohány Street was clearly not the only yellow-star house in Budapest where parents realized they had to organize child care themselves to replace the previous educational infrastructure.

For Margit, working with children gave her the opportunity to spend less time in an adult environment, so that she could avoid at least some of the many conflicts that arise when people are forced to live together. The non-adult environment, supervising the children, playing with them and dealing with disciplinary problems were all good for Margit because they distracted her from other, more serious problems. Her position within the adult community was strengthened by her role as a non-professional kindergarten teacher. She made many acquaintances among mothers, who were glad to hand over the supervision of their children when they could leave their forced accommodations for only a few hours a day. Kassai became so attached to the children she met in the kindergarten that she continued to try to find out about their fate after the war.

This experience as an amateur caregiver played a key role in Margit's being recruited by Sztehlo in early November 1944 to work in one of the protected children's homes. Margit had a knack for caring for children, and it is clear from her writing that she was deeply emotionally attached to them. We see her interest in psychology in her writing, as she also used psychological models to interpret the behaviour of the children in her care, as well as her own behaviour during the siege of Budapest. Although she doesn't state as much, her emotional attachment to the children may have been influenced by the fact that she had no children of her own during World War II. She also that the orphaned child she loved most could be adopted if her husband agreed:

> I've written such a lot about this little boy in comparison with others, but on the one hand I was very fond of him, much more than I have been of the later ones, so much so that I've often wondered if you'd agree to us adopting him after the war if his parents didn't turn up again. On the other hand, these small children's stories filled my daily life at that time, and I can only repeat that without the children my nerves wouldn't have stood up to this madhouse. (108)

The Good Shepherd Children's Homes survived the siege without major losses, with no children killed or deported, either by the Germans or the Arrow Cross. However, the long-awaited liberation and the arrival of Soviet troops proved particularly dangerous for the nurses and caregivers. Some of them were raped by Soviet soldiers.[13] And, as the fighting in Budapest came to an end, parents and relatives came to collect the children, and the number of homes dwindled by the day. The situation of the caregivers changed with the closure of the children's homes, since they now had to provide their own food, which was no longer being provided by the International Red Cross. Organizing this was no small task for the Jewish women who had become caregivers to save themselves. After her liberation, Kassai also feared starvation most of all.

On Kassai's Text: The Links Between Trauma, Identity and Language[14]

Margit's text occupies a unique place in the mass of Holocaust memoirs. This diary-memoir documents the story of the persecution of the Jews from an extraordinary perspective, which in many ways was a minority voice. Although there are many memoirs, there are still very few female voices, which is why Margit's text is extremely interesting from a gender perspective. As a resident of Budapest, she survived the persecution of the Jews in a metropolis, which was a

13 For more on the vast sexual abuses committed against Hungarian women by Soviet soldiers after the liberation of Budapest, see Andrea Pető, *Das Unsagbare erzählen* (Göttingen, Wallstein Verlag, 2021) and Andrea Pető, *Elmondani az elmondhatatlant. A nemi erőszak története a Magyarországon a II. világháború alatt* (Budapest, Jaffa, 2018). See also Gergely Kunt, "Wartime Sexual Economy as Seen through a Hungarian Woman's World War II Diary," Feminist Studies 43, no. 1 (2017): 108–33.

14 For more, see Gergely Kunt, "Ironic Narrative Agency as a Method of Coping with Trauma in the Diary-Memoir of Margit K., a Female Holocaust Survivor," *Hungarian Cultural Studies: E-Journal of the American Hungarian Educators Association,* no. 7 (2014): 28–40.

very different experience of persecution than was had by those who survived the death camps. This text was written by a woman who was involved in the child rescue work of Christian churches. And finally, it is a text that is unique not only because of the stories it tells but also because of the language in which it is told. The main feature of this particular language is irony. In discussing the function of writing and irony in trauma processing, my aim is to shed light on why the language in which Margit told the story of her persecution is extraordinary.

Margit's text is in three parts: the first is an introductory letter to her husband, followed by a memoir in which she discusses the period before the daily notes, and finally the diary. The memoir is the longest part of the text, about two-thirds. The memoir covers the events of the period between April 1944 and February 1945 — roughly the period between the German and Soviet occupation. The retrospective perspective of this section is also referred to by Kassai when she calls it a "posthumous diary." The memoir is much longer than the diary, which she kept from the liberation of Budapest, from February 1945 until the beginning of May.

Kassai focused actively and intensively on writing down her personal experiences of the Holocaust, as evidenced by the fact that she wrote an introductory letter to her husband on March 6, 1945, concluded her memoir in mid-April, and finished her entire manuscript by the end of May. The fact that she wrote her text at such a rapid pace is significant in itself. Psychological research, primarily the work of James W. Pennebaker, has long noted the role and importance of post-trauma narration and writing,[15] which allowed Margit to communicate the events to her husband so as to aim for no longer having

15 James W. Pennebaker, *Opening Up: The Healing Power of Expressing Emotions.* (New York: Guilford, 1997).

to bear her pain alone. She concluded her diary in April with the following words: "The siege diary was hard to write, but I feel good that I did it and managed to get a lot of stuff out of my system that was weighing me down. Try to read between the lines. Goodbye, Kispipi, I will stop now!"

In her memoir, Margit selected the events pertaining to her and her milieu carefully and systematically, an arrangement that was also justified by the genre, since a memoir allows greater freedom in selecting specific events from the past than a diary, which is more narrowly defined by the time period it allegedly represents. Margit's introductory letter to her husband states her reasons for writing her memoir and diary and dedicating them to him, describing the rupture of her life narrative brought on by traumatic experiences as a *caesura-komplexum* (caesura complex), a term she coined by apparently confusing the words *komplexus* (fixation) and *komplexum* (complex). Her explanation reads as follows:

> By now you may have heard that some things have happened to me, to Budapest, to the Jews, to Hungary, etc., that can't be called either trivial or insignificant, and I have gradually developed what I have concisely named a *caesura complex*. I'll explain in a moment what that means, but it's certain that this year has caused a caesura, a break, in your life just as it has in mine. This year cut me off sharply and pitched me against a completely different situation, in which I too became something completely different. Surely the same applies to you too, doesn't it? The essential part of the caesura complex is the fear that the new Kiskas and the new Gregi may no longer suit each other. (3)

Regardless of the confusion in the term's coinage, the function of new term is significant inasmuch as it allowed her to name and summarize her fears brought on by her separation from her husband and the rupture in her life narrative due to her traumatic experiences of the Holocaust. In the excerpt cited above, she used the adjective "new" to refer to both herself and her husband, which means that she realized both of them had been fundamentally altered during their period of separation due to their experiences of the Holocaust. She expressed her fear that their old identities and relationship could no longer correspond to their new selves by using the verb "cut off" to denote an irreversible process, where the action of cutting can also imply the infliction of a wound, which is the original meaning of the Greek word trauma. Using the verb in this sense is further confirmed by the attributive structure "cut me off sharply" to suggest no continuity between the old and new selves that left both Margit and her husband with ruptured and irreconcilable life narratives. Due to the persecution of Jewish residents and the siege of Budapest, Margit was forced to reconstruct her life narratives to be able to integrate the time period covered by the typescript and her experiences into her life history in order to process her trauma and share her burden with her husband.

Although Margit's introductory letter to her husband makes it clear that the Holocaust was a traumatic experience for her, she attempted to process her trauma by constructing a euphemistic, mitigating narrative, a striking example of which is her ironic enumeration of eleven negative experiences that she claims did not happen to her between April 1944 and February 1945. Such narrative devices inform us that, right from the beginning, Margit attempted to recount her experiences of an untellable period by constructing humorous stories and using ironic language, thereby shifting the focus from the original, painful and cruel experiences.

Margit's self-reflexivity is shown by the fact that she tried to name the fears and doubts that oppressed her. Drawing on her readings in psychology, she described her own mental state as suffering from a caesura complex. Being able to articulate what was troubling her was an important function of being able to summarize her fears, making them definable for her. Today, we would most probably call her mental condition PTSD, or post-traumatic stress disorder. Coping with the caesura complex, she saw writing as a means of creating a text of her choice about the traumatic period, so that it became narrative and removable for her.

The Memoir: Irony and Euphemism

Kassai admits in her introductory letter that her experiences of the Holocaust are difficult to narrate and even refers to her memories in another section as a vast jungle or a six-volume adventure novel that cannot be told even when broken down into smaller segments. She does provide a structure for her memoir to facilitate her narration. She divided the traumatic period between April 9, 1944, and February 23, 1945, into eight segments or chapters of different lengths: Az Egymás Után Zuhogó Pofonok Korszaka (The Age of Uninterrupted Slaps in the Face); A "Csillagos Ház"-ban (Miksa utca) (In the Starry House (Miksa Street)), in which what she refers to as "starry houses" were the yellow-star houses; Október 15. és vidéke (On and Around October 15), October 15 being the date of the Arrow Cross's rise to power; Bujdokolok (I Am in Hiding); Nemzetközi Vöröskereszt és a Kiskas (The International Red Cross and Kiskas); Ostrom (The Siege); Buda halála (The Death of Buda), and finally, Pest, where she recounts the end of the siege of Buda, her own liberation and her crossing over from Buda to Pest to find her parents. The first six chapters contain her memoir and the last two chapters contain her diary entries.

In writing about her own experience of persecution, Kassai had several intentions. She had in mind to put into words, to form into history, to reassess and reinterpret this traumatic period of her life history, which was part of her identity. Storytelling plays a particularly important role in the processing of trauma. As Margit Kassai saw it, this is the only means by which traumatic stories can be reintegrated, understood and processed. In addition, her writing is addressed to a reader, her husband, in whom she has complete trust and to whom she can be completely honest. The narrative also serves the purpose of attempting to reframe the unity of her life story, her narrative identity, by telling stories.[16]

Kassai's memoir is characterized by the use of ironic word compositions to reduce the tragic and solemn nature of her post-trauma narrative of the Holocaust. For instance, she referred to the lunches prepared specifically for Jewish employees at her workplace as a starry meal (*csillagos ebéd*), to the Jewish curfew as starry free time (*csillagos szabadidő*), and called the phenomenon of Jewish residents being forced to wear the Star of David starfestation (*elcsillagosodás*), even though the Hungarian word *csillag* (star) primarily stands for celestial bodies rather than the Star of David. This ironic double wordplay can also be understood in the case of the invented word *elcsillagosodás* (starfestation) to mean the approaching darkness that began in April 1944. Similarly, Margit refers to the introduction of regulations on wearing the yellow star as the premiere of the stars (*csillag premier*), to the clothes she wore during the siege as a siege dress (*ostromdressz*) and to the siege of Budapest as the Great Dance (*Nagy Tánc*) or the Great Hoopla (*Nagy Hecc*), the latter two terms likely inspired by the fact that World War I had often been referred to as *Nagy Háború* (the Great War) in Hungary. These ironic word compositions allowed Margit to euphemize and mitigate the events of the traumatic period and facilitated the narration of her memories.

To keep the positive tone of her memoir, Kassai used humour, mitigating language and ironic rhetoric to construct episodes relating to certain discriminatory measures. One of the narrative strategies that allowed her to present herself in her memoir as an active, positive protagonist was structuring episodes of her life narrative in ways that converted negative experiences into positive triumphs over systemic oppression, such as standing up for herself when she was

16 Daniel L. Schacter, *Searching for Memory: The Brain, the Mind, and the Past* (New York: Basic Books, 1996).

harassed on the street in Budapest. To mitigate the humiliation of persecution, she recounts an episode where she was walking down the street when a drunken man mockingly told her: "What a lovely streamlined star the young lady has." Margit continues the story: "I take one corner of the star between two fingers and with a sweet smile offer it to the man: 'Do you want it? I'll give it to you if you fancy it so much.'" The man falls completely out of role, awkwardly mutters something like he doesn't need it because he's thankfully not a Jew and quickly hurries off. Margit's description shows her pride in her witty retort and resourcefulness that allowed her to emerge from the conflict as the victor, thereby reinforcing a positive self-image and presenting herself to her reader(s) as an active agent rather than a passive sufferer.

Despite the narrative methods and rhetorical strategies discussed above, which all served to produce a euphemistic and ironic narrative, her memoir does betray the deeply traumatic nature of her past by the conspicuous absence of negative episodes and any mention of Margit's own humiliation and suffering, which by no means indicates that there had been no such instances but rather that her narrative serves as a unique defence mechanism. She purposefully created a narrative devoid of horror in order to construct a new past of carefully selected anecdotes that shifted the focus away from the pain and suffering of the period, which also facilitated her remembrance of painful events.

According to historian Sándor Bazsányi, one of the most important rhetorical methods for approaching trauma with euphemism in narrative and language use is through irony, as is evident in Margit's narration of her persecution but also in well-known works like Imre Kertész's novel *Sorstalanság* (Fatelessness). Kassai recounted her persecution and the siege of Budapest as her own success story rather than a narrative of suffering, and such an interpretation is justified inasmuch as Margit and her parents managed to survive the Holocaust.

The Diary: The Brutality of the Present

In the same way that Kassai tried to write about tragic events in the memoir part of her text in a brief and ironic way, mostly creating stories with a positive connotation, she also did not write the persecution and the siege of Budapest as a story of suffering. The memoir part is followed by Kassai's diary from the end of the siege of Budapest. The question arises: what was the function of this particular hybrid genre in dealing with trauma? And what are the differences between the narrative techniques and thematic elements of the memoir section and the fragmented diary section?

In Margit's typescript, her memoir is followed by a section that contains her actual diary kept from February 11, 1945 until mid-April 1945, and since the original manuscript has not been found, we can only presume that she had edited it thoroughly before she included her diary after the memoir to which it stands in sharp contrast in terms of narrative methods and language use. Margit began keeping a diary shortly after the Soviet troops had occupied the entire capital of Budapest at the cost of incredible damage and civilian casualties. The euphemizing narrative methods used in the memoir disappear entirely in the diary and the themes discussed in the diary are also different, which shows the advantages of constructing a desired past within the genre of the memoir in contrast to the more strictly defined genre of diary-writing. There are enormous differences between the two parts, which clearly shows that when we consider daily events, the siege of Budapest and the period of persecution were not as bearable for Margit as her memoir's descriptions suggest. In my analysis of the memoir, I have mentioned ironic wordplay as one of Margit's narrative strategies of mitigation, but when we compare the memoir to her diary it becomes clear that these ironic word compositions were all constructed after the fact. It shows that in processing the traumatic period in her life, mitigating painful episodes and using irony were only possible in retrospect. In reality, the period of danger during World War II may have been even worse than the period recorded in the diary since the diary begins after the arrival of the Soviet troops, which to Margit signalled the end of World War II and her consequent liberation from persecution.

While Margit's primary narrative strategy in her memoir was to omit negative events, construct episodes with positive outcomes and write of her persecution and the siege of Budapest as a series of trifling and ridiculous events rather than a narrative of suffering, the diary describes death in greater detail, since the specificities of the genre forced the author to concentrate on the events of a single day. The resulting difference practically divides the typescript into two parts, where the diary entries are far more realistic and horrifying than the memoir in which Margit was mostly hiding in Buda while working at a children's home operated by the International Red Cross. After the siege of Budapest ended, Margit's diary begins and it recounts her attempt to cross over from Buda to Pest to visit her parents, which was made difficult due to the fact that the bridges connecting the two parts of the city had been blown up by the retreating German army. The spectacle of dead bodies was a pervasive experience in the days after the bloody and prolonged siege, and Margit's diary discusses them in great detail, almost every day in the course of her crossing from Buda to Pest.

Although Margit's memoir and diary are vastly different in terms of themes and narrative strategies employed, her attempts at presenting a positive self-image and searching for self-definition remains consistent throughout her typescript, in which she described herself in any situation as someone who was always safe from harm. There is a sharp difference in word choice between the memoir section and the diary section. The ironic words and wordplays are only in the memoir part, with the exception of the word *ostromdressz* (siege dress), which meant the clothes she wore during the siege of Budapest. So the language play is all retrospective, constructed weeks or months after the events. This also makes it clear that it was only possible to imbue the traumatic period with irony in retrospect.

Many decades have passed since the manuscript was completed in 1945. Margit has produced two different versions of the text, the main difference being that one of them includes her own drawings. Both are typed and bound in book form and are identical in text. One is owned by her daughter, Frances, and is the one that includes the drawings as illustrations to complement the text. The other version was taken by Kassai as a Canadian citizen in the 1970s to Budapest, the place of her persecution. The text-only version was then purchased from her by the Metropolitan Ervin Szabó Library in Budapest for four thousand Hungarian forint. The manuscript can be found in the Budapest Collection under the reference BQ 0910/374 and is freely accessible. The volume consists of 271 A4 pages, mostly typed in black and blue, with double spacing. I found this volume in 2009 as a young doctoral student, and it was finally published in Hungarian in 2020 in full by Magvető. This English edition is a translation of the published Hungarian edition.

I am glad to have connected with Margit's daughter, Frances, and to have played a part in bringing this fascinating and important work, with its unique voice illuminating a dark history, to both a Hungarian and now an English readership.

Gergely Kunt
University of Miskolc, Hungary
2024

BUDAPEST · 1944

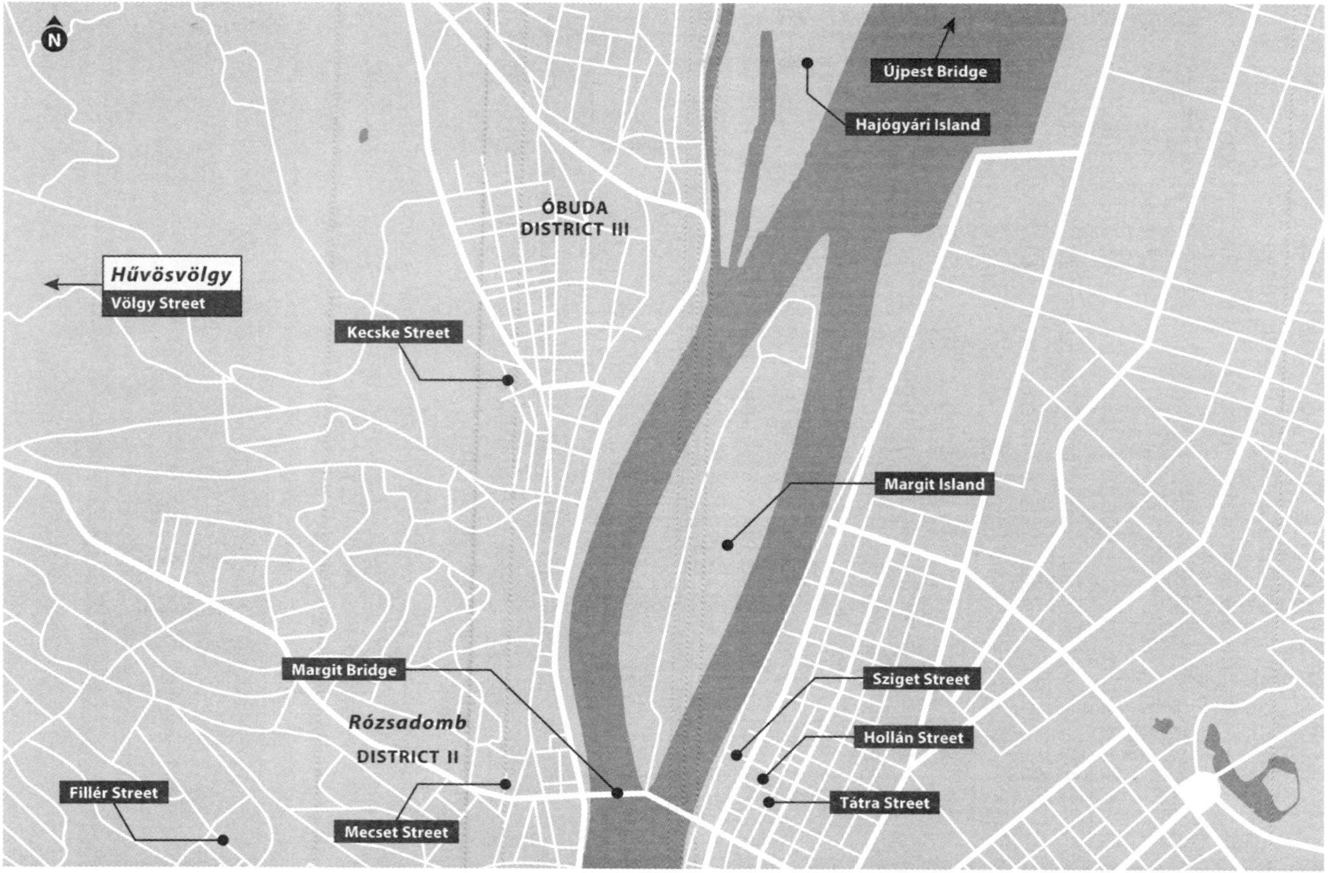

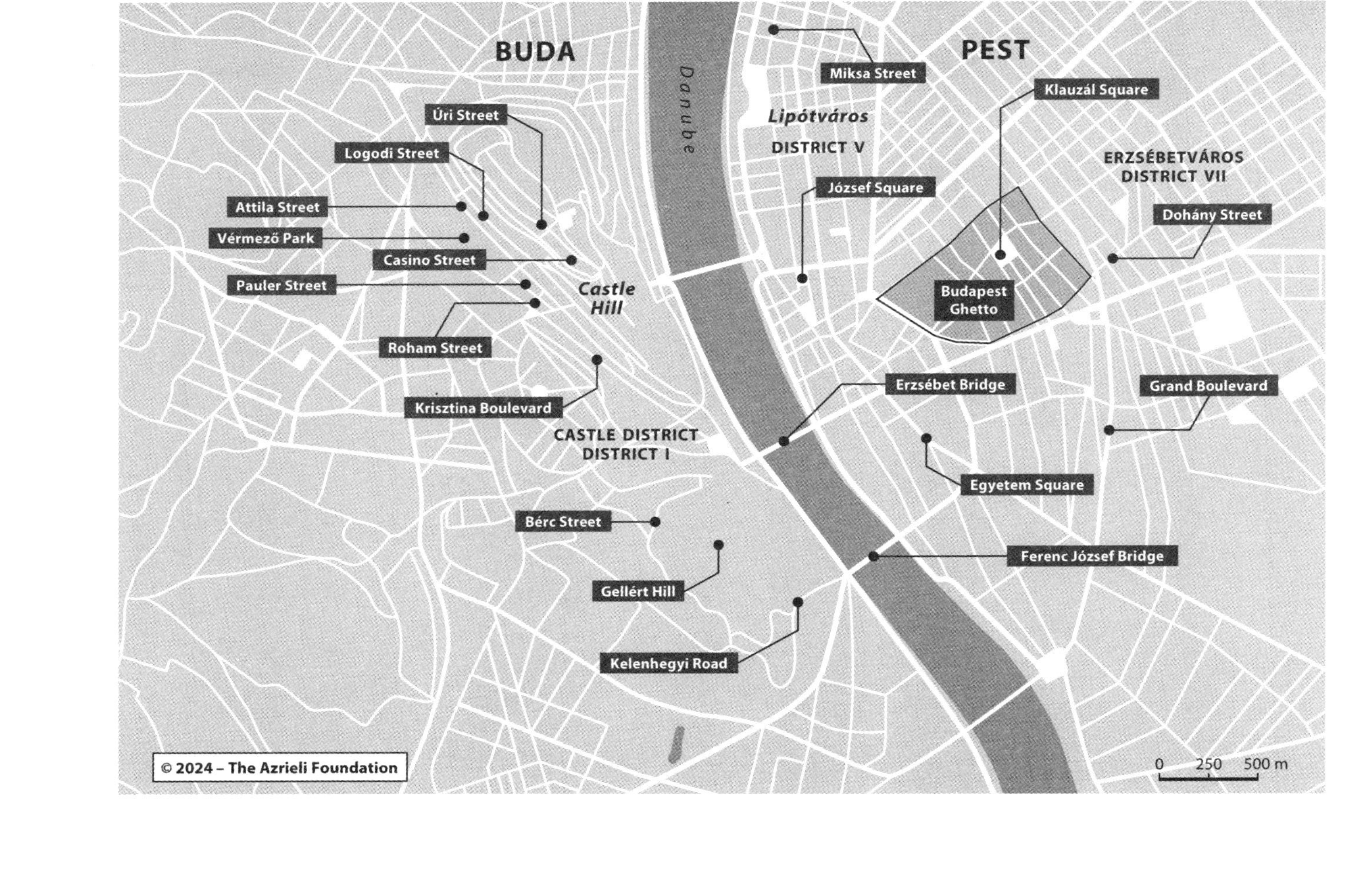

BUDA
PEST
Danube
Miksa Street
Klauzál Square
Úri Street
Lipótváros
DISTRICT V
Logodi Street
ERZSÉBETVÁROS
DISTRICT VII
József Square
Attila Street
Dohány Street
Vérmező Park
Casino Street
Pauler Street
Castle
Hill
Budapest
Ghetto
Roham Street
Erzsébet Bridge
Grand Boulevard
Krisztina Boulevard
CASTLE DISTRICT
DISTRICT I
Egyetem Square
Bérc Street
Ferenc József Bridge
Gellért Hill
Kelenhegyi Road
0
250
500 m

The Age of Uninterrupted Slaps in the Face

Pest!!!!!!!!! Tuesday, March 6, 1945

My dear, sweet Pippancs,[1]

It has been more than six months since I was last able to write you a diary letter as I used to do when I added a few lines to the page every day, keeping you informed of every insignificant and trivial thing that had happened to me. It seemed almost as if keeping a continuous process going was no problem at all. By now you may have heard that some things have happened to me, to Budapest, to the Jews, to Hungary, etc., that can't be called either trivial or insignificant, and I have gradually developed what I have concisely named a *caesura complex*. I'll explain in a moment what that means, but it's certain that this year has caused a caesura, a break, in your life just as it has in mine. This year cut me off sharply and pitched me against a completely different situation, in which I too became something completely different. Surely the same applies to you too, doesn't it? The essential part of the caesura complex is the fear that the new Kiskas[2] and the new Gregi may no longer suit each other. I've often imagined that having been

1 One of Margit Kassai's pet names for her husband, Dr. György Tolnai; others were Pipus, Pipsi, Pippancs, Pipik, Pipi, Gregi, Kispipi.

2 Margit Kassai's own pet name. Kiskas is a wordplay from the word *kis* (little) and the first three letters of Kassai, the family name (*kas* means hive). Her family nickname was Kas.

God knows where during this time you have found another woman to get used to. That would be quite natural, and something of the kind could also have happened to me, although not so easily, because you know how many men were exterminated around here. Then I also imagined that one day you would come home, there would have been no other woman and the new Kiskas would suit you, but you would suddenly ask what had happened, what it had been like. You would expect me to tell you about the whole year, and I would stand there not knowing what to tell. How could I tell it, what could I tell, if the biography of every single person who has come through it alive is a six-volume adventure story? One day we would walk down the street in Budapest together, and I would point out some passersby who seemed so insignificant that at other times we wouldn't even see them but, believe me, each of them is the hero of a novel — and what's more, the hero of a very thrilling novel.

Note: Don't expect a historical account from me. Other people could explain the historical, political, and strategic side of the affair much better than I could even trying my hardest. I only want to report what happened to ME, what the whole thing was like for ME. And — I repeat — I'm doing it to resist the caesura complex.

My dear Pipus, it was April 8 when we said goodbye last year. You patted my cheek with a typical Pippancs gesture and said lightly: "Try to stay alive. Okay?" I said (less lightly): "Okay." Well, I did try, and I suspended all spielbergerisms. I'm not saying that I don't owe a lot to trying. But that wasn't all. If I'm here today it's thanks to

1 Béla,[3]
2 Béla,
3 Béla,
4 the traditional bad luck of the Spielbergers, which always turns into good when faced with a question of life and death,

---

3 Margit's cousin Béla Nádas.

5 an astonishing series of lucky coincidences and
6 my indestructible nervous system.

Dear Pipus, you once said — or wrote to me in reply to a very depressed letter — that the prescription for coming through alive was keeping your cool and your collar clean. As for the cold blood, I can proudly report that I never lost it, but I must admit that toward the end the clean collar caused me quite a lot of trouble, and when I broke down — though that happened very rarely and only for brief spells — it was always the outcome of a collar affair.

My Pipus, listen carefully: Not only did I survive the whole disgusting business but

1 I was never abducted
2 I was never beaten
3 I was never in a labour camp
4 I was never in an internment camp
5 I was never in a ghetto
6 I never saw an Arrow Cross man from close up
7 No relation of mine was hurt
8 I did not know any starvation in the strict sense of the word
9 No Russian soldier ever messed with me
10 I never even had a cold, let alone a real illness throughout the period
11 I can't show as much as a scratch from a splinter on me

To understand all this, you would of course need to know the circumstances better. But believe me, there are very few people, or indeed any we know, who can say the same. The reason I stress this is that I don't want you to start reading with the idea of looking for the heroic epic Kiskas has written about herself. I want to be clear that, precisely because of the facts above, no one can claim more objectively that this year was terrible than me, and I have, relatively speaking, hardly suffered at all. Or let's say that I didn't suffer much more than some unfortunate Aryans who had been thrown by their bad luck into the cellar of the castle, where they remained under siege a whole month longer than the people in Pest. I had an easier time than the unfortunate Aryans whose blood froze when they heard the drone of the Russian fighter aircraft, which was music to my ears. On the other hand, it's true that the horror stories drifting out of the ghetto of Pest caused the Aryans less pain than me. All the time I was astonishingly certain that you were alive and would come back. I don't only say so now that a certain Havas has brought me your handwritten regards from Bucharest. All our friends and relations as well as my companions in the cellar of the Castle can testify that I had no doubts about this even on the nastiest days. Except that I wasn't always certain that you'd find me here.

I also had days of breakdown, when I was afraid that it would take years until you returned. But one thing I never did was to refuse to contemplate the possibility that something had happened to you. On the contrary, I often tried to imagine that you might have died. BUT IT DIDN'T WORK, I simply haven't got the imagination it takes. (I'll come back to this strange lack of imagination later.) I know that things happen only to strangers and not to Pippies, and in this respect even your mother's unrelenting pessimism passed by me like water off a duck's back. Something might happen to her son, BUT NOT TO MY HUSBAND. In the future, please be so kind as to bear in mind that you are no longer just the only child of Gizella but also the only husband of Kiskas, which makes quite a difference.

Unfortunately, I can only supply a retrospective diary, at least for the most part. I didn't start to jot down everything as it happened until the last days of the siege, and so you'll lose a lot of small details, which is a pity because they would have made the whole thing more truthful and it wouldn't have such a literary flavour (please forgive me this once!). There are too many of these tiny details, and I may tell you about them once you're home again. But the material is such a huge jungle that the only way I dare to approach it is by making a synopsis and dividing what I have to tell into small portions, as I used to do for the Hungarian essay lessons when I was a schoolgirl at the Veres Pálné gymnasium.

Hello, Kispipi. I begin.

The synopsis looks somewhat like this:

1944

April 9 to about July 1

1 The Age of Uninterrupted Slaps in the Face

a) Pipus Leaves

b) We Move from Kecske Street

c) The Belated Auction

d) The Great Relocation or the Death of Auntie Böske and Its Connection

April 15/July 1 to October 15

2 In the Starry House (Miksa Street)

a) My Nursery School

b) I Am a Photographer's Apprentice

3 On and Around October 15

October 23 to November 17

4 I Am in Hiding

November 17 to December 23

5 The International Red Cross and Kiskas

December 24 to February 12

6 The Siege

February 12 to 23

7 The Death of Buda

February 23

8 Pest

It will be best if I start with the evening of April 7 or 8, 1944 (I can no longer remember the exact date). I'm working in my darkroom on Kecske Street, enlarging my portrait of Péterke Lénárd — which had turned out quite well if I do say so myself — when Lilus blows in with the message that the troops are leaving for Transylvania tomorrow and I am to come and join you at once in Városliget Park. I grab my coat and run along with Lilus (leaving the photos in the fixing fluid for the days ahead), thinking that in corny films at this point FATE, in capital letters, invariably arrives in the middle of an idyll with the familiar opening bars of Beethoven's relevant symphony. In fact, I have been unable to stop thinking of these few bars ever since the Germans invaded the country on March 19. Now Pipus is leaving, and I know very well that this departure isn't like the previous ones, if only because now I no longer have to worry just about him but also about myself. But so far I'm not concerned in the slightest about myself. On the afternoon when you left, I ambled out once more to Café Gerbeaud in Városliget Park[4] to find out if you had gone, and from what people were saying it seemed that you had really left in the morning. It was there that I met the wives of Tárkányi and Kestler, who are in mourning and who hate me because I'm not in mourning. (For that matter, my Pipsi, this question will come up many times because I want to talk to you personally about why people hate everybody who doesn't react to things like they do.)

You were still at home during the premiere of the stars, but I don't remember if we discussed the fact that it had disturbed me very little emotionally, so to speak, and caused me no inconvenience of any kind. Nor did it later on, when the star also had to be worn in the office, sewn on our clothes. Some colleagues would make a wide detour along the corridor, clearly to avoid having to stop for a friendly chat

4 The famous café used to have a summer pavilion in the park; it was destroyed during the siege of Budapest. The main location in Vörösmarty Square remains.

with me as they had done before, even though they were aware of the dark secret of my birth. In our building on Kecske Street, the star hasn't essentially changed anything either. In the shops they are serving Nünüke[5] with more demonstrative care than before, putting the merchandise on one side so that she doesn't have to line up for it. In the office, the mood is mixed. Fränkel[6] is optimistic (poor little man, where is he now!); my boss is pessimistic and doesn't stop declaring that "NOBODY CAN GET THROUGH THIS ALIVE" (a saying I've heard a thousand times a day since then, whether about the Germans or the Arrow Cross, the bombing, the starvation or the epidemics).

I was in very bad shape. I was almost visibly losing weight and had somehow become so restless that even in the office I didn't have the patience to sit in one place but would rush around all morning without getting any work done. I can't write in any detail about this phase, because it was so long ago and so many things have happened since that I only remember it as a blur. All I know is that it was then that the worst time began for me, with anxiety, general discomfort, etc. In the night, I would wake up fifty times with a start and soaked to the skin, waking in the morning dead tired, and this went on until about July, when it slowly, almost imperceptibly, stopped. It was the deportation that had frightened me so, even though at the time I didn't understand what that meant and would never have believed before then that I could be so frightened of anything.

The next blow after your departure was having to move out of the apartment on Kecske Street within four (yes, four) hours. The "authorities" had forced the so-called Jewish Council to requisition the Jewish apartments for "bombed-out families," and the first one thousand such apartments included ours. It was a great problem to decide

---

5 Nickname for Margit's mother, Janka Beck (also called Nünü). The family nickname for Margit's father, József Kassai, is Püpüke.

6 Margit's colleague at the Hungarian General Credit Bank.

whether to appeal (which was still possible at that time) or to relocate at once into the planned ghetto area, so that my parents didn't have to move so often. Finally, I chose the latter and I had by chance done the right thing, because we wouldn't have been able to keep the apartment anyway (not to mention the fact that the building received a direct hit in July and this particular apartment became uninhabitable). So the old folks were spared the latest move. Leaving the apartment within four hours was such a terrible experience that I won't even try to describe it. It was so painful to see the old couple in the ravaged apartment that I DON'T WANT TO BE A HEAD TENANT[7] EVER AGAIN.

As soon as the changeover to the apartment on Miksa Street was over, we all went to stay for two days with Auntie Böske in Rózsadomb, so that we no longer had to look at furniture and luggage. Up there, at least, there was a garden and the sun was shining. About two weeks later, by which time my parents had recovered a little from the great shock, a city councillor "bombed out" of Pesterzsébet moved into the apartment on Kecske Street. While the "authorities" had ordered us to leave behind the most important pieces of furniture, bedding, kitchenware, etc., for three persons when we had left the apartment, the councillor demanded that we have everything removed from the apartment as well as the cellar within twenty-four hours because he wanted to have the place redecorated. Of course, this meant even more stress, worry and expense, because we didn't know what to do with all the furniture. I finally got some odd-job men to spread the furniture along the staircase and the steps leading down to the cellar and then I literally squandered away the stuff, letting people have the

---

7 Refers to the primary tenant whose name is on the lease and who is in charge of the rental unit.

pieces for whatever they offered. I called a *handlé*,[8] who paid forty pengős for wardrobes and superb mattresses, ten pengős for clothes by the kilo, and I threw in kitchenware for nothing as presents, and so on. This happened on May 1, and to me it was perhaps even more terrible (because of my parents) than the first move. At that time we had still been able to ask some friends to help us because such events were few and far between. But once the Great Relocation was under way, nobody could help anybody because everybody was busy with their own troubles. I was having a very bad time. I hated our new accommodation. I could see at once that it was infested with bedbugs, the toilet was full of cockroaches and the people who already lived there resented having to give up one of their two rooms (although later they were decent to us, and we got on well, unlike others who were forced to share their accommodation).

At that time the office was the only place I felt reasonably happy, since everything there was more or less as it had been before. Jews were still allowed to use the cafeteria, for which no special rules had as yet been announced. But when the supply to Jews of animal fats and other items became differently organized (we couldn't eat anything that contained fat because Jewish food coupons were only exchangeable for oil and because Jews weren't entitled to eggs, poppy seeds or other rare foodstuffs), the "starry meal" came into being. We Jews were treated, for example, to scrumptious potatoes in sour cream, while our "Aryan" colleagues were served potatoes cooked with the paprika commonly used at the time, which was unbearably hot, as everyone knows; or we were given delicious cottage cheese pies, while the others had to put up with pasta coated in poppy seeds, which in turn were not available to Jews. For a laugh I would offer to lend my star to my colleagues, assuring them that it gave me pleasure to do so, when I saw them wistfully eyeing the Jewish lunch. Later on,

8 Hungarian form of the Yiddish word *hendler*, meaning junk merchant.

however, we were no longer allowed to use the cafeteria, and after the Great Relocation the bank dispensed with my services by means of an official letter. The successor to my boss, Szentkirályi, tried for a long time to keep me on and eventually enforced my right to six months' notice, so that I was finally fired with effect from February 1, 1945.

Meanwhile my anxiety attacks continue. I get such palpitations when I see the notice on the walls ordering Jews to join the forced labour service that I almost faint in the street (even though this doesn't concern me personally since I no longer have anyone who can join up). Then there are the rest of the graphic monstrosities with which the streets of Budapest overflow: the posters showing the English or American pilot dropping bombs, the Russian bogeyman tearing the cross from the neck of the crying Hungarian virgin with his hairy hand, the despicable spy whispering horror stories into the ears of brave Hungarian patriots — and they all have crooked Jewish noses.

I think I wrote to you several times that I feel as if I've — unfortunately — stuck my head in a noose that is becoming tighter and tighter around my neck. Every day new orders, new inflammatory posters, new restrictions. One day all Jewish shops are suddenly closed and seized. At 11:30 p.m. the radio announces a law that came into force on the PREVIOUS DAY but wouldn't be reported in the official paper until the day after. On the next morning the Jewish shopkeeper opens his shop without suspecting anything, because at 11:30 p.m. on the previous day he had been fast asleep (and in any case his radio had been confiscated long before, immediately after the German invasion). He is at once taken away and interned. It's becoming more and more fashionable to round people up under a variety of pretexts[9]:

9 In the first days after the invasion, several hundred Jews were rounded up in the streets of Budapest, followed in subsequent weeks by some two thousand more. They were confined in the Kistarcsa transit camp and on April 28, 1944, taken to Auschwitz-Birkenau as the first group of deportees from Hungary.

I feel sick to my stomach if Nünüke gets home even a few minutes later than she promised, and every evening we heave a deep sigh of relief when we see the family together with no one missing after yet another day of worry. We hear constantly that X, Y or Z has been arrested on some trumped-up charge. A young girl I know goes down to the rationing office on the next street to sort out a question about food coupons and never comes back; eventually she manages to send a message from the detention centre, asking for clean underwear. A grandmother dies and every member of her large family turns out for the funeral, but they never get to the cemetery because the gendarmes drag them off the Rákoskeresztúr streetcar and lead them away. Only a child of ten is left behind to be looked after by the people living in the building. About the same time, Mrs. Vera Csillag Bálint[10] disappears. We believe for a long time that she has been kidnapped, and her relatives spread the same story; but as we discover a lot later, she had made herself disappear. Lívia also disappears at about that time (she "steps on oil," as the saying goes in Budapest) but in this case we know that she has bought false papers for about ten thousand pengős and is employed as a governess by an Aryan woman, who incidentally knows about her background and treats her well.

I'm constantly inventing fantastic escape plans (which of course aren't serious but rather like daydreams) but always end up by realizing that they are impossible because I haven't got any money and because I can't leave my parents. I get restless when I hear that somebody or other I know is escaping or preparing to escape. But then I decide complacently that — by pure chance — I have coped better than anybody else we know because I neither spent thousands on

10 Vera Csillag (1909–1997), a graphic artist and illustrator married to the left-wing journalist and critic György Bálint (1906–1943), who was murdered as a forced labourer in 1943.

forged documents nor escaped a lot sooner than would have been absolutely necessary. I could have waited two more weeks before I disappeared from Miksa Street, but on the other hand the two weeks' delay didn't cost me a penny because I was kept by friends. That, however, is a matter for later chapters. What is characteristic of this period of my life is that I am constantly choked up on the verge of tears and would from time to time, whether I am in the street or on the streetcar, suddenly start sobbing for half an hour at a stretch (these aren't strictly "crying fits" because I can suppress them if I really want to, but I generally don't want to because the tears relieve the spasms of anxiety a little). If I were asked about the immediate cause of the tears (*ad analogiam*: the "immediate cause of death"), I could only answer that I am sick, sick, sick (of the press, the posters, the colleagues, the Jewish housemates, everything and everybody). But now I know that it was my fear and my anger that made me cry. I was angry because I could be so afraid. If I think about it, this was not at all surprising given that day by day newer and newer restrictions are announced in the official paper, more and more disgusting inflammatory posters appear on the walls, the Jews get together to torture each other with horror stories, and I try to contradict them but I know that even the most savage horror story may not be a match for the truth.

Toward the end of May, our relatives in Bős write that they have had to leave their nice little house, garden, farm and plot of land that two generations had saved up for and have been deported to the ghetto in Dunaszerdahely. They write a few more times. Initially their situation is bearable. They live in one room with a kitchen. They have a small yard, where Mici's little boy, who is a few months old, can get some fresh air. They are allowed to keep some chickens and a cow, and their Christian friends from Bős bring them food by bicycle.

Then, from the first week of June, no more news. Later the wife of the doctor of Bős writes to the family that on June 14 they were transported to an "unknown place." By that time Mici's husband, Jóska, is a forced labourer. He works somewhere near Karcag, and we exchange a few letters. Poor Bandi had been picked up with the rest, and no one knows for certain whether (or not) they were deported together. The doctor's wife did know that the baby had died even before they were all loaded into the cattle car wagons.

One day I run into Margit Braun in the street. She works in the office of the Jewish Council's executive team and tells me that the council applied to the "relevant authorities" for permission to send its own workers to one of the Budapest marshalling yards, where the notorious sealed wagons containing Jews forcibly removed from eastern Hungary had stood *alla rinfusa*[11] in the infernal heat for days. The council intended to have the wagons opened in the presence of a representative of the authorities, the human waste and dead bodies cleared away, and those still alive given fresh water, but the request was flatly refused. The wagons were left standing in the marshalling yard until they continued their journey. This came from Margit Braun, the famous optimist, who dislikes even listening to bad news let alone spreading it. I firmly decide to commit suicide by whatever means rather than ever getting into such a wagon. (This time I consider my options carefully and seriously and am not merely toying with possibilities as is my well-known style!) I abandon this plan when Magda Belcsák, who happens to be in Budapest, calls on me to discuss the situation. Her mother and sister have been deported from Komárom, and she headed home to Losonc, where her husband was waiting for her at the station and told her to turn around immediately and stay in Budapest until he comes to fetch her or sends for her. In Losonc, some little functionary took a private initiative, and as a result they started to deport the Aryan spouses of Jews without giving a damn about any relevant legislation. Magda has no idea what will happen to her children if she can't go back to Losonc because Laci could be called up at any minute. But she doesn't despair in the slightest, and

---

11 Italian: haphazardly.

I am a little ashamed. Magda and I agree that we must survive this, because it can't last much longer (!!!!!!!!!) and that it might even be a good idea to get into the wagon because the tables could be turned at any moment. (A few days later the self-appointed miniature ruler of Losonc is fired, and Magda can go home to her family.)

Meanwhile, everybody is fervently fixed to the radio (the neighbours' or friends' radios, since the Jews have long since had theirs confiscated), frantically trying to hear the English news. About this time, word gets around that Turkey has joined the war[12] and there are those who know from an infallible source that the Turkish embassy has "already moved out of Budapest." There is also the gossip that Russian radio has promised Budapest a seventy-two-hour air raid and reassured the people of Budapest that when they come up from the cellars they'll find the Russian army waiting for them. Under the impact of this news everybody climbs down to the cellar and up again five or six times a day loaded with four-to-five days' food and drink instead of the usual air raid defence food parcel. Come to think of it, the Russians kept their promise, because (wait a moment while I add it up: *achtmal sieben: sechsundfünfzig, sechsundfünfzigmal vierundzwanzig = tausenddreihundertvierundvierzig*)[13] after an air raid of 1,344 hours in total they were really here. (But we had to wait four or five months for this.) Finally, I spent 1,344 hours in the cellar. Admittedly, the people of Budapest spent 672 hours less there, but I don't envy them for this because I believe that every hour spent in the ghetto during the war counts threefold. But I don't want to get ahead of myself.

---

12 The rumour referenced here would not have been true, since Turkey remained neutral until February 1945, when they entered the war on the side of the Allies.

13 In German: eight times seven = fifty-six, fifty-six times twenty-four = one thousand three hundred and forty-four.

Now I'll try to depict the mood of the GREAT RELOCATION. If I remember correctly, the ultimate deadline by which every "individual obliged to wear the yellow star" (as the term of endearment applied to the Jews in the order had it) was required to have moved into one of the so-called starred buildings designated by the authorities was June 25. There were not yet any ghettos and these starred buildings were scattered over all the districts of Budapest, with great care being taken to ensure that there should be at least one of them in each block. There was a widespread superstition that the British wouldn't bomb a Jewish building, and this was repeated not only by types below that of a custodian but also by an intelligent Christian acquaintance who tried to make me feel better by telling me how much she would have preferred to live in a starred building. When I asked how she imagined the thing was technically executed, I think she answered that the British had perfect instruments and would be bombing from a low altitude. Naturally, these starred buildings are only too few relative to the number of Jews, so that each apartment is shared by two or three families. The Jewish families who have lived from the beginning in one of the buildings that were now being "allocated" could call themselves lucky, while the less fortunate families were begging them for a share of their apartment, offering to do any kind of housework and promising gifts of food in return. Everyone prefers a relative or friend to move into their apartment if possible, but you can't imagine how they regret it later. We are happy because 11 Miksa Street was chosen, so that we don't have to move again, search for an apartment, etc. Of course most of the moves take place on the last day before the closing date, when furniture left on an open cart in the street is ruined by a cloudburst that goes on for hours. The movers are cashing in. They are in such furious demand that they can charge an arm and a leg and expect to be offered special rewards for their work. I can't describe the general mood. In the streets people with pale, tortured faces carry furniture to and fro, crying loudly, and there are so many suicides that the hospital on Szvetenay Street can't cope with all the bodies. All this is mainly about display cabinets and Persian rugs, which makes me swear that if I survive these things I'll never want to be a head tenant because it goes without saying that such a suicidal panic only rages in the circles of head tenants.

My poor Aunt Böske is a special case; we know that she would have had a tragic end sooner or later. They tried everything they could to stay put where they were. They tried to have their building declared a starred building, so they would be able to stay if they took in two or three other families. But it didn't work. They were finally obliged to look for an apartment in one of the starred buildings. While Old Béla[14] was out looking for an apartment, Aunt Böske started to pack. For a whole day she packed and prepared an inventory beautifully and systematically, but early in the evening she suddenly stopped even though there was still a lot of time before dinner. Meanwhile, Old Béla came home, they had dinner together and lay down to sleep next to each other in the *Ehebett*.[15] In the morning it wasn't possible to wake Böske: she had taken a huge amount of sleeping pills. It wasn't until midday that she could be taken to the Rókus Hospital, too late help her, and she died toward the evening. On her bedside table she had only left a note, which said "Let Young Béla pack. He knows how," and a handwritten cookbook in which she had placed a slip of paper with "For Margit" written on it.

Old Béla suffered a complete mental collapse. He turned into a helpless, wailing, dotty old man in one day, and Young Béla is suffering so hellishly that you can hardly bear to watch him. One moment he makes cynical comments, the next he sobs loudly. The funeral is delayed because the dead are numerous and those in charge of the cemetery don't want to bury suicides in consecrated ground. Old Béla insists on the opposite. Finally, the funeral takes place on June 22

---

14 Béla senior, Margit's uncle, Dr. Béla Nádas.

15 German: marriage bed.

(Böske died on the 18th) in Farkasrét cemetery. It's a gorgeous day. It's marvellously quiet out here. No posters, no placards, no German soldiers, and forgive me, my dear Pipus, but I must stress that the birds are singing beautifully, because all this goes with the terror of the whole. The cemetery is working flat out. The dead are buried as if on a conveyor belt.

People often talk about "such a beautiful corpse, as if she were only asleep," but I really can't forget poor Aunt Böske's face. She turned fifteen or twenty years younger in death. Her face is smooth, the unpleasant suspicious expression around her eyes has gone, and although the livid marks of death are now clearly visible I can't help thinking how beautiful she is. There are very few people at the funeral because everybody is busy with their own troubles. Old Béla's sorrow is even more repulsive than his normal behaviour. I simply can't be sorry for him. After the funeral he sits all day on a chair and groans.

The authorities have declared that all those selected to move must be in their new accommodations before midnight, and anyone found in their old home will be interned. The two Bélas don't move until the very last moment, and the mover leaves them in the lurch. At half past seven in the evening the van is still not there, so Old Béla simply ambles across to his room at 4 Szent István Park with a single umbrella in his hand. He doesn't even take the briefcase with the essentials that Young Béla has prepared for him, but lies down on the floor in his clothes and falls asleep, waiting for good luck. Good luck from now to the very end is represented by Béla's Irén, who finds a mover after the deadline (more easily and for one-tenth of the charge) and completes the move by giving the superintendent a bribe for not noticing the late arrival. The Kassais made an effective contribution to the packing and moving. I helped them pack, made an inventory and gave things away to anyone we saw, which I must say was almost as painful as it had been to break up our own household, because, in case you didn't know, Aunt Böske's apartment had been renowned as an outstanding example of its kind, which, equipped with the most beautiful, most costly and most practical objects available, had been run, even without a maid, as smoothly as the most accurate Swiss watch.

So all this is what I have to get rid of. She had a huge amount of exquisite clothes, some of which she had never worn but bought as a reserve, and now they have to be given away for nothing. We were in such a dispirited mood that it didn't occur to us to keep anything for ourselves. I only mention it as a curiosity that Aunt Irén's daughter Kató, my cousin, who is married to a Christian veterinarian in Kunágota, came up to Budapest for the funeral. We gave her everything that she could carry because she was the only Christian in the family. But her husband had forbidden her to bring home any Jewish possessions (this was also forbidden by law: Jewish property belonged to the Hungarian state). It pained me to watch poor Kató in her agony, until she finally simply couldn't leave the genuine lace and crepe de Chine slips and nighties, the brand new crocodile handbag, the unused gloves, the silk stockings, etc., etc., behind. It reminded me of the famous Andersen tale (I think it's called "The Lighter")[16] about the soldier who finds a lot of copper coins in a hollow tree, fills his pockets with them, then going deeper comes upon silver coins but as he no longer has anywhere to put them throws the coppers on the ground to make space for the silver, and finally, deeper still finds gold, so that he throws the silver out of his pockets. So it happened to our Kató. With a lot more agony she sorted the things and took them off to Kunágota from where — I must jump ahead here much as I dislike upsetting the order of the tale — she had to flee with nothing but the shirt on her back when the Russians arrived in September.

From your trunk in Aunt Böske's cellar I took out everything I could, leaving only useless stuff behind, like gas masks, ancient blankets, bad old shoes, a bedpan, etc. — boxes and all, they were where

16 The English title is usually translated as "The Tinderbox."

they had been. You can see the outlines of where they sat, at any time you wish. As for the six-place dinner service we were given by Aunt Böske as a wedding present. Its history: it only took a moment after glimpsing it in a shop window in the city centre to fall in love with it, but then I lusted after it for months and always made sure that I walked that way to see if it was still in the window. Aunt Böske's question as to what kind of present I wanted for my wedding couldn't have come at a better moment. We bought it together the next day and had it immediately taken to Rózsadomb, which seemed to be the safest place at the time, and it was so to speak never unpacked from its crate. Let me tell you what it looked like: it was made of smooth snow-white porcelain, with one narrow and one even narrower coral-coloured stripe at the edge. Every item was a very simple and beautiful shape. I once saw something like it with a green stripe and I remember you also liked it a lot. So this service was hidden for us by our market stall keeper friend, néni[17] Gólya, and her family in a woodshed in their orchard on Szemlő Mountain. A week ago I scraped it out of the shed, which had been blown to smithereens, with only one soup plate and two cups without handles left in one piece. But if I think that of poor, brave, kind néni Gólya even less is left — she is buried five steps from the shed, where the bomb hit her — and if I further think of what a narrow escape I myself had, I say: "The devil take the dinner service. One day, perhaps, I'll possess an even more beautiful one." But come to think of it, the devil take all the possessions in the world, I don't want to see any possessions, either beautiful or ugly, I've had nothing but stress and worry and no pleasure from possessions for years.

I spread your clothes, and mine also, all over the place. With yours I made sure that everywhere there was the right kind and the right

---

17 The Hungarian *néni* (aunt) and *bácsi* (uncle) are used as terms of respect for an older woman or man, especially by children or when there is a large age difference. The editors have kept these terms untranslated when the individual is not Margit's direct relation.

amount of everything you need to be dressed from top to toe. I hid your Transylvanian woven suit, your brown shoes, two shirts, two pairs of pants, socks, suspenders, ties, pyjamas, towels, handkerchiefs, soap, etc., together with your small black travel case in the cupboard of my colleague Károly Kiss in the staff cloakroom of the Credit Bank and kept the padlock key. Of all this I now have only the padlock key and your ugly little brown hat, the latter I found a few days after on the floor in front of the locker which had been broken into and robbed. I'm sorry I always jump ahead of myself. In brief, this age ended under the sign of anxiety, fear of death, the hiding of possessions, liquidation, etc. It was about this time that I had my hair cut short because I expected to go on a lengthy and crammed package tour in a sealed wagon.

In such circumstances there is little worse than having to live crammed in among Jews, who are constantly torturing each other with horror stories and each of whom looks paler and more miserable than the other. And they are meaner to each other than ever. They're all passionate guzzlers. Stuffed geese and ducks fetch extortionate prices within minutes, butter is paid for through the nose, and everybody boils, steams, fries, bakes, roasts and gobbles. We take no part in all this, because we haven't got the money. As a result, the people in the building (the grocer, the book hawker, the shoe accessory seller, the textile dealer, the jeweller, the estate agent) no longer respect us and do not even hide their mild contempt.

In the Starry House (Miksa Street)

Now I'm going to describe Miksa Street. You have moved houses many times in your life. You never stayed long in the same place and if my memory is right you never lived in Buda. I'll have a difficult job making you understand how a resident of Óbuda, and one as hungry for fresh air as I am, feels when she has to move not just to Pest but straight to darkest Erzsébetváros with its narrow, nasty, stinking and noisy streets, and that in the middle of summer. (Do you remember how I never knew what to do with myself on a Sunday if I couldn't go out to hike, ski or at least take a walk?) The source of the dirt, smoke and soot was the Athenaeum printing press across the street, but the source of the stench is still a mystery to me, and that of the noise, to a small extent, the traffic of the boys selling and delivering newspapers, and to a large extent the Metropol Hotel on the corner, which had by then been well established as a German military *Durchgang-Versorgungsstelle*[1] and which directed all the essential transport of persons and goods along our street, and later on, all the essential transport of hand grenades as well. These were the components of the noise out of doors during the day. At night the leading roles were played in the house by the Kulacs Bar, the local prostitutes and their clients, the drunken German soldiers.

---

1 German: transit supply point.

I'm not bothered by all this, least of all at night, when I am busy sweating and waking up with fits and starts, oblivious to any external noise. At the most I am irritated by my father, who complains all day about the unpleasant surroundings and wishes he were back on Kecske Street. Nünüke shows once more who she is. I should really devote a separate chapter to this, and perhaps I will do so at the end of the diary because even I was surprised to see what a wonderful person she is. She immediately found her feet, became friendly with the neighbours, softened the people in the house, even the grumpy, rude house commander and the shopkeepers of the quarter. Both those in Rákóczi Square and those in Klauzál Square were eating out of her hand. I try to introduce a system whereby I will do the shopping for her if we go to the Market Hall together. I must realize how much better it is when she does it because however modestly she joins the long line, at its end the salesman will jump out of his hut and bring the shopping to her, shouting across to the others who are complaining that such a grey-haired old woman can't waste her time here for hours. Nünü also does her cooking with great ambition. The whole of 11 Miksa Street gathers to admire her buttered sweet buns. She invents all kinds of specialties so that she soon becomes the culinary authority in the building on whom everyone calls for recipes and advice.

Initially it seemed strange to us — to me and Nünü — this close coexistence of the people in the building, with everybody knowing everybody, with everybody knowing everything about everybody. We had lived on Kecske Street for sixteen years and didn't even know our immediate neighbours.

I seem to remember that at that time people wearing the star were only allowed to be out in the street between 11:00 a.m. and 5:00 p.m. Initially, of course, we obey scrupulously. Later we cover the star and are a few minutes late, then half an hour. We needn't worry about our superintendent, who is a well-meaning Franzstadt[2] scoundrel with a huge mouth, immeasurably impertinent and rude, but to my old folk infinitely kind. I stress this here because in those days getting home punctually, wearing the star or not wearing it, indeed the question of being or not being depends on the caretakers and house commanders. Our house commander is an elderly, stupid and frightened printer, so near-sighted that as far as he was concerned I could walk about not only without the star but naked, and he wouldn't notice it. His name is János Matrác, he is terribly ugly, his wife even more ugly. They don't have any children but have a dog to whom they both bear a striking resemblance. About the superintendent Káldy and his family I would need to write at greater length, but then I would never finish this diary.

From time to time, Nünüke undertakes an excursion to Óbuda to the Borszékis (the custodian on Kecske Street, if you remember him) and the Gólya family to get some unusual delicacies. She always brings back something good, from Mrs. Borszéki, for example, some butter at the highest price (!!), bread rolls, etc., and from the Gólyas some home-grown vegetables and fruit, for which néni Gólya would under no circumstances accept a penny in payment.

On one occasion, Nünüke gets home not after five o'clock but about six o'clock, by which time the whole building (where everybody always knows everything) watches breathlessly how anyone could dare to walk in the streets so late. At last, Nünü sweeps in, with her long black coat folded over so that the star is covered and invisible, although in the appropriate place the outline of a hexagram appears in snow white tacking. But Nünü is proud of how cleverly she had hidden the star and tricked the authorities. My first starless excursion beyond the permitted duration was connected with one of your

---

2 A German word referencing the Ferencváros district of Budapest (District IX), a working-class area notoriously home to antisemites.

letters. Once, when we hadn't had any news from you for a long time, Judit Kőváry at last received a black card, which only reached me late in the afternoon. I waited until dark and then went in a starless coat to your mother on Szalay Street.

You know, if I had written this report then and there I would have described the residents of the building in lengthy detail, which I think important because this was the first time I lived in a Jewish community and can categorically declare that I DO NOT ACCEPT THEM, cannot bear them, do not want them, have nothing in common with them and want to have nothing in common with them. I want to go to the other end of the world and deny my Jewish origin. Not that I was surprised that they are greedy, violent, loud, ill-mannered and stupid, although this was the first time I experienced it from so close up, through my own skin. But it upset me that they don't pull together even when they are in great trouble. They treat each other meanly and cause as much harm to each other as they can. I had really been prepared to give them the benefit of the doubt and not ask for much from them. But if I have survived the whole affair with my nerves and my emotions in good condition, I owe it to the children of Miksa Street, about whom I would love to write to you in detail, and the only reason why I don't is that I know that you aren't interested.

The environment meant a great deal at that time. In fact, I believe that all that happened later depended on this: if you entered the decisive weeks with damaged nerves you dropped out of the finish. You once told, or rather wrote, this to me, and you are not for nothing the cleverest Pippancs in the world. I would first take six Sedyletta[3] tablets a day for my anxiety and broken nights, but later this became totally unnecessary due to taking care of twelve children a day. The children started with the air raids when the poor dears had to sit for

---

3 A common anti-anxiety medication at the time.

long hours in the incredibly crowded cellar, and what do children do at such times? They torture their parents. I began to make friends with the children in the cellar, where slowly and automatically a small kindergarten developed around my seat in the shelter. As the direct result of this, the children became more bearable for their parents, so that one fine day a deputation of the parents themselves paid me a visit and suggested that I try to organize something like a kindergarten in the yard, which they would be willing to clean for the purpose, and they would also put together some kind of payment for me. To begin with, I didn't want to take this on because the children's ages (ranging from one and a half to twelve years old) varied too much for me to look after them together, but this problem was solved when a young girl named Editke, who lived in the same house, volunteered to help me so that we could split the group into two.

The other difficulty was that the parents wanted two and a half hours of kindergarten in both the morning and the afternoon, which I was in no circumstances prepared to do because I needed every minute of the time we were allowed to be without the star. In other words, I was only able to work within the "prison hours," the starry free time, and even then only if I had already cleaned our apartment. Under such circumstances I couldn't very well ask for payment. We finally agreed to run the kindergarten from ten to eleven in the morning (at eleven we were allowed to walk in the street) and from five-thirty to six-thirty in the afternoon, and to leave the question of pay hanging in the air, with me declaring that I wouldn't accept any money. (In the end I didn't lose out because the parents gave me butter, eau de cologne, toiletries, genuine peacetime Lux soap, books, sugar cubes, etc.)

My Pipus, it did me a lot of good to be with the children, and of course I had my favourites, even though I tried very hard to hide it. However, there was also an extremely clever and extremely spoiled little girl of three who hated me and whom I hated and with whom I had a lot of trouble. The children were so good for me that I developed a system whereby between the end of afternoon tea and the start of supper they could come up to me in pairs on a schedule changing from day to day to draw and chat, which Nünüke enjoyed as much as they did. The exclusion of a child from one of these occasions was regarded as the worst punishment. As a special reward, I was sometimes allowed to take one or the other older children into the city or on one of my Sunday excursions to the Gólya or the Borszéki family.

I am again very tempted to write about the children one by one, but I know that it would bore you. I have now made a more informative list of them: they are all alive in spite of the ghetto, the house under Swedish protection, the starvation, and most of them are even in a relatively good condition. I don't know how they digested these times, and the experts don't yet know either. But I must make a note of two small scenes that are characteristic of these children.

1 Jutka Sós, my two-and-a-half-year-old "protege," in an unguarded moment, slips out of the gate and is brought back by the superintendent of the neighbouring building. She is given a spanking by her frightened mother and precociously rebuked by her three-year-old playmate: "Don't you know that a Jew is not allowed out in the street alone?"
2 Péter Boczán, my four-year-old student, friend and persistent admirer, sits next to me in the shelter whenever there is an air raid. If he sees me reading, he either keeps still and gazes at me devotedly or stares straight at the ceiling with his legs pumping up and down like a cyclist's, a sure sign that he is meditating on something.

On one occasion, about midnight, I am reading and Péter has been staring at the ceiling with his legs pumping away. Suddenly, he asks with that funny singsong voice of his: "Néni Margit, and what is that — peace?" (From the "and" I guess that he must have arrived at that question after a lengthy and obviously very interesting reflection and I would love to know what he has been thinking; later I try to take him back over his memories, but in vain.) There are roars of laughter. Péter looks around, about to take offence, but seeing that I remain serious he calms down and waits for the answer.

I wasn't prepared to answer such a difficult question at about midnight after running down to the cellar three times on one day, but I tried to make Peti understand as well as I could that one day all Daddies will come home and will stay at home, nobody will be wearing a star, everybody will come and go when they like, you'll be able to get anything you want in the shops, you won't have to line up for bread, there will be chocolate again (he still remembered that), and everybody will go back to their own houses. This answer supplied little Péter with so much material for ceiling-staring and leg-pumping that he wasn't heard to say anything else that day.

Talking about the character of Miksa Street, I must add that I spent the whole summer fighting, in vain, the residents' habit of spitting apricot stones, apple cores, melon rinds and any muck of the season into the yard. The superintendent told me that he had been trying unsuccessfully to stop this for years, but I thought they would refrain from spitting at least while the kindergarten was in the yard. Pigs might fly. My mother watched our neighbour, the shoe accessory salesman Mihály Kertész, resting his elbows on the balustrade of our shared passage and throwing the apple core he had just finished nibbling down into the yard. Nünü asked him politely not to do that because there were children playing in the yard. Mr. Kertész indignantly remarked that he hoped my mother didn't think he was aiming the apple core into this yard. No, he had aimed it into the neighbour's yard. (Because he knew what was right and proper.)

I am not going to say anything about what the people on each of the four floors of the building joined to ours throw into the yard daily. There will be more to report later. That house was also a "starred" one, full of unruly teenagers who gathered in their passage and watched our games with longing in their eyes but with no hope of joining us (even though their parents would have been willing to pay) because, as I have said, the kindergarten sessions took place during prison hours and it was impossible to get from one building to the other without stepping into the street. So instead they tried to disrupt our games by shouting and throwing things. There were also many adolescent boys living in that house and all were in love with Röné from our side. She was a gorgeous twelve-year-old snotty little Rose of Hebron, intelligent, flirtatious and very attractive, whom I have not been able to locate since the Great Hunt but whom I am still hoping to find.

The kindergarten, to put it in one word, was a success. Everybody was happy, especially the children, and I also got my reward. Initially we had fun with the familiar old songs and games. Then I started to invent a variety of entertainments, of which the most popular turned out to be the Funny Gymnastics Race and the Silent Orchestra. The winner of the first was the first person to catch up with me either after running backwards or hopping on tiptoe with feet crossed. The Silent Orchestra needs no explanation, but this was the game that amused me most and for me the greatest amusement was always the conductor.

Once when I had run out of tricks I went to see Éva Vajna for advice, but her books had recently gone missing and she couldn't tell me much from memory.

In the early days I often tried to see your friend Gyuszi, because I somehow feel that I ought to consult a male acquaintance before I embark on an important enterprise. The devil knows why, because in the end I do whatever I think is right. I am told that many women without a man to help them are in the same position as I am. But eventually I stop trying to reach Gyuszi because he hasn't behaved well. I often call him or leave notes at his apartment about wanting to see him, but he never gets back to me. In times like this such behaviour bothers me twice as much because he can move around freely and I can't.

The period of hiding things also belongs here. As you know, on March 19, the day of the German invasion, I discreetly began to separate our valuable possessions from the rest of our things. At first I systematically placed them with various acquaintances. But later, when we had to vacate the apartment, I suddenly threw them all where I could and where people were prepared to accept them. Take, for instance, the woman who lives on Kecske Street whom we don't know, but who is still keeping our serving carts, our lace tablecloths, our most precious vases (I didn't even think of going to fetch them back or to look whether they are still there). Two cases of old clothes left with my colleague Károly Kiss had to be brought to Miksa in September because Kiss needed the space in his cellar. At the Borszékis' we deposited Dénes's underwear, boots, ski boots, suits, and at the Gólyas' a dinner service set, tablecloths, etc. I started an inventory reminding me of what was where, but later this had to be destroyed at the express and understandable request of those affected. (The laws threatened those hiding Jewish belongings with harsh sanctions.) When jewellery had to be registered and deposited, I sent it to the Belcsáks in Losonc by post, sewn into linoleum board games, of course after discussing the matter with Magda. In midsummer Laci Belcsák came to Budapest with the intention of returning the jewellery, because in Losonc the gendarmes had begun to beat the soles of wealthy Jews with iron rods to make them confess where and with whom they had hidden their valuables. The Belcsáks were also hiding property of their local Jewish friends and were afraid that somebody would betray them, and their building would be searched. The jewellery was so well hidden in the curlicues of the ornamental carved chandelier that Laci himself could hardly find it again, but in any case the gendarmes had by then become wise to such practices. Luckily, Juci Lénárd happened to be in Budapest and took away the items that Laci had brought back. Touch wood, everything was still there, with the exception of Nünüke's six-gram wedding ring, which she had swapped for eight kilograms of flour at a moment of dire need during the weeks after the siege.

I've just remembered a significant detail: In Losonc a wall poster listing the cinemas and screenings that Jews were allowed to attend was first displayed on the day Jews were forced into the cattle cars that were to deport them. The wealthy Jews had been so badly beaten that they were unable to walk to the trucks and had to be conveyed to the station by their fellow Jews on wheelbarrows, many of them dying. When I hear this, I turn our room on the Miksa Street side into a slum so that no gendarme gets the idea that the Kassais are hiding valuables and to beat us until we hand them over. I spread ragged covers on the tables and make everything disappear from the apartment that might suggest that we ever knew better days.

I forgot to mention something else that is typical of these times. My cousin Béla joins up in Jászberény. There he claims to have some heart weakness and is sent back to Budapest. In Budapest he is found to be fit and sent back to Jászberény. By this time the deportations in the provinces are going strong. When Béla gets back to Jászberény, the men he was joining up with the first time have already been taken away to the notorious camp in Bor (you probably know what happened to most of these). All this takes place in mid-June. The patients declared fit present themselves in Jászberény, the commander gives them leave until July 10 and sends them back to Budapest. These young men know what this means and beg to be allowed to stay with the company until the end of their furlough, but the commander declares that he is not a Jew-hiding institution and sends them home, although he believes that they would be incredibly lucky if they actually get there.

He says this openly and talks about the July 10 return with a skeptical smile. Béla sets out for home but reckons the gendarmes are obviously waiting for Jews on the Hatvan railway line (as the *Drehkopf*[4] of a gendarme says). Accordingly, he follows a diversion in the direction of Szentmártonkáta and is proven right because at Hatvan the forced labourers are taken off the train, waved into the ghetto and

4 German: literally, knobhead; used by Margit as an insult meaning something like "idiot."

a little while later deported with the rest of the Jewish population. These people all ended up in Auschwitz. And exactly the same thing happened to Imre Bolgár.

Béla gets home and starts to plan his subsequent wanderings, but hiding is not the right word for that because what he has done is unique. On June 17, it is finally decided that the Nádas Villa cannot be declared a starred house and they have to move out before the twenty-fifth. On June 18, Aunt Böske commits suicide and is buried on the twenty-second. From the twenty-second to the twenty-fifth, Béla liquidates the Villa with minimal help from Irén and us. On July 9, he takes his leave from everybody, saying that he is going back to Jászberény to rejoin his company. In full forced labourer's outfit, he leaves home, calls at Irén's apartment where he changes into civilian clothes, then crosses the Danube with his luggage to Buda, where he rents an elegant room at number 10/c Hattyú Street as a sub-tenant USING HIS OWN NAME AND WITH HIS OWN DOCUMENTS and lives there in the lap of luxury.

I repeat, he lives under his own name right up to the end of the siege, when Hattyú Street, in its entirety, is suddenly flattened by the explosion of a nearby ammunition dump. The only building left intact is number 12 (right beside 10/c), which is still under construction. Béla and his family had moved into its shelter — God knows why — quite a while ago. When building number 10/c collapsed, there were nine people staying in its shelter, out of which only one was still alive when Béla burrowed through the rubble on his belly, which took him twenty hours of miserable work, and dragged that person out. I don't like to skip ahead in the chronological order, but I want to mention now that Béla survives many nasty things unscathed. He evades all attempts at catching him by possessing innumerable forged IDs to dodge the marching orders. When the police, ignoring any orders, storm from building to building, apartment to apartment, or (in the last weeks of the siege) cellar to cellar, rounding men up to dig trenches, he pretends to be running upstairs to get his documents, climbs down into the yard of the neighbouring building and disappears from there. He is twice arrested and twice released by the GPU.[5] But this Béla, who has cleared away so many ruins, who has dug out so many human beings, both alive and (more) dead, I say, this Béla finally ran out of luck while he was digging a grave with several of his comrades in a yard one Saturday before Easter. As they were digging he picked up a small object shaped like a sugarloaf and painted red. He examined it from all sides, shook it thoroughly and threw it away. At this point the small object, which was later recognized as some kind of signalling device, exploded, and our Béla is still lying in the Siesta Sanatorium heavily wounded, with a million tiny splinters in his body, losing a lot of blood and chewed by bedbugs. It looks unlikely that his leg can be saved and will probably have to be amputated from the knee down. And in the midst of all this, Irén is very close to the joys of motherhood and they are broke.

The next chapter will be about my short career as a photographer's apprentice:

In September the kindergarten gradually came to an end of its own accord. The weather was turning too chilly to play in the garden, and in the crammed apartments there was no room for a kindergarten. At that time, I heard from many different people that there was great demand for photographers' assistants due to the mass call-ups to the army.

I offered my services several times to an Arrow Cross photographer on Rákóczi Street, who was photographer-in-residence on a repulsive publication called *Harc*[6] but who said he was nevertheless

---

5 The abbreviation for the fomer political police in Soviet Russia. By this time, the Soviet NKVD had succeeded this body.

6 *Harc*, meaning "fight," was an antisemitic periodical. The masthead read: "The official magazine of the Hungarian Institute for Researching the Jewish Problem."

prepared to employ me, star and all, from a quarter past eleven until a quarter to five daily. The deal fell through because on three or four occasions when I called on this photographer he was out, and meanwhile another photographer had heard from one of Cini's apprentices that I was looking for a job and sent a message to my apartment urging me to present myself at his studio immediately because there was lots of work. That was how I found myself at the Schweiger establishment in Egyetem Square, which doubled as a photographer's studio and a shop selling specialist photographic equipment. Naturally, the sales section was closed and sealed according to an earlier order providing for the confiscation of the stocks of Jewish shops. The superbly equipped studio behind the shop displayed magnificent cameras, reflectors, aluminium foils and modern film cassettes: everything most practical, up to date and in perfect condition. A wooden staircase led to the upper part (which I can't really call a storey) where there was an equally well-equipped lab with drying machines, cutting machines, touch-up fluid containers, giant tanks and the photocopier that unfortunately brought the wife of my boss with it. Now listen. During the first couple days everything went beautifully before I met my boss's wife, who hadn't been around because she happened to be ill. My boss, Mr. Schweiger, is an extraordinarily charming, intelligent, refined gentleman with whom I got on very well from the start. We first agreed to a ten-day trial period. I said that I could cope with an assistant's work although I wished to be contracted at the level of an apprentice. As I said, the first two days everything went well, but on the third day the boss's wife appeared. She had specialized in photocopying — which was a hot potato at the time, and we could hardly keep up with the amount of work. She didn't know anything about photography but had something aggressive to say about everything and argued from morning until night with the staff or with her husband or with the customers As a result, I began to make lots of mistakes the moment she appeared. During the ten days of probation, I achieved the following: I dropped and smashed a glass plate, which carried a reproduction that had at last turned out well after many attempts. I copied a whole day's material too dark, so that it had to be thrown away and redone the following day. Redoing it was worse than throwing away because we mostly manufactured pictures for IDs, which were all urgent. Then I underdeveloped eight shots that turned out so thin my boss actually tore out his hair (I had never before seen such a thing; it had only been a saying until then). In the lab, the rubber pipe slipped out of my hand and I spilled water on all the cassettes and the almost dry urgent negatives, and as we were preparing the ornamental picture of the little girl in the ball dress I put the film into the cassette upside down.

Nevertheless, at the end of the ten days of probation I was hired with a starting wage of fifty pengős a week (which was very high pay for an apprentice in those days). I owed this high wage to the fact that my boss was absent from the studio for long periods of the day, which he spent running from one government office to the next chasing after exemptions by the regent. In addition, the young girl who had been working there for eighteen months also as an apprentice had suddenly fallen ill, so the entire studio was left for me to look after. I took and processed pictures on my own.

My boss made no secret of how moved he was by my pictures, and we went to the craftsmen's corporation to draw up the apprenticeship agreement. The officials required that I produce a statement from the medical officer that I am physically fit for the occupation in question. But such certificates were only available from the offices of the eleventh district after showing a revaccination certificate. As I didn't have such a certificate, I would have to be revaccinated. I was prepared to undergo even that, but then Szálasi arrived and put a stop to the whole affair. This photographic business turned out to be very good for me. I learned a lot and I enjoyed all the activity there. I often had to "serve the clients" in the store, which meant handing them the photocopies of documents. Working there, I met many people I knew, and all our doctors put in an appearance: Klauber, Zádor, Sebestyén. With Zádor I had a very pleasant conversation. I had finished his photocopies well before the deadline. He asked about you. He was very friendly, and I once went to see him in their shared apartment in Újlipótváros, but only the wife was at home.

Speaking of exemptions by the regent, I'm not sure whether you know what that was. The regent was entitled to release certain "meritorious personalities" from the obligation to wear the yellow star and from some additional stipulations. The application had to be submitted to the Cabinet Office and apparently any kind of specious "merit" was accepted as a ground for exemption so long as the applicant was supported by the right influential person. Now, one Sunday morning when I was busy exterminating lice on Miksa Street (this was my occupation every Sunday morning and often every Sunday afternoon: I scraped out and dismantled the room facing Miksa Street down to its atoms, sprayed, fumigated, daubed and traced every crack with the finest of knitting needles, wearing the appropriate clothing), Reverend Mihály Hőgye, a protestant reverend whom I had met in the street a few weeks ago and who had emphatically advised me, as we exchanged addresses, to store a week's food and several days' water since the population might well have to spend two weeks in the cellar (!!!!), appeared on Miksa Street. I was obliged to receive him in the lobby, which was slightly awkward because our roommate, Mrs. Bözsike Spanyol, was constantly running in and out of there in her underwear.

I agreed with Hőgye that I should submit an application in your name (I forget what merits you were supposed to have, but Hőgye and I invented something between us) and a separate one in Nünüke's name, while Hőgye himself would make sure that we received the exemption out of turn and at record speed. You also have a claim through your mother and I through Nünüke and my father. A further step would have been bringing you back from Transylvania. We expected the matter to be closed by October 16, *nebbich.*[7] It wasn't until after liberation that I realized how lucky we had been not to get the exemption. When the Arrow Cross went on the rampage they had lists of the "exempt" in their hands.

The exemptions remind me that I also fell for the mass hysteria that overwhelmed the Jews of Budapest in the middle of June. I was running around after a Swedish *Schutzpass* without any conviction, only because everybody did the same. I wasted long mornings on Gellért Hill in the heat of high summer, hanging around in the garden of the Swedish embassy, paying sixty pengős and having photos taken with no result whatsoever. I can say that I hated the whole affair with the *Schutzpässe* and didn't believe in it for a minute, particularly since by that time the Swedish embassy looked deceptively like the Jewish Council's housing office on Síp Street or like the tax office of the congregation of Buda, full of loud-mouthed, rude, inefficient and corrupt Budapest Jews. In Budapest, you could always find a bunch of opportunists who thought it most important to suck up to a person in some superior position who would protect you. If you noticed a face in the Jewish Council's housing office in May or June, you will probably recognize it later "working" in the Swedish *Schutzpass* office, or you might come across it in the office of the Association of the Christian Jews of Hungary, then at the International Red Cross, and if you were still interested, in the offices of the British or American Military Missions.

Strangely enough, when Cini got the Swedish letter of protection and Lili Havas the certificate of exemption, I had a strong feeling that my fate did not depend on whether I was protected or exempt and was even more convinced that I would breeze through the whole affair without such things. There was no reason why I should feel that way. I was trying to satisfy my conscience that I was doing what

---

7 Yiddish: alas or it's a pity (often spelled *nebekh*).

I could — not only fighting for Swiss assistance — when I heard a false report based on a misunderstanding claiming that your unit had been brought back here, to Ráckeve, and I was afraid that you would be taken out of the country and in the worst case sent west like the rest of the forced labour companies.

At that time everybody was still convinced that those who had a protective letter would not be deported. (My cousin-in-law in Bős, Jóska, is another victim of this error because although I obtained a Swedish Red Cross letter of protection for him with the help of the Éliáses, the poor young man is missing.) At a critical moment a Swiss *Schutzbrief* for the whole Kassai family was delivered to Miksa Street by the postal service, but I had disappeared far from there by then. Your brother Laci managed to organize a Swedish passport for your mother at some point in the autumn as a result of my application in July, and it was thanks to this that we were able to place Gizella in the Swedish hospital, which in the difficult months could be such an El Dorado for elderly people. I want to stress here that in the early days of January the residents of numerous Swedish and Swiss "protected" houses were executed by the Arrow Cross and most of the others herded into the ghetto (where, e.g., the Wiener and Laci Winter families almost starved). But even those who were neither executed nor forced into ghettos (e.g., the Hercegs, who were under Portuguese protection) had an extremely difficult time because they had to live in incredibly cramped conditions for months and because the majority of "protected" houses were on the Danube embankment on the Pest side and therefore most exposed to the siege.

I have not yet written about the conversion mass fever, which began to assume serious proportions when the church offices started to list the individuals who had converted by a specific point in time. That specific point in time was August 1, 1941 (God knows why), and I, as you know, held my own head and at the same time the head of a practice pipi under the baptismal water on August 31, 1941. I wrote to you about this listing business at the time and even remember getting a letter from you telling me off — something like "Now, now, Kiskas." Of course you were right, since apart from the fact that to this day nobody knows what they wanted to achieve by these lists, many people we know are resting in peace at the bottom of the Danube with bullets through their throats even though they converted in good time. Nevertheless, I appeared for listing purposes in the office in Deák Square, where people were pushing and shoving people, or perhaps I should say Jews were pushing and shoving Jews to get through doors bearing notices forbidding them from trying to do so until they had settled their tax affairs. Having read this, I panicked. I pushed myself forward, shoving my way into the tax office to pay both my and your tax, including arrears and getting rid of a tidy sum in the process. (I still suspect that the purpose of the entire listing affair was to jolt converts owing tax into paying.) After a long wait, I then pushed and shoved my way to the presence of the Reverend (whose name I have forgotten) and explained to him that I was baptized a few weeks after the crucial date but my husband was born a Lutheran and educated in religious schools. I also showed him our certificate of a church wedding, which impressed him greatly (say what you like, but you are the cleverest Pipi in the world). I could see that he wanted to help but didn't know how. He finally said that there was nothing he could do for me, although he told me to register you at Fasor Alley[8] even though members of the labour service were not required to be registered. This was done as recommended.

The conversion fever grew into a mass madness when the Association of the Christian Jews of Hungary was founded and issued identity cards to its members. (You got one too.) Lili Havas joined at once and works in an office. I also applied because that kind of work comes with many advantages, but thank God I was rejected and able to keep my time free to work as a photographer's apprentice.

---

8 Fasor Alley (Városligeti fasor today and Vilma királynő fasor in Margit's time) refers to the offices of the Protestant Church.

Around this time the priests of various denominations are beginning to preach veiled encouragements from the pulpits of their churches, clearly under papal pressure. Hőgye tells me that Bishop Ravasz, for one, is fighting hard for the lives of Budapest's Jews and resists the deportations arm in arm with Serédi.[9] I no longer believe in deportation but although I feel better in general and watch the things to come with a kind of cheerful indifference I do all I can to persuade my parents to convert. Initially they refuse to listen — my father categorically, but Nünüke also. It takes a hint in a newspaper that Christian Jews and Jewish Christians cannot possibly live together in the same apartment to make the parents nervous and toe the line, father still reluctantly but not willing to leave the splendid dramatic opportunities unexplored.

The groups of would-be converts are formed according to the buildings they live in, and the courses are held in the nearest schools. Nünüke is diligent, but father often ditches out on the lessons. I join the lesson once and sit between the two of them (there are about two hundred people in the group). They take turns falling asleep, and the one awake at any time will make fun of the other. I am having a whale of a time as a strict instructor subjects a row of District VII types to relentless questioning: Mrs. Kohn, Mrs. Blum, the grocer, the great industrialist, the grandfathers, the grandmothers. In addition, the whole conversion procedure has been made more rigorous. It takes about three months. It is difficult to register for the courses, which has to be done weeks in advance, and there is a strict exam at the end. Nünü and father were due to take the exam on October 20. They zealously studied the catechism. I would have liked it if they had turned to our religion, or at least to the Reformed Church, but the

---

9 László Ravasz (1882–1975) was a bishop of the Hungarian Reformed Church who spoke out against the Nazis' anti-Jewish measures during the German occupation of Hungary, causing him to be placed under house arrest. Jusztinián György Serédi (1884–1945) was a cardinal of the Roman Catholic Church who also condemned the deportation of Hungarian Jews.

Éliáses flatly refused, as did our people. The process had been made much more difficult and lengthier than it is with the Catholics. Lili Havas and her crowd managed to convert without studying and what is more even without any significant financial sacrifice. In September, Lili is rushing around with a huge gold cross hanging around her neck. By the way, this is often done by many who wear a Lutheran star. I am not prepared to do that because I have noticed that such ornaments are only worn by converted Jewish women.

The chapter called Miksa Street is about to end. I have only one or two trifles to add about starred houses in general.

When people moved into shared accommodations, most chose to live with friends or relatives, although experience proved that sharing with strangers was the best option. There were huge fights in every apartment, less so in the early phase of constant nervous tension and panic but much more toward the end of the summer when even the pessimists only talked sporadically and languidly about deportation.

The central issue of most fights was BUGS with special reference to who had brought them in and who had them already. This question was the constant topic of passionate debates between original residents and later arrivals. To us, the Kassai family in the Lehner apartment, there seemed to be nothing controversial about this: we had brought some and there were also a fair amount already present, as shown by the numerous spots on the wall, but either way we would have had more than enough material to fall out over. For example, when I was in the middle of a grand Sunday cleaning and bug-killing session one of the daughters of the house came in to watch, as I put it, and to learn, as she put it. I managed by a heroic effort to stop myself saying: "It's a pity you didn't learn five or six years ago. Who knows how many fewer bugs we'd have now." But I didn't say anything either when it was my turn to spring clean the kitchen and the daughters of the house were shocked to find that I didn't polish the hot-water heater that had been out of action for months and sandpapering it would have been the only way to clean it. I quite liked them otherwise, and there were never any serious problems between us. They were decent, honest people. In addition, they were very religious and kept a strictly kosher diet, so that we had to work at completely separate kitchen tables, but this didn't cause any friction either. I easily got used to cleaning toilets after complete strangers once a week without being disgusted. In fact, I have since managed to rid myself almost completely of the handicap of disgust.

A significant part in the fights was played by housework, and the mutual accusations of unfairness could be overheard by the neighbours: "You're sitting on your bottom all day while I'm working myself to death." In almost every apartment there were such scenes; brothers and sisters, sisters-in-law and friends were quarrelling and hating each other. In our apartment all hell broke loose when a couple related to the Lehners moved in. The man was bácsi Lehner's young brother, and the woman was half-divorced and had lived with him for years. She was pretty but stupid and vulgar. She hated bácsi Lehner's daughter, whom she constantly provoked. The two women came to blows more than once (which was not unknown in the other houses either) so that Nünüke had to separate them.

One early morning I am woken by Bözsike (as the vulgar beauty was called) wrenching our door open, appearing in our room, of course without knocking and with her hair in disarray and her emotions stirred up, roaring "just because I'm honest and don't gossip about the Kassais behind their backs like Erzsi..." Bang goes the door. Then it opens again and Erzsi appears with her hair in disarray, pale and screeching with excitement: "The Kassais know I don't say anything bad about anyone behind their backs!" Whoosh goes the door! I am strongly reminded of a cuckoo clock and wonder how soon the door will open again for somebody else to coo us their story.

Nünü and I look at each other. We don't understand a word of the whole business, me even less than Nünü because I'm still half asleep, so we think it best to burst into a demented silent laughter. But we can already hear the squealing from outside, and Nünüke runs out quickly to get the two women out of each other's hair.

It isn't easy to live in peace with Bözsike, but we even manage that. Bözsike is proud of how well she gets on "with that sweet old Mrs. Kassai," and it is pathetic how convinced she is that this is exclusively her, Bözsike's, achievement. I can't stop repeating what kinds of things we have to swallow without a word for the sake of domestic peace. We come up late from the cellar after a long air raid and we rush lunch to save part of the afternoon we have that's cut short for the Jews. Nünü puts our lunch to cook on one of the three flames of the gas cooker. On the other two flames the Lehners' and Bözsike's lunches are bubbling. Nünüke goes into the bedroom, thinking that she has finished her work and our lunch is cooking. When she comes out again, she is surprised to find that our lunch has been taken off the fire and replaced with Bözsike's basin of water, because Bözsike had been prevented from washing by the air raid and of course her wash is more urgent than our lunch. Nünüke and I agree between us that no housewife in the world would put up with such a thing in silence, but we also agree that we would rather have lunch at five o'clock in the afternoon than annoy Bözsike.

Another thing I don't much like is bácsi Lehner combing his moistened hair in the kitchen every morning, splashing the water from his hair in a wide arc straight into my breakfast, but I just cover everything somewhat demonstratively without saying a word, although he never notices my demonstration and goes on splashing. I don't even ask him why he can't do the same thing in the bathroom, which was actually invented for that purpose. The apartment contains a beautiful bathroom, which is squeaky clean but which the Lehners use mainly as an object for cleaning because they only take a bath for Shabbos. There are problems with the ancient and worn water taps, and when someone overstrains the damaged tap the water keeps running. At such times there is a great *Kreuzverhör*,[10] with searches for evidence,

10 German: cross-examination.

crafty cross questioning, and thrilling face-to-face "who damaged the tap" confrontations. Bözsike wants to discover who "broke" the tap because she is "not so stupid as to pay for others," while I explain to bácsi Lehner in front of the plenary meeting that I will be responsible for any damage occurring in the apartment that cannot be attributed to any specific person and which does not exceed ten pengős to repair, because I am tired of listening to the arguments. This shames Bözsi's "husband" to commit himself up to 50 per cent in place of his "wife," and so we manage to avoid such arguments to some extent.

I enjoy some respect in the building — although we clearly have no money — perhaps thanks to the kindergarten or to the fact that I don't make friends beyond always being friendly toward everybody. One exception is a young married woman I regularly visit on the floor below mine. She is from Vienna, speaks bad Hungarian and like all the women in the block has a husband in the forced labour service. She has an extremely sweet little girl of one and a half, and I get on well with her because she is not pleasant, but sharp, rigorous and abrasive, but still the most intelligent woman on the premises — and also the most orderly. She is the landlady of my four-year-old friend Péter Boczán, whose mother, Klári Bárdos by her maiden name, knows you well. She says that she was your colleague for a short time in a lawyer's office where you worked as a clerk. I have become very fond of this small family, although, if I think about it, it's not really so small: there is the husband, a textile mechanic called Földes (of course currently a forced labourer somewhere in hell), his wife, Manci, and two charming little boys, naturally called Péter and Tamás (the countless Péters, Jutkas, Tamáses and Zsuzsis of the Jewish houses were an agreeable change from the Csabas, Leventes, Attilas, Emeses, Emőkes and Ildikós of Kecske Street). But even the grandparents — bácsi Petschauer, a cobbler, and his wife — are very nice. The only reason why I haven't become closer with Manci Földes is that she is too domesticated and motherly to talk to about anything else. But I still drop in on them because I am very interested to know how they are getting on. The husband has disappeared after being taken away west. In the kindergarten, the younger boy, Tomi, was my favourite, or let us say one of my favourites.

Another typical little episode from the life of the building on Miksa Street. The trash has been piling up for days in the corner of the passage at the rear staircase close to our kitchen window. Since we haven't had a custodian for some weeks, the tenants on the third floor expect the superintendent to take it away, as has been the custom until now. But the superintendent is a big shot who doesn't relish carrying garbage and because the biggest garbage heap is on our floor he climbs up to our window and delivers a rant about how terrible it is to have such inconsiderate tenants, who could really take away their own trash when they saw that his wife was ill and it was impossible to get a custodian. Whereupon the often-mentioned Bözsike of the Lehner apartment positions herself in the passage and with her hands on her hips to inform the superintendent in a sonorous voice that "we were neither born nor brought up to carry trash" (*ipsissima verba*[11]). The superintendent turns on his heels without saying a word to Bözsike and departs. The garbage is finally taken away by my father, who has had enough of the smell and the argument. Bözsike is so proud of her speech that she tells everybody how well she told off the superintendent.

An episode with the yellow star in the street before October 15:

Somewhere in the neighbourhood of Miksa Street, I believe on Nagyatádi Szabó Street, there is a school that is currently a German barracks. It seems that by some chance I must have always walked past this school without a star because, passing for once with the star, I make a little jump when a German soldier marching up and down with a bayonet and a fierce expression on his face (the snotty little

---

11 Latin: the very words, her exact words.

puppy) orders me to get off the pavement with a silent but unmistakable motion of his hand.

I have heard of such a thing from others, including my father, but this is the first time it happens to me. At first I don't understand what's happening because I was deep in thought and can see other people walking on the same pavement without any concerns, but then it dawns on me that on this day of all days I am wearing the star. I suddenly find myself laughing in the face of the soldier, thinking how funny it is that by now the British and American troops have reached Paris. I speculate that perhaps they should also have stood such grim snotty kids with bayonets along the Channel to order the British soldiers they didn't like to get off the continent. I am somewhat scared by my own laughter because the boy doesn't understand and is clearly angry, but then he turns around scornfully and continues his march.

Another street episode: On Dohány Street a proletarian-looking, slightly inebriated man is making loud remarks about the Jews coming near him. I walk a few steps behind him and when he turns and sees me he says in a tone that is both mocking and threatening: "What a lovely streamlined star the young lady has." I take one corner of the star between two fingers and with a sweet smile offer it to the man: "Do you want it? I'll give it to you if you fancy it so much." The man loses the plot, mumbles something about not needing a star because thank God he is not a Jew, and swiftly takes to his heels.

I should add that apart from the above I have only been abused like that in the street once, and that time by a woman. I was standing with Gizella on a street downtown when a woman who looked like a seamstress walked past us, turned back and shouted: "It's terrible that there are still so many Jews in Budapest."

And here I have to write about József Kromesch, the Swabian master joiner from Csillaghegy, whose whole story is so incredible that a separate fairy tale should be written about him.

Perhaps you remember him: he was the man in charge of the boat house that my little brother, Dini, used to row from, and they had met in Russia. Of course, Kromesch was a regular soldier, and it was through him that Dénes sent us the message that he was well, but since we weren't allowed to write to him we weren't getting any signs of life from him. When Kromesch got home he called on us. He wouldn't accept any present but asked if he could help us and offered to do any joinery work free of charge.

When the "starfestation" set in, Kromesch looked for us on Kecske Street, where he was told we had moved but was given a wrong address. Therefore, he went to Falk Miksa Street in vain, then back to Kecske Street, where he was finally given the right address, but he still came back looking for us several times in vain because on Sunday we weren't at home. After four or five attempts, he finally managed to locate us and ask if there was anything we needed or that he could do for us.

I wrote all this down in such detail because many people we know, who moved more freely without the star than we could wearing it, didn't make one tenth of the effort to ask us the same questions, although it would only have cost them a phone call. This man travelled from Csillaghegy into the city fifty times by suburban train, each time paying a fare even though he wasn't rich. We agreed that he would take Dénes's bicycle to Csillaghegy, dismantle it and hide the pieces in the attic. And that was what we did.

We didn't hear from him again until about the end of June, when we received a postcard asking me to meet him in the street to talk about an important and urgent matter. The important and urgent matter was that he offered to me, free of charge, all his wife's documents, as well as food coupons, shopping booklet, etc., so that I could flee. He took one of my photos to the local village hall to be provided with blank rubber stamps certifying his wife's personal details under my name.

And he was doing all this because he had watched the Jews of Csillaghegy being herded into the cattle cars and immediately thought of us. He decided that if he couldn't help the three of us, he would at least save me. When I asked him what his wife would do without any food coupons, he told me not to worry and he would take care of it. I thanked him very warmly, saying that I might come back to the question but that for the time being I would not escape because I wouldn't abandon my parents. He said that the papers were ready and as soon as I sent him a message that I had made up my mind he would come at once to fetch me.

I worried for days that I might have let my last chance go. About that time Laci Belcsák happened to be in Budapest. Early one morning he turns up on Miksa Street with a marvellous food parcel and asks straight out if we need any money. I say no thank you (I was still getting my wages and father his pension), and he leaves. But next morning he is back. He has been thinking and had come to the conclusion that the reason I had refused his offer was that I find it embarrassing to accept money. But he has decided to leave some with me, whether I agree or not. Now I accept a thousand pengős, at that time still a lot of money, without any hesitation, all the more so because Kromesch's offer has come between Laci's two, and it occurs to me that if I do decide to flee the money would come in handy.

By now we have reached the last stage of the deportations (although of course we didn't know that it was the last). The people loaded into the cattle cars are not only the Jews of Greater Budapest (Újpest, Kispest, Csillaghegy, Kelenföld, etc.) but all Jewish workers, male and female, serving the war industries around Budapest.

Now let us stop for a moment.

The year that has passed was characterized by the Jewish intellectuals' desperate search for ways to survive the disaster. There was a phase when they were chasing a Swedish, Swiss, Papal or Portuguese *Schutzpass*, fanatically believing and trying to make others believe that such a document was the one and only instrument that could save their lives. Then the rumour spread that the workers in any industry of importance to the Hungarian war effort would not be taken out of the country. Whereupon the Jews of Budapest — men and women alike — stormed the relevant premises and would have sold their father or mother for a job in any one of those strategically significant factories. Of course, it took no time for a number of agents to appear and earn tidy sums for "placing" Jews in such positions. The whole Zinner photographic studio[12] became military workers, and Lilus too "found herself a position" in a factory in Rákospalota. The only thing that saved me from such a fate was the Spielberger vein. The Jewish workers in the war industry were living in their factories, and you can imagine what the hygienic conditions were, bearing in mind that there could be no question of coming to work from home because Jews had long since been forbidden to travel on the local suburban railway. Cini was lucky not to have to live in her factory because it was in the city, and Lilus happened to be ill at the critical time. They were saved by lucky coincidences, but Stefka Mándy,[13] who worked in Csepel, Feri Lendvai (Laci Lévai's friend and an electrical engineer) and many other people we know have unfortunately disappeared. At that time, everybody still disapproved of me for not running after such solutions. Later it became fashionable to get a job with the Association of the Christian Jews. In hindsight, this proved to be less a matter of survival, and looking at it with my eyes of today or even yesterday I don't think it very important. Generally, I was already beginning to see that there was no point in jockeying for position and wondering what would be good or bad to do, because everything always turns out to be completely different from one minute to the next than anyone would have expected. If I were not a descendant of a notoriously fatalist family, I would have had to learn to become one now.

12 Erzsébet (Cini) Zinner (1909–1977) was a well-known photographer and close friend of Margit.

13 Stefánia Mándy (1918–2001), a poet and art historian, survived Auschwitz.

On and Around October 15

This is how it started:

On Sunday, as is my habit, I am giving the apartment a big clean. As I shake out the duster I happen to glance through the window and see something strange. In front of the Metropol Hotel on Miksa Street a German officer is giving orders to some German soldiers carrying bayonets, who then spread out and sidle singly toward us, that is, toward the corner of Dohány Street (we are in a corner building that pays its taxes under the title of "55 Dohány Street" and appears under the same title in the list of starred houses, although its gate carries the inscription "11 Miksa Street." Our yard is the twin of a yard belonging to the huge block of apartments numbered fifty-seven. I spell all this out in such detail because it will become important later).

The German soldiers take up positions facing the gates and next to all street corners on the opposite pavement. I go out to the kitchen to report to Nünüke and the others, naturally expecting the worst. The kitchen window opens onto the passage, where all the residents have gathered, talking at the same time and falling around each other's necks, laughing and crying and shouting from one building to the next. We learn from the shouting what has happened: apparently the war is over. Regent Horthy has addressed a statement to the people through the press and the radio to the effect that "er war eigentlich immer dagegen."[1] Whatever happened had happened exclusively under German pressure, but now Hungary is asking for a separate peace or armistice (as Romania had done, with success, about a week ago). I am also infected by the collective insanity for a moment, but then I remember the German soldiers with the bayonets in front of the gates and suspect that we are not going to have such an easy ride.

What went before: About a week ago a hand grenade had exploded in the state school on Wesselényi Street, where German soldiers had been stationed from the first moment, whereupon all the residents of the starred house opposite were indiscriminately rounded up and transported to an unknown destination. This event caused great concern in our neighbourhood.

About the same time some kind of census took place in the country, and Béla had to disappear from the apartment on Hattyú Street before somebody recognized him as a deserter. He left the apartment under the pretext of having to travel out to the countryside on official business, where he would be included in the census, but of course he stayed in Budapest, where Irén and another person took turns hiding him. On Saturday, October 14, he came to us for dinner, and we expected him to stay the night. We were all very nervous because people living in Jewish households could always expect a visit by the forces of law and order, which end in abuse and violence.

We were sitting at the dinner table when — BANG — there was an enormous explosion in the immediate neighbourhood, followed by the sound of falling roof tiles and shards of glass. Then, total silence. I had no idea what was happening, but I quickly hustled Béla out of the apartment and told him to get away from the building, because at best there would be a raid. Leaning out of the window, I realized from the shouting not only that something had been blown up in the Metropol Hotel but also that this "was once again done by

1 German: He had actually always been against it.

the dirty Jews; why don't they just kill them, what are they waiting for?" Because what such a mass of Jews is able to produce jointly in the way of fright is not something that I can describe.

On that day we were prepared for some serious measure to be taken toward our extermination, e.g., deportation or similar, but nothing happened. (The other people in the building are watching the Kassais with a little suspicion and hostility because it's clear that in comparison with the other residents we are not at all frightened.)

The next day we heard that some German soldiers had dropped something that they were carrying and that was what had blown up.

I continue on October 15: People are dementedly celebrating the news about the armistice, wildly tearing the star from their clothes, and somebody runs down to the gate to remove the prescribed board with the overdeveloped yellow star.

By now the superintendent is not our friend Káldy but a man called Ökrös, who is also well meaning but a coward and not a bolshie[2] as the Káldys were.

The street is silent. The German soldiers are standing poker-faced in front of the gates, and so far it's only forbidden to enter through the gates, though coming out through them is still permitted. But at two o'clock in the afternoon they are locked, and now there is neither in nor out allowed. It's interesting that so far this is the case in the side streets alone, as we hear from people shouting across to us. The residents leaving that building suspect there is something fishy about the armistice. They climb over to the yard of the building on Dohány Street and escape through the Dohány Street gate. Likewise our fellow residents, the Lehners. We, the Kassais, decide between us that we have neither anywhere to escape to nor any real intention of escaping, because our nature is such that we don't seriously believe

---

2 Slang term for Bolshevik, referring to communists, from the name of the faction that became the Russian Communist Party.

anything bad could happen to us. That lack of imagination seems to be a family idiosyncrasy.

So there are only four of us left in the Lehner apartment: the Kassais and Miklós Katz, who had escaped from hard labour service when the Russians dispersed his company in mid-September in Transylvania. He then came to Budapest with regular release documents, but rather than reporting to the military authorities, he has been hiding with the Lehners ever since. He is a simple, wily, provincial Jewish youth, but brave, good-humoured and by no means an unpleasant roommate. We have been feeding him since the Lehners disappeared. The Lehners have a small piece of land somewhere along the outer Stefánia Road with a small woodshed in which they are hiding. There is no bed and they can only sit up in it. They bring with them food and water for a few days. This is something that they tell only us, and we have to tell everybody else that we don't know what happened to them.

What makes things complicated is that Erzsi Lehner was the apartment supervisor in our apartment and she would have had to report all such disappearances to the house commander, but since she has herself disappeared, nobody reports anything to anyone. (According to regulations, in every Jewish apartment there had to be a supervisor who was personally responsible not only for the apartment from the point of view of health but for each individual resident. The supervisor has to report daily at five o'clock in the afternoon that all the residents of the apartment have come home on time and none are missing. They really look after us like some treasures.)

In the afternoon the automatic weapons open the proceedings from the Grand Boulevard. Frightened people run from the shooting into the side streets. Nobody knows what is really happening. I hope in secret that there will be some serious movement, because I have long heard whispers that in the Hungarian leadership there is significant opposition to Germanophilia.

The shooting lasts all afternoon. The streets are restless, people are running, trucks speeding with teenage boys in civilian clothes and guns at the ready. The affair may well be called a little *unheimlich*.[3] I'm in an "I SAY, WHAT'S GOING TO HAPPEN HERE?" mood. I'm not afraid, only very, very excited. My stomach climbs up and down, as it will do whenever I catch the "whiff of freedom," as I have dubbed an ambiguous emotional state in which every more than average noise from a weapon awakens new hopes in us and whenever the street grows silent we look at each other in horror.

By the evening it is known that Szálasi has seized power and made a speech on the radio. Panic breaks out in our building. I don't despair because the Russians are already very near, and on the front line the Hungarian divisions will immediately surrender. The whole circus will only last a few more minutes.

I hear that local people at the battle line on Dohány Street watched the residents of the Jewish house on the opposite side being dragged away and the Arrow Cross looting their abandoned apartments, while armed louts pushed around Jewish men, women and children, their hands held high as they are loaded onto trucks or into forced marches. I don't want to believe this. It's the beginning of overt mass deportation,[4] looting and beating. Several days later we hear that the Arrow Cross "Brothers" had been granted forty-eight hours of unimpeded robbery, during which many of our friends lost everything they had. We are no longer allowed to step out into the streets, but this would not be advisable in any case. It is forbidden to look out of

---

3 German: ominous, unsettling.

4 Although Margit refers here to the beginning of the deportations of Jews in the city of Budapest, the most devastating phase of the Holocaust in Hungary had occurred earlier, especially between mid-May and early July 1944, when the majority of Jews outside the city, about 437,000 people, were deported, nearly all of them to Auschwitz-Birkenau, where most were murdered.

the window, and therefore we leave the blinds down, and that way we can push the curtain out a little to see what is happening in the street.

Here I must once more talk about Nünü. In the middle of the greatest street shootout, when every self-respecting old woman crawls under her bed in fear, I have to pull her back from the window because she is determined to see what is going on.

In the evening, we don't undress, because in the whole neighbourhood the residents of Jewish houses are being dragged away, although we hear from time to time that they were brought back unharmed and that the whole rigmarole had only taken place so that the Arrow Cross could loot the apartments undisturbed. But those who had been taken away like that could certainly expect a thorough beating. I hadn't been beaten for a long time and I didn't remember what it was like. I would probably have borne it quite well, but I wouldn't have liked to see the old people beaten. Nor did I believe they would have liked to see me beaten, and so I tried to think of some tricks to avoid it, but basically I still couldn't imagine that something like this would really happen to the Kassais. I eventually came up with the following plan: our escape would begin in the Lehners' maid's room, which could be reached by way of the kitchen or directly through a door set in the same wall as the kitchen door. A person entering the kitchen might easily overlook the second door, because there was a water pipe between the two doors and above them a hot-water heater, and because I had made the semi-dark space even darker by fixing a second shade to the kitchen light hanging from the centre of the ceiling. The window of the maid's room opened onto the *Lichthof*,[5] as did that of the toilet. In the maid's room stood a wardrobe painted white like the door frame, and its door opened into the kitchen. I would

---

5 German: literally, lightwell; refers here to air shafts, a narrow vertical space that provides natural light and ventilation to the inner-facing rooms of an apartment complex.

lock Nünü and my father in the maid's room from outside, with some food and water, a candle, matches, a chamber pot, blankets and some of our most precious other items, and push the wardrobe in front of the door, which would be completely invisible from outside (I even put some suitcases on top of the wardrobe). Then, with the help of an ironing board laid across the *Lichthof*, I would clamber from the toilet to the maid's room to join them, pull the ironing board out of sight and shut the windows. An unmade bed and some unwashed pots and pans would make it seem as if we had only fled a few days ago.

I was lucky, because Miklós Katz, our deserter inherited from the Lehners, volunteered to lock the door on us from outside and do the climbing in my place, so that finally I had nothing to do except saunter with the old people into the maid's room.

But all this only happened a few days later. We spent the intervening nights fully dressed, taking turns lying on a sofa in the tidy room trying to guess when it was our building's turn from under the blinds. This was never boring. The street was interesting. All appeared completely dead and quiet, but the moment a vehicle turned onto Miksa Street six flashlights lit up, German soldiers jumped out of the dark, stepped onto the running boards and demanded papers. Or we heard from Dohány Street how they were hurrying the Jews down the stairs, naturally not in the kindest tones. Nonetheless, when Miklós took over from me I slept like a baby until morning, when I noted with satisfaction that another day had passed and still nobody had been taken away. I celebrated by having a divine breakfast. (I remember the kind of honey and butter sandwiches I gobbled up without counting, plus a few grapes. If only I could have a little of that now.) The food was brought to the building by the superintendent and the Christian friends of certain residents. The maid's room was kept in readiness for the next night.

We had constant visits during the day from the residents of the building, particularly the women and children, who kept coming to us for reassurance because they could feel that we didn't believe in misfortune and were not afraid. The children asked a thousand times: "Néni Kindergarten, are you sure there won't be any trouble?" (The name "néni Kindergarten" was given to me by a child who could hardly speak a word.)

The following evening things became serious. As early as eight o'clock I hear and see soldiers with flashlights walking up and down the passage in the Dohány Street courtyard, banging with their rifles, kicking the doors and shouting "Aufmachen!"[6] All this happens in pitch darkness, but we knew this: they had already raided every building in the neighbourhood. The only people who had not yet been dragged away and beaten were those from 11 Miksa Street (we didn't discover until much later that the Arrow Cross visited the starred houses on the basis of the houses' official listing. On this list there is no 11 Miksa Street as such, since it's only there as 55 Dohány Street, which is not written on the door).

In our building, everybody rushes into their own apartment, some women lose their heads and run down into the cellar with a child in their arms. They want to hide down there, but the house commander orders them back. I consider that the time has come for us to tidy up the apartment and move into the maid's room.

Everything goes as planned. We are sitting in the dark. At about ten o'clock the bell rings, but we don't move. The ringing goes on for a good ten to twelve minutes, then silence again. We are tired and sleepy because God only knows how many nights we have spent fully dressed like this. I am perching on a stool on which I have piled cushions and snoozing with my head resting on my knees (my usual air raid position). Since the maid's room window is completely blacked out we even turn on the electric lights from time to time. In the only bed in the room (bácsi Lehner's bed in normal circumstances), Miklós Katz and my father take turns sleeping. Miklós Katz even snores.

---

6 German: Open up!

Around midnight, Miklós climbs over to the toilet to do his business. Before he climbs back he tells us all to do our business in the chamber pot and hand it over through the window so that he can empty it before he climbs back. This happens, but Nünüke and I are laughing so much that I am afraid we can be heard through the *Lichthof*. Katz climbs back and goes to sleep again. There is no noise from outside. In the morning when all my bones are stiff from the position I was in, I climb back into the apartment, thinking *what will be, will be.* I lie down on the sofa and sleep until late morning. Nünüke wakes me at eleven o'clock by telling me that last night's bell ringer was a Jewish resident who wanted to set our minds at rest with fresh news. He tells us that forty-eight hours of free robbery was granted to the Arrow Cross to celebrate the successful putsch and that the forty-eight hours had finished at midnight. He also tells us that the previous day, late at night, a transport of Jews had been on a forced marched along Dohány Street, when an old woman collapsed and died at the corner of Miksa Street. Her body was taken to the nearest gate (our gate) with a policeman standing guard over her. (As you know, nowadays the only worthwhile thing is dying!) When the Arrow Cross thugs and German soldiers turned up and tried to force their way in on the pretext of looking for partisans, the policeman, who knew that the free looting ended at midnight, dragged out the time and talked them out of going in by showing them the dead woman. After midnight, police on bicycles went around the Jewish houses and told the residents that from now on the doors must be kept locked and only local officials were allowed in. If I remember rightly, we are not allowed to leave the building at all or perhaps only for an hour's shopping a day. Bread is brought to us by the superintendent. Béla visits us faithfully, surviving numerous identity checks with his forged papers. I hear that identity checks are most prolific on the bridges.

The powers that be are collecting men from the Jewish houses to clear rubble. One morning at half past five, the superintendent tells everybody to dress quickly and report down to the courtyard. I hastily put on a dressing gown, peep out into the courtyard and see that only men are supposed to be collected, but the policeman and the armband-wearing Arrow Cross "guards of the nation" are searching the building from top to bottom for "hidden weapons." (On October 15, some soldiers were allegedly shot at from a starred building in Teleki Square, after which the Jews were dragged out into the square from all the buildings in the area and shot, one by one.)

Nünüke and I become somewhat nervous because of the forced labour refugee about whom even the superintendent doesn't know anything. First we want to hide him in the maid's room, but then we get cold feet. The policeman is already here inspecting room by room, asking about weapons and warning us to hand them over because otherwise there could be great trouble. Then he enquires about the men. We tell him that father is seventy-three, and we also produce Miklós, but the policeman doesn't care how he got here and what he is doing here. Since he is of the prescribed age, our policeman takes him down to the courtyard. Meanwhile the Arrow Cross men deduce from the list posted on the gate that there must be six men of the right age to be taken away to clear ruins. They are a little surprised to find an extra one. The surplus is of course Miklós Katz, who shows his marching order and explains that he arrived yesterday late at night (the superintendent doesn't make a squeak) and that he is very tired and doesn't have to report until tomorrow. This all happens on October 18, with the marching order dated in early September near Kolozsvár, but the Arrow Cross men accept his story without further ado and then send him back into the apartment as somebody they are not concerned with.

A tall Arrow Cross man then addressed a garbled speech to the residents to the effect that they should not be afraid for the men who have been taken away and who will not be harmed if they behave themselves, just as the Jews will not be harmed either if they behave themselves and, in his opinion, things wouldn't have reached this point if they had behaved differently in the past. We left it at that. The

Arrow Cross departed, and the women remained at home frightened and wailing.

All that time I had kept in close touch with Lili Havas and her family, who lived near us, at 5 Hársfa Street. Every afternoon, if only for five minutes, I would run up to their apartment because it felt good to get together with friends. Lilus also always knew some relatively reliable news, either through Déri or through the Association of the Christian Jews, where she worked in an office. She often brought us some food, because in the weeks before Szálasi she had been granted the "regent's exemption" and therefore didn't have to wear the star, walked about freely and, most important, was able to shop. At Lili's apartment I often used to meet Kati, who also lived near us and who also used to come to Lili to have a bath, as I did. All this time Kati prophesied darkly that we were all going to die and there was no point in getting upset. "We can't get through this alive," she would say as she signed her name to the Palestine immigration list, for which in those days you needed a great deal of patronage. Her parents had been deported from Miskolc. Her younger brother, a doctor in Debrecen, had narrowly avoided the cattle car by escaping to Budapest. Kati got him a "job" with the Gestapo, where she also turned up later and from where both were taken to Germany. We always greeted Kati with "When are we going to die?" although by September she didn't believe in dying either, so much so that she was outraged when Lili wore a cross around her neck. She was angry with every Jewish convert.

After October 15, I am cut off from everybody because it's no longer possible to run across into the neighbouring street. I only discover much later that such Arrow Cross and German atrocities only occurred in our district. In District v, neither Cini nor your mother knows anything about it. Being cut off and locked up like this makes me nervous. We are constantly being checked and counted several times a day to see if we are all here. They are guarding us as if we were some treasure. I'm not afraid but rather relieved that, at last "jetzt geht's los."[7] What we had been afraid of for years had arrived. It was happening and there was no either-or about it. By now they wouldn't deport me anyway, but at most put a bullet in me and strangely enough I find this much more acceptable than being dragged away. I am glad to see that the old people aren't afraid either. Nünüke is once more going about her daily chores calmly and imperturbably. My father of course doesn't leave any opportunity for dramatics and unpleasantness unused. He is talking all day about "a bullet in the back of the head" to those who are most afraid of that, and about "deportation" to those whose weakness this happens to be. But he isn't afraid either.

I can't help it, but however many innocent persons fell victim to the Arrow Cross putsch it didn't give me an impression of being anything serious. Rather, it recalled children playing cowboys and Indians. I think that is one reason why I couldn't be afraid. I'm sure that the Germans were also laughing their heads off at the infinitely stupid Arrow Cross, who blustered and fired off rifles to frighten the Jews but basically did nothing.

7 German: here we go.

I Am in Hiding

THE POSTER that ordered every Jewish woman aged between eighteen and forty to join up for labour service appeared about October 21.[1] We were to report to the KISOK sports field at 8:00 a.m. on October 23 with full equipment (knapsack, boots, etc., just like you). In our building there are hysterical scenes because almost all the women have children and their husbands are away on forced labour. What will happen to the children? The poster doesn't say anything about that. The women run to and fro dementedly. Everybody asks for advice, borrows or lends a knapsack or a pair of stockings, and they all argue furiously about whether to take the children with them or leave them behind, and if they leave them behind, who would look after them. The young mother of a two-year-old little girl runs up to the third floor and is about to jump. The other women pull her off the sill, and she lies for hours in bouts of tears.

October 22, Sunday, exactly a week since Szálasi's putsch. I am getting ready to report for work. I'm packing and in a good mood. Going to work seems like an interesting adventure. In my stupid

---

1 Many new announcements appeared around this time calling on either men or women to register for labour service, and the required ages stated changed periodically. One announcement appeared on October 22 requiring all Jewish women between eighteen and forty years of age to report for so-called recruitment, and about ten thousand Jewish women were recruited at this time.

head I imagine being taken away for a little while to dig trenches or something of the kind, like you were. By the afternoon I have finished packing, when my cousin Béla arrives and urgently advises me against turning up for work. He says that this is my last opportunity to escape and to hide with some friends for a "short period" while people think that I reported to work as ordered. The Russians were only a few minutes away, and I would be mad to walk into the hands of the Arrow Cross now. This makes me extremely nervous, and my stomach starts dancing when I once more smell that whiff of freedom. Nünüke is frightened and doesn't want to give any advice. I explain to Béla that I am a helpless coward, unsuited to hiding, afraid to take any action and so clumsy that I would be caught on the very first day. Béla assures me that I would be at no greater risk from running away than from obeying the order. The matter is decided by my father coming in and with his customary solemnity declaring that he regards escaping as unsuitable: "I say, my daughter, that you should report for work like the others."

I immediately decide to escape because I know from experience that it is always advisable to do the opposite of what my father says. But on this Sunday afternoon I must finally decide what to do, because I have to discuss the details with Béla. We cook up the following plan: in the morning I will leave the building with the other women reporting for work but drop out at a street corner, possibly with the help of a woman to whom I will tell the truth and who will cover for me. Béla and Irén will be waiting for me on a side street and take my luggage while I go out to the Mátés' in Óbuda and wait there until Béla brings forged papers (there is no time to look for Kromesch). I agree to meet Béla at seven-thirty the next morning on Nagyatádi Szabó Street in front of the Beszkárt building. Béla goes away. I pace around the apartment full of tension. Nünüke is sad.

At first some daunting complications arise that almost make me turn back. The superintendent and the house commander are personally responsible for seeing that every resident of the house obeys the order to report. Mr. Matrác, the house commander, wants to escort us personally and hand us over at the KISOK sports field (obviously for a receipt, as is the custom with such valuables). He announces therefore that we must assemble at seven tomorrow morning in the courtyard. In the evening, he walks from one apartment to the next and lists the women who are to be escorted. God knows how he misses me, but he doesn't come in to see us, and I hear from the others that I am not on the list. Nünüke and I look at each other. She probably thinks like me that this is the Finger of Fate with two capital Fs.

This night none of us sleeps for long, and we get up very early. I must dress so that at a stroke I can change from a Jewish forced labourer into an Aryan woman out for a walk. I solve this problem by putting on my dirty raincoat with its yellow star over my elegant navy spring coat (the latter, poor dear, long since dust and ashes — may it rest in peace). Then I wrap a silk scarf around my head in the style of a peasant, which I can later use fashionably around my neck. On my feet flat shoes and white socks turned down over stockings give the impression that I am going to the work camp. All this comes with a brand new knapsack, on which I've embroidered my full name for entertainment during many hours of inactivity in the cellar, and a large shapeless handbag full of civilian things that I shall need at the Mátés'.

At 7:00 a.m., I step out of our building, running into the superintendent in the gateway. I tell him without being asked that I have to have a broken belt repaired at the belt maker next door and will be back in half an hour. In the first empty side street, I slip from the starred raincoat into the navy coat with a pair of elegant blue gloves. Off with the headscarf. I adjust my hair, put on some makeup and stand the knapsack and my handbag on the ground. Béla appears on time and picks up the knapsack, while I travel out to Óbuda to the Mátés' with my other bag. They receive me very kindly. We agree that I will stay with them until I get new papers and a job. They too believe that the whole thing will only last a few days.

Later, I hear that on Miksa Street nobody noticed that I had disappeared because when the women were gathering to report for work the house commander had an argument with them and left them standing there, saying that it served them right and they could go and report for work on their own. That same evening, Mr. Matrác walked from one apartment to the other to see if everybody had given themselves up and that nobody had stayed behind. The poor devil got a furious reaction when he asked Nünü where I was, and she exploded that it was he who should answer that question because he had taken the women away. Many of the women came back the same day, asserting their right to do so while their husbands were away on forced labour. But I know of many others who were nevertheless held and sent off to the countryside the same day. So I can flatter myself that I escaped at the right moment, and not a second too soon.

Two weeks later, without exception, the wives of the forced labourers, even those who had young children (e.g., Klári Erdős), were also taken away.

According to the poster, those who had protective documents from another country were exempt from reporting. When my Swiss *Schutzpass* was delivered by the post office on behalf of our unknown guardian angel, Nünüke was delighted to bring it out to the Mátés' in Óbuda, saying that I could now come home to Miksa Street without any problems. Naturally I didn't go because I listened to Béla who never stopped arguing that a *Schutzpass* is only a piece of paper that can be lost, torn up, invalidated — in other words, it was better to be a phony Aryan than a real Jew with the most spectacular *Schutzpass*. You would also hear from various friends how the Arrow Cross men simply tore up such protective letters and dragged away their owners or shot the residents of the "protected houses."

So I didn't go back. For a week or ten days I lived quietly with the Mátés on Selmeci Street. But I couldn't just sit on my backside. After a while I had to find a job and somewhere else to live with the forged documents that Béla was organizing for me. I travelled all over the city, often by the No. 72 streetcar, and only realized later how bold I had been to mix with people I had known by sight for many years since they must have known me at the time of the yellow star. But more by luck than good judgment I never ran into any dangerous acquaintance. The Borszékis, the custodian of the apartment building on Kecske Street and his wife, knew where I was living. Mrs. Borszéki even came to see me one day at the Mátés' and brought me a goose. But I only learned how dangerous they were six months later when it was discovered that Borszéki and his son were active Arrow Cross members who betrayed, robbed and executed Jews, several of whom lived in the buildings for which they were responsible. It was rumoured that they had killed a woman, and her child, whose valuables were hidden with ours. I repeat, to us they were always kind. I still can't believe this horror story, but it seems that it was proven and the old man is still in prison while the son has disappeared west. I will relate somewhere else how fabulously they treated us. I also asked the Borszékis to let me sleep in their apartment but they had already hidden three old Jewish women there, and the situation could have become dangerous for me because one of the women, the most dangerous from my point of view, had been living in that particular wing of the building on Kecske Street that had been almost uninhabitable and uninhabited since July.

I agreed with the Mátés that I would live in a zigzag pattern, spending three or four days of the week with them and the remainder looking for different accommodations. At the end of the discussion, my friend Juci Lénárd comes home from the countryside where she was staying with her children. Although they are very easily frightened — particularly Ernő who doesn't like to do anything against the rules (who does?) — they readily agree to let me stay with them. Juci invites me particularly nicely to lunch or dinner at their home whenever I am in the neighbourhood so that I need not go to a restaurant where I might be recognized.

That was the time when I turned to disguises. I plucked my

eyebrows and bought for thirty pengős a pair of spectacles with black frames and clear glass to walk in the streets. Meanwhile, an offer came from Kosana (Lívia's Serbian sister-in-law) who lives at 7 Csalogány Street in a gorgeous apartment with all comforts and whom I hardly knew beforehand. She very kindly invites me to stay with her at any time except that I should come after seven o'clock in the evening because she is not at home earlier and leave before the cleaner arrives at eight-thirty in the morning. Each time she treats me to a tasty meal.

Other offers of accommodations: your mother has an ownerless sofa in her room and a starless gate, through which I come and go, but not to the cellar during air raids because the house commander is a colleague of mine from the Credit Bank. Your mother is very kind to me when I need it and treats me with great care and concern. The Hercegs have no objection to me as a temporary sleeping guest, only Klári asks me to bring my Jewish documents along and to leave them behind in case a Christian guest is found in their apartment during a raid. This is forbidden by law.

I also use the Bolgár family's apartment on Uszály Street as a base, in which Béla's Irén stayed for a long time as a co-tenant. Boci had only occasionally returned home to sleep because the neighbours were beginning to suspect that there was something wrong with her background and she was afraid of being reported to the authorities. Sometimes several people turned up on Uszály Street to sleep: Boci, Irén, Béla and I, Renate (Mrs. Bali Bíró) and at times several pairs of Jews were even sharing the leather armchairs, but everything was fine, except that it was a very, very cold apartment with no firewood anywhere and a gas water heater that worked very badly.

Boci had brilliantly survived with the trick of pretending from the beginning that she wasn't a Jew. She didn't sew on the star, didn't move in together with other Jews, didn't leave her apartment and never registered for labour service. It's true that this was easy for her to do because she had carefully hidden her Jewish heritage all her life.

However, in the dangerous season she didn't dare to sleep at home, particularly since one night Arrow Cross men had come up to the apartment to inspect their documents. The idiots wanted to take Irén with them because they thought her documents suspicious, as they all came from 1941, but finally the two women argued so much with them that they neither arrested anyone nor looted the apartment.

Once I slept in the apartment of the woman for whom my friend Lívia worked as a nurse under the pseudonym of Mária Kutassy. That is a different story, but on the same day (in early November) Margit Bridge blew up. All the bridges had long been mined at conspicuous points and were only waiting for the command. Owing to some technical fault (a short circuit?) one midday at the busiest time the bridge exploded. This created an indescribable panic in the city. And it wasn't just a momentary panic but a long-lasting one. On the one hand, the destruction of the most important bridge paralyzed all traffic, including food supplies. On the other hand, people came down with bridgephobia, that is, a pathological fear of stepping on a bridge. The worst damage was done to the traffic of heavy vehicles, which could only move at a snail's pace on Ferenc József Bridge. Once I had to travel from the National Theatre to the Margit bridgehead in Buda, which took me an hour and three-quarters. It would have been much faster on foot.

I think the bridge was blown up on November 5.[2] I was due to meet Béla in front of the Bem Apóhoz restaurant at about 1:30 p.m. I knew that he was coming from the Pest side, and I was reading the ads when three huge explosions took place very close by. As the sirens had just finished warning of approaching enemy aircraft, everyone thought a bomb had been dropped. Some people ran for safety toward

2 The explosion destroying the eastern section of the bridge occurred on November 4, 1944.

the shelters while others shouted that the Margit Bridge had blown sky-high. I believe neither story because a further explosion seems unlikely and the explosions just heard did not sound like bombs.

I set out toward the bridge to see what is going on. By now more and more passersby come running in my direction, shouting that the bridge had been blown sky-high. I still can't believe it. Who did this? What for? How could this be? Now I see the bridge that looks like a matchbox squashed underfoot. The pillars are still standing but the remainder is hanging down into the water. From the No. 6 streetcar people are trying to climb out through the windows, some are swimming and clambering onto beer barrels (it seems that there was a beer wagon full of empty barrels on the bridge, which fortunately saved many lives). Suddenly, I feel that I am running with tears in my eyes along Zsigmond Street toward the Chain Bridge, obviously with the intention of reaching the old couple before the other bridges are blown up.

Luckily Lívia, who is coming toward me, stops me and warns me that everybody at the bridgeheads and in the side streets leading to them has to show ID and it would be wise not to be around just now. Lívia's boss, Mrs. Maca Gajáry, lives nearby at 29 Zsigmond Street opposite the Mercy Hospital. We go straight there, and they don't let me leave for the rest of the day. I sleep in the maid's room, where it is very cold and I am freezing. Lívia (who must be called Mária, as in her forged papers) drops in every minute with another blanket. God knows where she gets them from. My teeth are chattering. I am convinced that Béla was on the bridge because he should have been there to meet me in front of the restaurant at the critical time. When Lívia has piled so many old coats and blankets over me that I have almost stopped freezing, she suddenly appears again, ceremoniously opening a beautifully folded document, which she also puts on top of me. She says that Béla left this a minute ago but has already gone. It was my brand new forged birth certificate, which presents me as having been born of ag.h.ev.[3] parents, with the rest of the details corresponding to the facts. The blank forms (rubber-stamped in Kassa) had been bought by Béla for three hundred pengős. He never let us buy any other document thereafter. The family still lives on what Béla did not allow us to waste.

The blowing up of Margit Bridge caused me further complications by creating a very unpleasant atmosphere in which people became extremely nervous and even more afraid than before. Those who had been quite willing to provide accommodations were visibly less so now. Everybody urges me to regularize my situation and get a properly registered address because it's becoming more dangerous every day to live in illegality. Naturally, the whole city knows for certain before the end of the day that the bridge had been blown up by the Jews.

I am looking for a job that comes with room and board. I almost get into a Swedish girls' home, with the help of Lotte Nádas, who is now called Eszter Kovács. (These new names drive me mad, and if I run into someone I know I make a detour, because I don't know what to call them today.) Lotte is very difficult to reach because she is the secretary of Countess Tolsztoj, a repulsive old bag who has me thrown out ten times, so that the eleventh time I have to bribe the superintendent's wife to call Lotte down to talk to me. The Swedish girls' home is full but there is another possibility: for a pittance I could stay in Gusztáv Gratz's[4] villa in Marczibányi Square with people who know who I am. But I miss this opportunity because suddenly things change. Lotte's parents and Lívia's mother must urgently find somewhere to stay and take the remaining spaces there.

Meanwhile, I frequently meet with Hőgye, chiefly to ask him for

---

3 Lutheran; abbreviation of "Ágostai Hitvallásu Evangélikus," referring to Lutherans following the Augustana (in Latin) or Augsburger (in German) creed.

4 Gusztáv Gratz (1875–1946), a Hungarian liberal politician, MP and minister of Foreign Affairs in 1921.

advice. Once he offers me some money, but I don't accept it. I can only see him if I turn up at the pastor's office on Pozsonyi Street at 7:30 a.m. to take part in the morning Bible lesson and to help with the psalm singing.

The Margit Bridge has only been destroyed on the Pest side. The Buda side is still intact as far as Margit Island. Soldiers have built a pontoon bridge from the island to Pest. Elsewhere, for instance between Pálffy Square and Rudolf Square, the traffic is carried by ferries, but using them is a miserable, time-consuming affair. It's constantly raining and you have to stand for at least half an hour waiting for the ferry to pick you up or to complete its crossing with you on board. Every small errand has become a major undertaking, because the streetcars can't be relied on. The service has been badly curtailed and, on some lines, completely cancelled. The crowding is terrible, there are obstructions all over the place and accidents are frequent.

From the beginning of November, I don't like to walk in the streets because the fun in the brick factory[5] has started: at every step on the ferry, on the pontoon bridge, in the streets you meet long lines of Jews — old men, women, children, with bundles and knapsacks, painfully dragging themselves along. They are escorted by Arrow Cross men in uniform or with armbands, who treat them atrociously.

One day, in driving rain, I am about to take the ferry from Buda to Pest when I see such a march approaching in Zsigmond Street. I watch them from behind my umbrella. They are young women, each with her complete *Ausrüstung*,[6] and there in a knot among them are the women of Miksa Street. Soaked to the skin, they pass by me with no more than five paces between us, but luckily none of them looks my way. I feel ashamed, although I am not sentimental and know that

---

5 Jews were forced into the brick factory in Óbuda before being sent on a death march.

6 German: gear, accoutrements.

it would not have made their lives any better if I were marching with them. But it still spoils my day.

Every day on Bécsi Road, old Jews, dusty, dirty and some barely able to crawl, are chased in and out of brick factories. It's even rumoured that whoever can't keep up with the march will be shot *stantepede*.[7] I don't believe this for a long time, but then I see here and there bodies along the edge of the road, covered with brown paper and with only their shoes showing. I can't tell whether they are Jews or not, because I can't see the star behind the paper, but it's strange that these bodies are strewn along this notorious route.

When I see the old people in the street, herded back from the brick factories, I decide not to let Nünü and my father be chased like this. Whatever happens, I will help them escape from Miksa Street. I sell Nünüke's precious diamond earrings to buy forged documents for the old couple. Thanks to the Rapochs, I can do a reasonably good deal. I think that the earrings are worth about thirty thousand pengős and that the experts generally want to get them for eight-to-ten thousand pengős. I let them go for fifteen thousand.

While I am hiding, I am constantly in touch with the Rapochs. They had disappeared from their apartment in Buda at the time of the Great Relocation and were hiding for weeks in the apartment of a friend somewhere along the József Boulevard. While the friend and his family were staying in the countryside, everybody in the building thought that their apartment was empty, so the poor devils staying there hardly dared to flush the toilet or go to the cellar during air raids. Eventually somebody managed to get them the necessary papers (of a deceased couple, refugees from Beregszász) for a fortune, and they rented a holiday apartment on Gugger Hill, where they lived

---

7 Latin: literally "with one's foot standing still"; a medieval juridical term meaning "on the spot, without having left the court," used here to simply mean "on the spot" or "where they stood."

quietly and very well for a while. In November, they fed me an unforgettable meal of young goose, not to mention the apple strudel or the genuine black coffee we drank afterwards. (Toward the end of the Great Hoopla, Gugger Hill proved to be a very bad place, but it was taken by the Russians fairly quickly.)

Hiding also has its lighter moments. The Mátés were entertaining one evening while I was staying with them. I had often heard them mention the name of a counter-intelligence lieutenant, Kemencey, who was a good friend and drinking companion of Jancsi Máté. On this occasion, Kemencey turned up with his wife, and I immediately recognized him as a classmate of Dini, who came to our apartment frequently at that time. When we were introduced, I mumbled something unintelligible and still don't know whether he recognized me or only pretended not to, but I don't believe in any case that he was capable of deliberately hurting anyone.

I very much enjoyed my stay with the Mátés because they treated me kindly, thoughtfully and considerately. The only disadvantage of the Selmeci Street quarter was that the toilet is in the middle of the garden and one could see from the neighbouring garden who used it and how many times. The owner of the neighbouring building, an upright old Swabian woman, was kind and harmless. We discovered later that she knew from the start who I was and why I stayed next door from time to time in spite of all my fairly plausible fairy tales (that I live on Csillaghegy, that I am unhappily married, or that I help Kató with the sewing), but there are other residents in the building who might also be kind but not so harmless.

Béla and Irén often come to see me at the Mátés' and on one occasion they bring Mrs. Borszéki with them.

Hiding with Kosana on Csalogány Street is also pleasant and fairly safe. I never meet anybody on the stairs and have never seen the superintendent. Csalogány Street is very romantic because I can only go there on dark evenings, but I still know better than most people how dark an evening in November 1944 in Buda can be.

Once I was walking alone in heavy rain from Béla on Hattyú Street to Kosana just after a siren warning of approaching enemy aircraft, in complete blackout. Heavy rain is all right, enemy aircraft is all right, complete blackout is all right, crooked, cobbled, totally deserted Csalogány Street is also all right, but you could say that all this together is a little *unheimlich*. (By the time of the deportations, I no longer dared stay with Gizella.) Hiding with Juci is almost as good as being at home. When I get in that evening, soaked, freezing and depressed, having achieved nothing, she is waiting for me with a hot bath and good food. She comforts me, and I feel that she is genuinely on my side.

At the beginning of November, my cousin-in-law Jóska (the husband of my deported cousin Mici) turns up in Budapest. His unit is working in the salt stores somewhere near the Railway Connection Bridge, but he has lost all his friends and relations. I visit him twice, early in the morning, taking food and cigarettes. It's interesting that Béla does not volunteer for this because he regards it as dangerous, even though he has done much more dangerous things without batting an eyelash. Béla gets a Swiss *Schutzpass* for Jóska. At the same time, I get him a Swedish Red Cross protective document from the Good Shepherd organization with the help of Emil Hajós. Irén takes the document to Jóska, but this is the last time we hear of him. He must have been sent to Germany with his colleagues, like most members of the "protected" class.

Meanwhile, I walk until my feet are sore to find a position using my forged papers. Mrs. Rapoch wants to place me with one of her Christian friends, who is rich and has always had a governess for their only child but who is without one at present. Mrs. Viktor Hornyánszky owns the printing press of that name and lives in her own mansion on Pauler Street. Listen well, Pipus, because this will be important later.

I go to see the woman, who is sympathetic, refined and beautiful, as is her little girl, and the apartment is beautiful and welcoming. The woman knows exactly who I am because I told her. She tries hard to help me, but her husband and mother-in-law, who are not in the know, object that they can't employ any more staff because of the food shortage. Mrs. Hornyánszky's good friend is the wife of Count Arz Roderik, and they are supposed to be at their country estate in Vasegerszeg (close to the western border). They have two children and the countess harasses Mrs. Hornyánszky daily to get her an intelligent and reliable person to look after them. I could actually be on my way with Mrs. Hornyánszky's recommendation, but I can't tell the count and countess the truth by intercity telephone and don't want to risk being kicked out if the countess isn't prepared to hide me when I tell them face to face. But not telling them at all is even more dangerous because I would only get around the alertness of the local gendarmerie with the help of the count and countess, not to mention that in Vasegerszeg the war will be over a few months after it ends in Budapest and that I can't go so far away from the old couple. All the same, I toy with the idea for days. I see Mrs. Hornyánszky several times because she is trying to enrol other friends of hers in helping me. By now the telephone is so unreliable that I rush there personally each time.

The day the connection to Mrs. Hornyánszky finally fails and her last friend has given a negative answer, I ask Mrs. Hornyánszky why there is a Red Cross on the gate. She explains that they had offered their building to the International Red Cross, which immediately made use of it for the protection of children by converting some rooms (up until now the elder Mrs. Hornyánszky's boarding house) into a children's home. I ask her who looks after the children. She calls in one of the caregivers and introduces us. This is when I hear for the first time of Gábor Sztehlo, the Lutheran pastor who from the Red Cross office at 60 Fillér Street directs the different children's homes set up in various parts of the city, and on whom everything depends. The woman encourages me to go to Sztehlo, who is a very good man and who may accept me as a children's caregiver.

You must know that everybody I meet gives me at least fifteen wonderful tips as to what I could do, who I could turn to, who I could use as a reference, etc., and that by now I have gone everywhere in vain. I will also mention that Dóri once gave me a recommendation to the Red Cross office and another big shot on Baross Street, and said that I could consider myself employed, because she was asked about a perfect office worker. She had first wanted to bring in Lilus, but since Lilus already had a brilliant job (at the neurological department of the Szent István Hospital as a nurse, where she could work with an altered birth certificate), Dóri passed the excellent position on to me with the condition that I let Lilus take it as soon as she needs it.

I'll be short. The brilliant job kicked me out. The big shot threw the letter of recommendation away and the whole office on Baross Street was full of snotty conceited Jewish busybodies who kept me waiting for hours and who sent me here and there before they finally turned me down, saying that at the moment they can't take on any more people. After this you will understand that I didn't trust that woman's tip for one moment, but somehow the name and address got stuck in my head. I tried in many other places over the subsequent days, mostly running around in heavy rain, and was sent away from everywhere. I came to the bitter conclusion that one could only achieve something with patronage and nepotism, but I had access to neither.

As I say, I was soaked to the skin and as thin as a rake, saddened and deadly tired too. What the hell, I climbed up Fillér Street which is a long way from any streetcar line. I had to climb up Rózsadomb all the way to Pasarét but luckily I didn't know that in advance or I wouldn't have started in the first place.

In the lobby of an elegant villa, a large crowd was waiting for Reverend Gábor Sztehlo. I sat down to wait without any conviction, because at last I was somewhere warm and it didn't matter where I was because nothing would work anyway. I saw to my surprise that the Baross Street mentality outlined above did not exist here. Once in a while, some kind of male secretary goes round to everybody in the order of their arrival and extremely politely asks who we want to talk to and what about. There is no question of conceit, no sense of superiority. I can hardly believe my eyes.

Soon, believe it or not, I AM SITTING OPPOSITE THE REVEREND, who receives me kindly as if he had known me all my life. He comes around to me and asks what he can do for me. All my life I have stood up to being kicked out without batting an eye, but now I immediately burst into tears. I tell him that I have been hiding for four weeks and that the situation is getting worse, not because of me but because of my friends, whom I can't expose to danger much longer. I had heard of his actions and would like to be a caregiver in one of his homes, which apart from everything else I would very much enjoy because I have always liked being with children. I tell him about the kindergarten on Miksa Street and can see that he likes it a lot. He takes me to another room and hands me over to a woman called Mme Barrée,[8] saying: "This young lady would like to work with us. Put her name down on the list." At the same time I get a glimpse of myself in the mirror opposite: the young lady's grey hair is hanging into my eyes, she has deep furrows in a wan face reminiscent of mine, and she looks even older than my thirty-five years. I start bawling again, but Mme Barrée is already writing down my details and telling me to come back in two days to hear what has happened. She can't promise me anything because there are large numbers of applicants and by now only a few new children's homes will be set up.

At other times I would have been discouraged by something like this, but it made me realize that while I was in the waiting room I saw many women dismissed because the Red Cross only places children

8 In Margit's original typescript she spelled this woman's name incorrectly as Mme Barrey. The editors have followed the Hungarian editors in correcting the name and have also made the honorific consistent.

and not adults. About ten to fifteen women were sent away like this, including some whose children had already been securely placed in homes and who would have accepted any kind of work to be able to stay with them. I cling so desperately to this solution that no other will do. I rush to Brother Hajós and to Hőgye, begging them to push the matter. Hajós thinks that it's completely hopeless; Hőgye promises to try to find an approach to Sztehlo. Meanwhile, I meet Lotte Nádas (a.k.a. Eszter), who also tells me not to waste my breath because Vera Nyilas, for instance, mobilized the whole parish of the Good Shepherd to be accepted and still didn't get in because you either need a great deal of patronage or you have to gift a serious amount of money for the purposes of the institution. Two days later I report to Mme Barrée, who tells me excitedly that they expected me yesterday. I was placed in the newly created home on Casino Street. Sztehlo selected my name from the list of applicants and gave me preferential treatment. They are already typing up my employment contract and some sort of document declaring that all my belongings are the property of the Red Cross and that I'm allowed to remove them from the starred building.

The rest belongs to the next chapter, but I just remembered a few small details from the period when I was in hiding. For example, I used to arrange a clandestine meeting with my parents whenever I wanted to see them. On one occasion, I waited for them at a restaurant on Rákóczi Street while Béla and Irén brought them over, and we had dinner together. Another time, shielded by a wide-brimmed hat I'd borrowed, I saw Nünüke as she was leaving Miksa Street for the market hall. I sidled up to her and whispered in her ear to follow me to the Kővárys'. The poor thing covered her star as soon as she reached the corner of Wesselényi Street (we always concealed our "insignia" on our way to Juci's place), where we had a great chat. However, suddenly Gyula Kőváry bursts in, he is beside himself because the Arrow Cross is conducting a raid in the building. I try to calm him down by saying let them come, all my papers are in order (on my photo

ID from the Credit Bank Béla gave my religion as "ag.h.ev.," and he signed it as the director of personnel), and we'd tell them that Nünüke was there to clean the apartment. All that was to no avail. Gyula kept on ranting, at which point Nünüke and I left, although evidently that was the stupidest thing to do under the circumstances, because anyone who was trying to leave the building was automatically suspect. But nothing bad happened, except that I felt awfully sorry for Nünüke for the rather humiliating and embarrassing situation. There was also the time when Nünü came to Buda to the Bem Apóhoz restaurant, and we had dinner there. The new superintendent at Miksa Street was very decent to my parents, letting them in and out of the building without their stars on whenever they wished.

Before I launch into the chapter titled THE INTERNATIONAL RED CROSS AND KISKAS, I need to tell you about how my parents escaped. As I have already written somewhere, in early November people wearing the star were being made to march back and forth, particularly the old ones, because most of the younger ones had already been deported from Budapest under the pretext of labour service. This kind of scene was most frequently seen in the region of Óbuda. Threatened by Arrow Cross men, people in dirty clothes, deadly pale with tortured faces, were dragging themselves back from a brick factory to the gathering place on Síp Street and from there to another brick factory. The sight of bodies lying by the roadside, covered in brown paper, became less sensational day by day.

While I was trying to deal with my own affairs, I was also looking hard for someone to hide Nünü and my father, if I could help them escape. For my father, I already had an excellent hiding place with the Szabós at 2 Klauzál Square. Of course you ask: Who are the Szabós? Two weeks ago I wouldn't have known them either. Sándor Szabó and his wife, née Anna Kiss, were stallholders in the Klauzál Square Market Hall. The husband was once a cobbler, the wife was from the region of Béla's Irén and was her motherly good friend. One day Irén asks her if they would be prepared to let the old couple move in with them. They are willing to hide one of my two parents but can't take both in an apartment with one room and kitchen and a young girl, some sort of relative, already living there. I visit them to discuss the financial side of the matter, but they wouldn't hear of accepting any payment: "After the war," they say. The apartment is squeaky clean even though the woman is busy with her own occupation from morning until night. Their house commander, a friend, is let in on the secret, and there is nothing to fear from the building's superintendent.

By that time Nünü and my father have impeccable birth certificates from Debrecen courtesy of Béla, my cousin. Two blank forms cost six hundred pengős. They were filled in by Béla acting as a Debrecen priest in 1872 and 1873 respectively. We need to reserve the Szabós for my father, who is the greater worry and needs to be placed in such a way as to make him unable to give himself away.

I run around for days to place Nünüke. Mrs. Borszéki is full up, the Gólyas live in the German SS ring and a family we know on Testvér Hill refuse because all their neighbours are members of the Arrow Cross, with whom they don't get on. Finally, based on "something will turn up," Ernő Lénárd agrees to let me bring Nünüke to them until I find somewhere else for her, but I must promise that it will only be for a few days. I do this with a heavy heart because I have no idea what else to do with Nünüke. Without the Szabós, I would never have dared to embark on the escape, but now it is becoming more and more urgent, because in District VII people are being deported from one building after the other. In the early morning the Arrow Cross men gather in the squares where they form units to tackle the starred buildings one by one. Béla and Irén volunteer to help with my father and Nünü's actual escape. We agree to meet at the Szabós in Klauzál Square.

The great day is November 17. That morning the Arrow Cross gathered in Klauzál Square, which gives me a terrible fright thinking that we had missed the time for the escape. I will never forget this horribly long morning, waiting until Béla appears in his slow way, by which time I am half dead with horror because I am convinced they have both run straight into the Arrow Cross and been taken away. But the reason for the delay was that Nünü and my father had invited Béla to lunch to celebrate their escape and were having a relaxed meal on Miksa Street, while people from the next street over were being herded to the brick factories. Béla reports all of this to me when he at last appears in the afternoon at the appointed meeting place: the Szabó apartment, without Nünü and my father but at least with the first transport of possessions. I must beg Béla to hurry back and collect the old couple because I am afraid that if there were a race the Arrow Cross would win. About four o'clock Nünüke arrives back with Irén. She helped to smuggle their possessions out of the apartment. At last Béla gets a move on and instructs some movers to bring out the suitcases with the most important items. A few days later he goes back to the apartment. He has everything packed into crates and taken into the cellar. The contents of the pantry are taken to the Szabós'.

Since you can't be clear about conditions at the time, I must explain to you what Béla was risking by helping people escape and even more by hiding their possessions. The least punishment he would have received would have been internment, if he had happened to be a pure Aryan with a clean military record. But in his circumstances it would have been much worse. The delayed rescue of the possessions was a foolhardy and insane enterprise. I would never have asked Béla to help. He did it of his own volition.

We leave my father with the Szabós. Irén stays with some friends in Klauzál Square. The three of us — Nünüke, Béla and I — start out together. We just catch the last ferry and afterwards have dinner in a restaurant, then we accompany Nünüke over to the Lénárds'. Béla accompanies me to my new home in the Castle District. My mother is calm and looks pleasantly excited. My father is afraid, not of the Arrow Cross but of the change. If you ask him, he would hold out to the end in the starred house waiting for the things to come.

The International Red Cross and Kiskas

Protected by the Red Cross

The words quoted above were written on the front doors of the buildings in which I lived from time to time after November 17. The first stop was 1 Casino Street, the mansion of the actress Mária Lázár, which faced the Bástya Promenade, Casino Street and Úri Street respectively on its three sides. The actress lived on the first floor, the children's home was accommodated in one of the ground-floor apartments, and the other ground-floor apartment was rented by the newly appointed Arrow Cross deputy sheriff of Sopron County, Béla Somssich, who was moving to Sopron with his whole family (as was becoming the fashion in Arrow Cross circles). The actress stored the Somssich family's furniture in one of the four rooms of the vacant apartment and placed the other three rooms, unfurnished, at the caregivers' disposal, who could bring a wardrobe and a bed, etc., and I got Béla to deliver my sofa and my Biedermeier wardrobe, which I particularly wanted to save if I were saved. Who would have thought that the old trash I left behind on Miksa Street would survive the war unscathed while so many things I carried with me everywhere I went were lost forever?

At the children's home I'm received with amazing respect, not only, as I discover later, because Mme Barrée introduced me in very flattering terms but also because they mistake me for a specialized educator named Kassai who used to write influential articles in

Népszava.[1] I immediately connect with a young kindergarten teacher called Évi Bolgár. She is a good, sweet person, and we get on well together. We are both a little disappointed that the job isn't what we had imagined. The home is directed by Mrs. Lóri Leiner (daughter of the wealthy owner of the Leiner glue factory in Újpest). She learned to cook in response to the law passed in May — which forbids Jews to keep servants — and seems to feel that this qualifies her to run a home for infants. She shares the "running" with her daughter Lívia, a snooty eighteen-year-old and the most repulsive *Lipótváros jampezza*[2] I've ever known.

This home on Casino Street is really an infants' home, with the majority of children less than two years old, and those still being breastfed have their mothers with them. This is where I meet Palkó Demiány, who is five and who is here as a result of running away from home with his grandmother, his aunt and his aunt's six-month-old baby. Palkó's father disappeared in Ukraine, and his mother was deported for labour service. Palkó hates his grandmother and his aunt, and I must say that no child has ever had more reason to hate an adult. Palkó is a little gentleman, easy to handle and well behaved, but becomes a horror the moment he is left with the two women. He is the first motherless child entrusted to my care and so attractive that I carry the mother substitution somewhat too far. Later on, there will be a great fight over our separation, but believe me, it's difficult to keep within bounds, as I try to look after a child well enough that he doesn't miss his mother too much but at the same time not so well that he becomes too attached to me. With later children, I was able to keep some distance, to a large extent because I had lost some of my sensitivity and was no longer so sorry for each individual child.

---

1 Hungarian newspaper, established in 1873.

2 Lipótváros: a Budapest neighbourhood; jampezza (from Yiddish and Hungarian): a female dandy.

Initially, I would become deeply stressed and bawl if a child cried for their mother, but then I got used to it like a nurse gets used to blood. The food was very bad here, and I'm still angry when I think of the lousy meals Palika's granny and our Lóri, joining forces, managed to concoct from the copious, first-class raw materials.

It also annoyed me that there wasn't enough space to work or play with the children. There were a few older children, of school age, whose relatives had all been taken away. They were friendly, polite and well mannered and seemed to come from a simple background of Jewish craftsmen, but we soon lost touch with them and unfortunately couldn't find out anything else about them.

We had been on Casino Street for four days when Deputy Sheriff Somssich suddenly appeared and started an argument with the actress Lázár. Declaring that Lázár had no right to grant the Red Cross access to an apartment rented and not placed under notice by him, Somssich, HE EVICTED THE INFANTS' HOME WITH IMMEDIATE EFFECT. At nine o'clock in the evening, we were informed that we had to surrender the apartment by nine o'clock in the morning, *cleaned*. The next morning, in pouring rain, we moved "temporarily" to 7 Kelenhegyi Road on Gellért Hill. The beautiful, stately villa belonged to one of the counts Teleki, and the apartment she lent us for the purposes of a children's home was the property of Countess Márffy-Mantuano. Reverend Sztehlo had come to Casino Street early in the morning. Having tried everything to bring Somssich to reason but achieving nothing, he helped us personally with the cleaning and the move.

A few miserable days followed our move to the home on Kelenhegyi Road, because in this villa there was already another home with about twenty other children and almost as many caregivers. The director was Daisy Ullmann, and the caregivers were recruited from her circle of friends. They were rich and posh Jewish fashion dolls who didn't give a damn for children or education and were only interested in saving their own skin. It would have been better if they had hidden their intentions a little, at least by pretending to be concerned for the children. They made us feel right away that we were not wanted because it was more comfortable for forty people to live in ten rooms than for seventy. Besides, we were not a specially selected ensemble like they were. Among our mothers, there were some very poor proletarian women, whom some compassionate policemen had allowed to escape from the brick factory serving as a ghetto in the flimsy dresses they stood up in.

Daisy Ullmann further nourished some Aryan mothers and children in her bosom hoping that this would improve her prospects of saving her skin and preserving the Aryan character of the home. She therefore watched with disapproval as the Kelenhegyi Road home absorbed the home from Casino Street, where everybody had been Jewish, some with genuine, others with forged, papers. The behaviour of these women was so appalling that I wish I could forget them forever. I would have run away at once if Évi Bolgár and I hadn't kept each other going. Later I cheered up because all the children here were of kindergarten age, which is what I needed. Each was more charming than the other, although nobody had taken any interest in them and they were very grateful when somebody did. My position among the women also improved greatly later on because they came to respect my ability to control the children — while on Casino Street I had slept in one room with about eight to ten children who took turns roaring in the night, here the Casino Street "frame"[3] have been allocated a hall on the upper floor where only four of us caregivers sleep: Évi, me and Lóri with her offspring. It's true that the hall is at the same time used as a passageway but I still sleep well disturbed only by the infernal heat because the whole villa is terribly overheated. I am putting this here to boast because at that time nobody had any fuel.

One sore point of the move here in the pouring rain was the

---

3 *Frame* is an ironic reference to the soldiers guarding forced labourers.

Biedermeier wardrobe, which they had thrown from the coach into the garden of the villa on Gellért Hill and refused to lug it up to the villa even though I had prepared a place for it. There the poor thing was lying in the garden, and I must admit to my shame that I stood next to it and bawled. I wasn't sorry for the wardrobe as a possession but because I very much loved this piece and it was so old and so many people had used it before me. It was also very beautiful, and I had always imagined our future apartment with it in a place of honour. There was also something symbolic of mourning it, if I think carefully.

One thing I haven't told you about Casino Street was how kindly the superintendent of the Lázár mansion, bácsi Homoki, a retired street sweeper, treated us throughout our stay there. He was nice to the children; he helped us move; and you could see that he had his own opinion of Mr. Somssich and his behaviour. Nor have I mentioned the unforgettable air raids in the legendary cellars of the Castle District. Such a deep cellar it was, Pipus, you go down one flight of stairs, continue down a second flight carved out of the rock face, confront another flight down and then yet another, but I don't attempt the last because by the time I'm three floors down water is dripping on my head. I didn't see much of the actress except in the cellar during air raids, but she was decent enough to us, since she was an old friend of our leader, Lóri.

My short *séjour*[4] on Casino Street kept me rather busy. The errands for which I took the funicular down into the city included reassuring Nünüke, who was staying with the Lénárds, that things would somehow work out, asking Ernő for a few more days' patience, discussing the most urgent chores with Béla, shopping for the children's home, going to the pharmacy. So far I haven't worn the Red Cross caregivers' hat (a large grey triangular headscarf tied in nurses'

---

4 French: stay.

style and a Red Cross badge in the front and middle), which I believe to be compromising and dangerous because in this early phase you see masses of Jewish-looking women in Red Cross uniforms in the streets. I keep my old civilian woollen scarf with its multi-coloured checkerboard pattern and above my spectacles with their clear lenses under the scant remains of my plucked eyebrows. Juci (Lénárd) keeps moaning at me not to show myself in public because they would demand to see my identity papers, but on the one hand I have no alternative nose and on the other hand I am convinced that the matter is not resolved by the nose but by the way a person wears their nose. And it seems that I wore mine exactly as it was meant to be worn, because even Mme Barrée asked me why I was hiding and almost fainted with surprise over my Jewish origin when I told her that I was on the run from the starred house, that is, the labour service. When I asked her how, given that nose, she could have regarded me as a genuine Christian, she answered: "Many Christians have big noses, but very few Jews have discreet manners."

By the way, throughout that period I followed a method of my own; if I saw people in the street being ordered to present their identification documents I would walk straight into the middle of the uniformed group of Arrow Cross investigators, reach into my handbag and ask if they also wished to examine my identity. They would then usually send me on my way, unexamined and with no more than a dismissive wave of the hand. I would, of course, do this just as readily to the German soldiers, of whom I was hardly afraid at all, though I was even less afraid of the Arrow Cross. Pipus, I can assure you that my heart didn't beat a fraction faster when I walked through a detection unit because I never believed that I could be caught like others. An important part is played here by that lack of imagination that makes it impossible for me to picture that something seriously bad could happen to me or to anyone close to me. So I had an easy task because I was going for *ziheres*.[5] Deportation was something else, of that (not to mention roller coasters) I was afraid, and in the course of my future life I may find something else to be afraid of. Do you know the famous Grimms' fairy tale "The Story of the Youth Who Went Forth to Learn What Fear Was"? If you don't know it, I'll tell it to you when you are home and will also throw some light on the analogy.

Now I'll continue with the home on Kelenhegyi Road. The mansion is awfully elegant. From the huge oak-panelled hall you can get to all the rooms and the upper floor. The stairs are covered by a gorgeous carpet, on which I gallop up and down hundreds of times a day, but a little more slowly on the way down, where I am faced by a mirror that makes me feel like the lady of Manderley.[6] In the building I wear a headscarf and apron. To be honest, I should share the housework, like cleaning and washing up, with the others, but when my turn comes the mothers (with whom, for reasons I'll explain later, I'm extremely popular) will snatch the work out of my hand and do it all in my place, shrieking that I should lie down and rest. Naturally, I wouldn't dream of lying down, but I did escape the housework, which I admit I've never been able to enjoy. In those days, morning and afternoon snack was still fashionable in the homes and included jam sandwiches. I would set about spreading some *eráris*[7] (a despised jam at the time, but my God, how nice it would be to have some now, even if it were only a few grams) on my bread from the ten-kilogram wooden box, but the mothers would rush up to me, snatch the jam out of my hand and disperse in ten different directions to bring me some of their — God knows where and how — privately made Csabai sausage, goose liver, butter, cheese, etc. Food, then, is no

---

5 Hungarian term borrowed from the German *sicher* meaning "certainty."

6 Lady of Manderley is the heroine of Daphne du Maurier's novel and Alfred Hitchcock's film *Rebecca*.

7 Latin: treasury; slang term referring to provisions provided to institutions by the state.

problem. Even butter and Trappist cheese arrive from the Red Cross food storage at least once a week. There are *eráris* honey-macaroons and apples — you can still get the most beautiful Jonathan apples for twenty-four pengős if you find the *eráris* diet insufficient. Nevertheless, I am so thin by now that the whole home has heard of it, and when I wash myself the other caregivers come along specially to see the sight. You can actually count my ribs. The bathroom is always in great demand. Each of the two, that on the upper floor and that on the ground floor, on its own is as big as the whole apartment on Kecske Street. It contains a huge tin-glazed sunken bath, next to it a connected sitting bath, two gigantic wash basins, a bidet, two imposing wardrobes and windows everywhere. On each floor there are two toilets, four in total, but of these two are always out of order. I mention this in particular because one of my miseries, the toilet miseries, began here and have accompanied me to this day. The elegant mansion has no air raid shelter, only a basement with nothing but glass everywhere.

I owed my popularity among the mothers to the fact that even the naughtiest child would soon be eating out of my hand and nobody had ever seen me lose my temper. The homes and the mothers had a serious problem with non-eating or fussy children (a habit that eventually petered out, particularly toward the end of the siege of Buda) to whose condition we had to pay increased attention, especially considering their continuing development. So I specialized in children's diet, and with such success that I even surprised myself. There was a very likeable young woman who cried her eyes out every day because her two-year-old, otherwise very sweet, offspring simply refused to eat more than two spoonfuls of anything. When I took charge of the affair, and with complete success, this mum offered to clean my shoes so that I could spend even the time I had reserved for cleaning my shoes with her child.

I could tell you many pleasant details, but there is too much. Earlier I mentioned Palkó Demiány, who caused me a lot of trouble with his asocial behaviour when he arrived here and found himself among children of a similar age. He was always fighting or bullying those smaller than himself, so the other children disliked him and their mothers couldn't stand him, which of course made him even wilder. He also caused many problems over food. He was choosy and I was unable to convince him that one had to eat what there was. The most difficult thing was getting him to eat vegetables if he happened to notice that somebody was eating meat (the better-off caregivers used to order meat jointly from outside the home). Once I had to talk him into eating some kale. After the second spoonful, he protested desperately, especially once he realized that somebody was eating salami. I said to him: Look, at least eat half of what's on your plate. He said he'd eat half the vegetable, but would I please ask that lady for a little salami. I said I didn't want to ask her for any salami because she probably didn't have a lot, but to show my appreciation of his goodwill I'd go and bring him some of my own raisins. We finally agreed on this, and he began to eat the vegetables while I ran upstairs to fetch the raisins. Meanwhile the "lady" eating the salami had noticed Palkó's longing glances and put a slice of salami on the edge of his plate. As soon as I had returned with the raisins I saw the salami, but neither showed any awareness of it nor suggested that after what had happened we should amend our earlier agreement.

Palkó: "Will you still give me the raisins?"

Me: "Of course I'll give you the raisins. I promised, didn't I?" Whereupon Palkó took a deep breath, braced himself and — contrary to our agreement — ate *all* the vegetable.

I was very fond of Pali Heimlich, the son of the pianist with the same name. He was by far the most intelligent of all the children. He organized a proper children's republic with daily meetings, which I had to attend as honorary president, and I must say it was fun. There were also two little girls, cousins, about eight or nine years old, of whom at least one would remember once daily that she had been here long enough and wanted to go home to Mummy. She would then start sobbing bitterly, the other would join her, and if I didn't effectively intervene in good time, the whole children's home would be blubbering within half an hour, I the loudest.

One evening, when the children were already in bed on the upper floor and I was by chance the only caregiver left to walk down the stairs and join all the other caregivers at dinner on the ground floor, an air defence gun in the immediate neighbourhood suddenly began to roar, whereupon one of the children jumped screeching out of his bed, grabbed his clothes and rushed toward the stairs to the cellar. Within seconds the whole company had gone wild. Howling and bellowing, in nightshirts and bare feet, they all galloped toward the cellar. For a moment I was seriously scared because you can't imagine how scary a mass of children in such a state of excitement can be. Finally, shouting until my throat was hoarse, I managed somehow to restore a semblance of order, but the children wouldn't let me go back to dinner until I promised to stay with them for the night. I also had to let them sleep fully dressed because that was the only way to keep them more or less calm.

Then there was a very likeable young mother with a little boy of two. They were known as Irén Kássa and her illegitimate son, but she has told me her real name. We immediately took a liking to each other and would often chat in whispers over a cup of tea until two o'clock in the morning when the others were asleep. Her little boy always had a temperature. Nobody knew what it was, but it could have been some complicated kind of flu. Late one night, when in the silence of Gellért Hill it was no longer difficult to recognize the not-so-distant gunfire, Péterke remarked in an artificially deep voice: "Mummy, do you hear it? They shoot like a clown." We never discovered what he meant, but from then on the unit whereby we measured the intensity of the bombardments was the clown (although by January the intensity was no longer expressible in clowns).

Since I don't like to be confined, I volunteer for any errand outside the home. With large churns to fetch milk in, I go to the mansion at

25 Úri Street in the Castle District where the food stores of the children's homes of the International Red Cross are located. Then I take the little boys in threes to the barber to have their hair cut. The other women are reluctant to go out because we hear ugly news from the city. I'm not afraid of being seen because I've never been in this part of the city and there's really nobody here who could recognize me. Once a week, the caregivers meet in the children's aid centre on Fillér Street for a kind of conference, which I also attend. That's where I hear that the Reverend has set up some kind of secret home for elderly people, mainly elderly relatives of functionaries, officially registered as a children's home. I waste no time trying to get Nünüke accepted, which isn't easy because the home is full. The move once more causes a lot of stress. I can't leave the home in the evening, so I ask Béla and Irén to accompany my mother, but for some reason they can't go either. Suffice it to say that Nünüke climbs up Gellért Hill late at night in pouring rain with heavy luggage to the villa at 12 Bérc Street, which I myself found with difficulty in broad daylight. Luckily, I needn't be afraid for Nünüke: in the dark she stops a man to ask him where Bérc Street is. He takes pity on her, offers to accompany her, even takes her bags from her and carries them all the way to the gate, where they ring the bell. It's only when the superintendent appears with his flashlight to open the gate that Nünü realizes that the friendly gentleman was an Arrow Cross man in full uniform. Nünü had such adventures right to the end.

The home on Bérc Street has a telephone, but they won't let anyone near it. The only exception is the director, who can talk on the phone and pass on messages. Visiting is strictly forbidden, and the old residents aren't allowed to step out of the building, which keeps them out of sight of the Gestapo and Arrow Cross men ensconced in every villa in the neighbourhood. Nevertheless, I look them up at least once a week after sunset, invariably wearing my caregiver's hat. This is another elegant villa. Each huge room sleeps fourteen old people on wooden pallets and mattresses but each with their own bed linen. Everything is clean and tidy, and the food is out of this world, even by the pre-war standards.

Once I know that both my parents and I are relatively safe, I can relax for a few days. But the calm doesn't last. One day Béla turns up with the news that the Szabós (the market vendors who have taken Püpüke in) can't let my father stay with them any longer because their apartment in Klauzál Square has been included in the area designated for the ghetto. They have been ordered to move out at once and dare not take the old man with them to their newly allocated apartment (Wesselényi Street). So I must do something. And do it fast.

After a sleepless night, I call again on the Reverend, who picks up the phone immediately and despite the protests of the director squeezes my father as another supernumerary into the already overcrowded home on Bérc Street, where he is given as bleak a reception as one might expect. But by now Nünüke has become so popular that she is even forgiven for my father.

I heave a sigh of relief and now I really live a lovely peaceful life. (For at least a week and a half!) Meanwhile, I'm losing more and more weight, so there's hardly any me left. The children are very sweet, the cooking atrocious, the lodging and the surroundings I've become used to. Once a week, at seven o'clock in the morning, I nip down to the Gellért Baths (not quite two minutes from us) where I have a divine bath, followed by a hair wash, a massage, a pedicure, a dry steam, a rest, and I'm back home in time to give the children their breakfast. Now I'm only worried by the unending succession of new ordinances requiring even those who have so far been exempted under one order or another to present themselves. I'm afraid Béla will get caught. By now even Aryan male civilians are having a hard time in Budapest. For instance, one day I'm travelling on the No. 9 streetcar when the streetcar is suddenly stopped, all the men are ordered to get off, and the streetcar continues on its way with just the women, while the patrol examines the identity of everyone taken off the streetcar, one after the other, from the schoolboys to the grandfathers. Béla is continually adding to his collection of ration vouchers, with various riders listing the holder's personal details. Women are rarely expected to identify themselves, and raids on apartments are mainly directed against men.

It's about this time that the order appears for a list of all the residents to be posted with all their details not only on their apartments but also at the gates to the building (of course this doesn't apply to the Red Cross) and not only of the permanent residents but also of the temporary visitors; and the superintendent and house commander, who are personally responsible for everything, keep an eagle eye on it all. At this time, the only document I have, apart from the forged birth certificate from Kassa, is the one from the Credit Bank with my photo, with my Lutheran Christian religion entered and the last entry signed by Béla on behalf of the personnel department. I would also have my marriage certificate, but I can't use that because it says that I was born in Budapest (and not in Kassa). Otherwise, I use my true details everywhere and the initials are correct.

When we have put the children to bed in the evening, Évi Bolgár and I sit down together and, barely an hour after the normal *eráris* dinner, have huge feasts purchased privately by her. Évi escaped from the Locsodpuszta labour camp,[8] where the Arrow Cross made her "labour" until she came back with a lovely bladder catarrh and inflammation of the ovaries as souvenirs. She's been suitably starved, and it's now her who organizes our passionate food orgies, but even though we share the same diet we are surprised to find that she grows fatter while I become thinner and thinner. We still like each other and are good for each other. I am good for her because, even though she is a trained nursery school teacher, in her nervous condition she doesn't have the patience to concentrate on the children but I pretend that she does. And she is good for me because she builds up my prestige

8 The camp in Locsodpuszta near Pécel in Pest County was an internment camp.

as a nursery school teacher in the eyes of the — mostly horrible — mothers and tells everybody that although I have no official qualification, I am a recognized authority in professional circles, whom the best-known nursery school teachers will consult on the more complicated cases; she enthuses about the stroke of luck that brought me to this particular home and the pleasure that working side by side with me gives her, and she tries to calculate how many of her young colleagues envy her because of her relationship with me. We had to concoct all this because — although she had warned me not to let the mothers know that I am not a professional — whenever I was asked I had immediately blurted out that I was only an amateur. It was my blunder that we had to correct by means of this complicated story. Évi had been quite right because later I wouldn't have been able to cope with the many stupid mothers of Lipótváros.

By now the homesick children's snivelling leaves me cold: I'm used to it. But I still get very worked up one last time: when little Palkó Demiány falls ill. He looks very pale and sad, then he withdraws into a corner, and when I go to him he declares without being asked that he is unhappy here because everybody is a stranger. When I ask him why everybody here is a stranger, he says that it's because they don't know him and because he doesn't like them. I ask him if he doesn't like me either. After a short hesitation he says: "Only half." And he adds: "Mummy whole." (This was the first time he mentioned his mother during our whole acquaintance.) His hand is hot. I check his temperature, which is high. I put him to bed. We call the doctor. It's exactly the eve of Saint Nicholas's Day, and the whole building is preparing for Saint Nicholas's evening. I have to go to the children's aid centre on Fillér Street, the Reverend has summoned me and Évi Bolgár. (It's just as well that I don't know yet what for.) Palkó asks me very quietly and very seriously not to leave him but to stay with him, but he says this not in a child's pestering whine or a sick child's petulance but as if he had thought carefully about the matter and considered it important that I should stay with him. He doesn't cry even when I explain to him that unfortunately I must go out but will hurry back home. He nods sympathetically, but he has tears in his eyes and quickly turns his head away.

You know, my Pipus, how many children I have been and am friendly with, how fond I am of the little Belcsáks, for example, but I can't explain either to you or to myself how restless I was that whole afternoon and how I could hardly wait to be at home again with the children. Perhaps this little boy was more my child than the other small children I had met so far, especially because at that time he had nobody except me and he knew that. You will see how little the child could rely on his grandmother and his aunt if I tell you what happened when I got home and asked the grandmother what the child's temperature had been in the afternoon. She gave me a surprised look and said with some irritation that she had not taken his temperature. (She is the intelligent mother of a well-to-do merchant family, not some primitive prole.) Before I went to Fillér Street that afternoon, against my habit and conviction, I bought up everything that I knew would give Palkó pleasure and when I got home in the evening I was carrying a large parcel which I put in his bed. By that time he was feeling better and his temperature had also gone down. He didn't jump up and down with pleasure, but he let out a loud shriek, then looked at the items for a long time before he repacked them, unpacked them once more and finally packed them, saying that he would only play with these at home. (He was probably thinking that the toys were too good for the nasty surroundings.)

Unfortunately I missed the Saint Nicholas celebrations because of the meeting on Fillér Street, but it was worth it because the Reverend told us in confidence that we must disappear from the home on Kelenhegyi Road because there will be a major raid in response to the Ministry of the Interior's wish to see only pure Aryan mothers and children, with attendant caregivers living in Buda while everybody else is moved to homes in Pest. Sztehlo advises me to disappear on about December 15 and report to him a few days later, having tried to complete my documents, that is, at least adding refugee papers to my poor lone orphan of a birth certificate. By now Évi Bolgár has the complete series of papers in the name of Erzsébet Tóth and is transferred under that name to the children's home at 20 Csaba Street, where nobody knows her. Things begin to heat up a little when Béla, who is regarded as a kind of oracle in such matters, and not only by me, tells me not to stay in a marked building, whether there is a star or a red cross on the gate, which, at least in the eyes of the Arrow Cross, are the same animal, but to try to get a private job. In the home too it's soon rumoured that between December 15 and 31 there will be raids on the homes. Our suspense is rapidly growing and mixed with embarrassment as we try in vain to keep it secret from the Aryans present.

Béla comes out to us on Kelenhegyi Road late every night to clean up certificates with invisible ink, to complete forged forms or to give advice, and all that for free, even though it was possible at the time to make heaps of money that way. I gradually have my possessions taken away from Kelenhegyi Road, and finally I also leave, saying that I'll be back some time. But I've jumped ahead of myself again: The removal of the majority of the mothers to Pest caused a lot of commotion. Most of them were put up in the Lutheran high school on Vilma Királynő Road, and I wondered whether it wouldn't be wiser for me to go with them. I leaned toward this solution first because you had gone to that school and then because everybody was convinced that Pest would be in Russian hands long before Buda. In the meantime, I wouldn't have liked to fall into the hands of the Arrow Cross, even though — as I have said — my imagination doesn't reach that far. However, I had to think of the various possibilities.

The mothers begged me to go to the Vilma with them, but one day I woke up certain that I wouldn't go with them nor even stay with them here. I didn't tell this to anybody, but I helped those about to leave with their packing and at the same time ran to and fro attending to odd jobs of all kinds. I couldn't visit your mother at that time, but a very nice woman named Mária Anker, who lived on Horthy Miklós Road (not far from me), a good friend of the Baranyais, went to see your mother several times at the Bs' request and always kept me informed.

On the evening before the departure of the group due to move to Vilma Királynő Road, a deputation came running up the stairs, calling me to come with them immediately because Palkó was refusing to eat his dinner without me and was making a huge fuss because he believed I had gone away. I went down, sat next to him and his supper and told him (he and his relatives were on the list of those moving out the next day) that I had to go away for a few days and he should get used to having supper without me because if I were to hear that he'd made another fuss like that I wouldn't come back to him at all. He thought for a long time and then said quietly and deliberately in a slightly trembling voice: "If you go away I will… I will stop pooing" (without realizing what a great and profound thing he had said and how pleased Alice Bálint[9] would have been, not to mention old Freud. Finally, we agreed (generally it was possible to come to agreements with him, and he always fulfilled them handsomely) that he would stop pooing only if he learned that I went away when it hadn't been absolutely necessary for me to do so or that I had only gone because I felt like seeing some other children. I must add that he had never before shown any sign of affection for me, but just noted that I existed and that it wasn't his grandmother who looked after him, but me. It was clear that he preferred the latter, which didn't surprise anybody who knew the grandmother. But I must say I was afraid of tomorrow's farewell and had decided not to be around when the carriage left and if possible not to be seen at the general goodbyes either.

Unfortunately, my real farewell to the poor dear turned out to be

---

9 Alice Bálint (1898–1939) was an important member of the Budapest school of psychoanalysis, with a special interest in the development of children.

a great spanking because he had done the following: When all the adults were busy packing and carrying things to the coach, Palkó marched into one of the magnificent bathrooms with Andriska, the two-year-old squealer, who was already dressed for the journey and squealing, but whose squeals weren't noticed by anybody because he used to squeal most of the time, with or without reason. When the squealing had nevertheless become too much for me, I opened the bathroom door and found that Palkó had sat Andriska, fully dressed, into one of the sitting baths, carefully put the plug into the plughole and turned on the tap so that Andriska's head was underneath the tap but his shoes got wet also. When I stepped into the bathroom, the small creature was sitting under the tap and getting soaked, squealing but obeying. You could have knocked me down with a feather. Andriska's clothes were already packed and in the carriage, his mother was busy getting ready for the departure, they were due to leave in ten minutes, and here was a dripping wet child. As quick as lightning, I stripped Andriska completely naked, put him in a bed and his clothes to dry on a radiator before I went back into the bathroom and asked Palkó, who was still standing at the scene of the crime with a smug smile, how he thought Andriska might have got into the bath. Palkó informed me in his usual quiet way that he couldn't tell me what I wanted to know unless I promised in advance that he, Palkó, wouldn't be punished. I didn't promise him anything, but having told him what I thought of his behaviour gave him a spanking and stood him in a corner. He didn't cry, but stood in the corner with an embarrassed grin, not daring to look at me. I ran up to the next floor to continue my packing and never saw the child again. I don't know what became of him, although I tried to find him. At his old address, nobody knew anything.

My Pipus, I've written such a lot about this little boy in comparison with others, but on the one hand I was very fond of him, much more than I have been of the later ones, so much so that I've often wondered if you'd agree to us adopting him after the war if his parents didn't turn up again. On the other hand, these small children's stories filled my daily life at that time, and I can only repeat that without the children my nerves wouldn't have stood up to this madhouse. This reminds me of an amazed mother once asking me (when I had to make peace between, and calm down, a group of angry children) how I could love so many children so much at one and the same time. I forget what I answered, but I thought to myself: I love so few adults and so little, but there's so much more left for the children.

About December 15, I moved out of the home on Kelenhegyi Road with the last modest parcel in my hand, closing a relatively calm period of my life in hiding. Since the Reverend had advised me to return to privacy and stay with friends for a few days until a place is found for me in another home, I choose Juci and her family as my first hosts, in spite of the order for a list of guests to be posted at the entrance to the building and the risk of the maid, whom Juci is allowed to employ, forgetting her good intentions and blurting out that there is another visitor who is missing from the list.

Béla continues to urge me not to go back to a Red Cross home. He is only too right, even if the events justify me in hindsight. So I try to find a private job. Évi Bolgár's aunt, the doctor who used to come to treat the children of Kelenhegyi Road, takes a very kind and active interest in my problem and through of one of her aristocratic patients recommends me to an elegant middle-aged lady with bone tuberculosis who needs half a companion and half a nurse. I can't go to introduce myself for a few days because I don't even know what my name will be with the confusion over my documents, which I will explain later. I want to get the refugee papers, which can be used as substitutes for lost documents of origin and also be used to obtain food coupons. It was our good luck that Budapest was flooded with refugees from eastern Hungary, and both ID registrations and food coupons were in such chaos that it was impossible to check who was a genuine or a fake refugee.

Apparently, refugee certificates were only given to those who had jobs. So Béla gets me a war-worker certificate with a fake photo for three hundred pengős. For that only a fake registration is needed. We fill this in, and a friend of Béla's, a Jewish girl who escaped here from Bihar County, will get a refugee ID for me from the District VI administration. For that purpose she takes my only documents, the fake birth certificate and the beautiful new war industry certificate with her, promising to bring them back tomorrow with the addition of a refugee certificate and food coupons. Days full of suspense follow. One, two, three days pass, and the girl isn't seen again. I phone our friend Kromesch on Csillaghegy, who immediately comes here. I tell him that it's now or never to get his wife's papers. To get those, he has to travel to Nagymaros, which is no trivial matter at the moment. We say goodbye and never hear from him again. We discover later that he has been called up.

I occasionally visit the home on Kelenhegyi Road. One wealthy and rather charming young mother offers me a set of papers free of charge that she originally bought for fifteen thousand pengős but that she would let go for nothing because she has since bought some better ones. I take them with me and try to learn the contents by heart, but I don't like them. I might just about be able to convince people that my name is Erzsébet Balogh, but I would find it very difficult to make anybody believe that I am twenty-four at a time when I am lucky to be taken for forty-four. As far as the woman with the bone tuberculosis is concerned, I don't dare go to introduce myself to her because I still don't know what my name is. Neither can I turn to Sztehlo because the recommendation is personal.

Finally, after six miserable days, the girl turns up again bringing the fervently awaited refugee certificate. Since she accepts no money, I give her my brown sweater with the lovely turquoise angora decorations because no other sweater of mine fits her and because the poor dear escaped from the ghetto in summer without any warm clothes. At last I can go introduce myself to the sick woman. We very much like each other but the job has already been taken (I think it was 15 Hattyú Street, which has long since been destroyed, but I don't know what happened to the woman).

Meanwhile — out of sheer boredom and because I happened to have the time — I obtained the refugee documents for Nünü and my father. To get these documents, I first had to collect their baptism certificates from Bérc Street, so they were without any documents for two days. Then one fine afternoon I was in the area and the weather was good and I had time. I ran up Gellért Hill and dropped off the baptism certificates with the newly acquired documents. That night there was a raid on Bérc Street, and those whose papers were not in order were immediately taken away, and I still don't know what happened to those who were taken. This would have happened to Nünü and my father if I hadn't decided to pick up the papers that afternoon but, say, the following morning. Our lives depended on such fortunate coincidences all the time, from raids to bombings.

Once I meet Busi and Muki in the street. They are also living as refugees with forged papers in a furnished room somewhere in Krisztinaváros. They ask me to accompany them to the Kramolins at 23 Attila Street. They are not relatives of mine, but I knew Busi well as one of the Kramolins' little children. Her parents were divorced, and she lived with her great-grandmother as a kind of nobody's child, but was loved by everybody for her charm, which we also experienced during the long hours she spent at our apartment as a visitor. Eventually her mother married a rural royal prosecutor, and they had recently been transferred to Budapest.

It was to this couple that I accompanied Busi and Muki. I had a chat with their mother, Gizi, and told her about my situation. She was prepared to employ me as a governess and although she immediately agreed that I should be registered under her address and sleep there from time to time, there remained the insoluble problem of food. (Ernő Lénárd wanted me to sleep somewhere else from time to time.)

I often called on Sztehlo about my transfer, but because the Arrow

Cross raids were not yet over he advised me to wait until after Christmas if I could hide that long. I told him that I wanted to get a job but that every plan had failed because of the question of food. He told me to accept a job anywhere and not to worry about food, that he would make sure I was fed at the nearest Red Cross home. In the Kramolins' case, this would mean that I would have meals in the home at 13 Pauler Street (in the Hornyánszky Palace).

By that time, I knew that Vera Nyilas worked at that home as a caregiver. The Reverend also told me on that occasion that he very much wanted me to go back to the home on Kelenhegyi Road. He asks me if dare go back there. I say laughingly that I am not afraid of anything and will go wherever he wants me to go. He calls Kelenhegyi Road right in front of me and agrees with Daisy Ullmann that in due course he will transfer me to her but not until the expected raids have taken place. We say goodbye to each other, having agreed that I will come back in a few days.

When I go back to the headquarters on Fillér Street a few days later, the Reverend is not there. I have a long conversation with Mme Barrée, who tells me that the situation has become much worse, with the Ministry of the Interior constantly harassing and bullying the Red Cross, which it suspects of hiding many Jews. Arrow Cross men are reported to intrude into Red Cross homes at regular intervals and abduct not only the caregivers but also children. From one home in Budapest, all the Jewish children and children without documents were taken to the ghetto and crowded into a block, starving, covered in scabs and infested with lice. Mme Barrée also advises me not to report for transfer until after Christmas because the Reverend has many problems at the moment.

Meanwhile, it has turned evening. Feeling sad, I wander home, i.e., to the Lénárds. When Juci opens the door, I can see from her face that there are problems. Nünüke is sitting in the room immobile. She hasn't stepped out of her building since November 17. Today the authorities served strict orders for the home on Bérc Street to be vacated within forty-eight hours and for all adults to be excluded from the protected status. I feel as if I have been hit on the head. I have no idea what to do with the old folk. We can't leave my mother with the Lénárds for the night because of the maid and the lack of space, but since it is already dark I can't let her go back alone either. I gather my things and walk up with Nünü to Bérc Street, where we spend the night with other despairing, panic-stricken old people, whom I am not going to describe because that would be a task for a Russian short story writer or at least a French filmmaker, but whom I will never forget.

Nünüke and I share a bed, but we can't sleep. We squeeze each other's hand and in the morning we rush away to look for some accommodation for the old couple. My father is useless by then. We rush up and down, but there is nowhere to live and nobody wants to accept old people. Finally, on Béla's advice, I manage to find the former Lévai boarding house and rent a room there. Early on December 24, I pick up the old couple from Gellért Hill, where we collect as many possessions as the three of us can carry in our hands, and additionally on my back, leaving the rest ready in the villa, from where I intend to have it retrieved after the holiday.

By now the guns sound very near, but the traffic is still almost normal. We take the streetcar to the boarding house, which is freezing cold. There is generally no food in the restaurants, let alone in the boarding houses, where not even a breakfast cup of tea is to be had. The guests' documents are examined at once, but it seems that all are in order. Luckily, Nünüke is immediately popular wherever she goes. A maid, for example, brings wood to light a fire in their room and even promises them some hot water for washing. As I leave them, I am desperately worried because it is so terribly cold and I can't imagine what they will get to eat in the few restaurants that may still be functioning but are also not cooking during the holiday.

All this on the morning of December 24, which was a Sunday. That same day I have a meeting with Évi's aunt, the doctor, about my own matter in the home on Csaba Street. From there I go to have lunch with Juci and then I plan to drop in on the old couple in the afternoon. The ferry is too slow for me, so I gallop across the pontoon bridge each time I cross the Danube.

Juci and her family are getting ready for the holy evening. They are decorating the tree. Juci has collected Stühmer sweets in twenty-gram units, lining up in the terrible cold for hours for every ten grams so that the children might have the kind of Christmas they are used to. She bakes splendid Christmas biscuits out of hoarded ingredients. There will be roast goose brought by Ernő from an adventurous journey to the country, and the whole apartment is beautifully cleaned for the holiday. In the early afternoon, as I leave to see the old couple, Juci runs after me and places a big parcel in my hands, saying that she is sending this to the old couple for Christmas.

Pipus, I am afraid that you won't be able to understand, but to me this parcel is an act of true humanity. It only contained small amounts of flour, sugar, walnuts and sweets, but all of which Juci had collected with considerable effort, freezing while standing in the line for hours, and anxiously guarded for her own children. Unable to tell her what I thought — and still think — of her gesture, I broke down in tears and mumbled something that might or might not have sounded like "thank you."

I ran across to Pest where Nünüke and I wrapped up one-third of these gifts for Gizella, and I took it across to the Swedish hospital for her. Gizella was pleased to see me and what I was bringing. But I didn't see her again until the end of February — that is, after my own siege.

From Gizella, I was happily walking back to Buda on the pontoon bridge in the beautiful moonlit night. The Danube bathed in moonlight and the festive excitement on the streets in spite of the otherwise miserable common atmosphere were very beautiful. The streetcars were still running when I got home to the Lénárds, where they were waiting for me to return before they lit the candles. There was a present for me under the tree, and everybody was so kind to me that I ran out to the toilet to howl. Ernő had now done a month's military service in Pápa and had only come home for three days at Christmas. We go to bed late. I am somewhat comforted about my parents but their diet remains a great worry. We don't get much sleep that night because toward sunrise the detonations become so powerful and so close that they blow us out of our beds. Juci goes down to the cellar with the children while the maid and I stay in the apartment. Ernő runs up and down between the cellar and the apartment.

In the morning, I try to get to the old couple on the other side of the river, but I am not allowed to step on the pontoon bridge, in front of which there is barbed wire, and which is guarded by soldiers. I panic. What's going to happen to the old couple over there without anything or anybody? In the afternoon, I discover that the ferry is still running, so I decide to go and fetch the old couple. These are the few days when it looks as if — despite all expectation — Buda will fall first into Russian hands, since the Russians surprisingly invaded the city from Hűvösvölgy. The ferry crossing is not much fun. There are shells hitting the water beside us with a hiss. When I get there, the old couple are slumbering calmly and can't understand why I am trying to hurry them so. We must catch the last ferry, which leaves for Buda at 5:00 p.m. I quickly pack their things, and we rush to the ferry. This time I almost collapse because unlike yesterday I have to carry not only their parcels but also my own essential possessions on my back, given that I was leaving Buda and might be marooned in Pest.

As we board the ferry, a mine explodes in the water near us. We throw ourselves on our stomachs, and the situation gets worse and worse. Nobody knows what is really happening, but it's rumoured that the ring around Budapest has been closed, the Russians had already occupied the region of Hűvösvölgy-Pasarét-Farkasrét, and everybody realizes that now the real fun and games are beginning.

Darkness is falling when we reach Buda. My father finds the speed hard to bear. We have to stop or leave him behind. He is complaining about dizziness, and I am afraid that he will be sick. We climb up to the Gül Baba Boarding House, which you know. Luckily, they have a room available. The owners take a long time sniffing at and objecting to the old couple's papers, but Nünüke's confident manner seems to dissolve their doubts. Before I go back to Juci and her family, I explain to the old couple that tomorrow I will get my new posting from Sztehlo and come back to them sometime later.

All this happens on December 25, the first day of Christmas. On December 26, the firing is even more vicious. Margit Boulevard is beginning to be pounded, the mood is terrible. We cannot get a mover, let alone a van, to collect the things left behind on Gellért Hill even though these really are the old couple's most important things: their few bits of clothing and some bedding. In between, I hear that Fillér Street is already in Russian hands, so that my next posting is kaput: I can't reach the Reverend.

On reflection I decide to go back to my registered lodging, the Kramolin apartment, and try to get myself into the home on Pauler Street. Since I have no posting, Juci tries to hold me back. She tells me not to leave them now that the Russians are here. The whole thing won't last two more days, so I might as well stay. But I don't let myself be persuaded, mainly because, whether or not the siege ends, there won't be any food for a long time, and I don't want to eat the supplies meant for Juci's children.

(I discover after the siege how wise I was not to stay there. On the next day the local unit of the Arrow Cross Party moved into the building because their headquarters had been shot to pieces.) I run upstairs to the boarding house to say goodbye to the old couple and to leave all the food supplies, tin cans, etc., that I had hidden with Juci to them. Then I slip into the siege dress, which I will describe later, load my most important possessions on my back and set out toward Attila Street in savage shelling.

I am free to choose where I want to walk: Krisztina Boulevard, to the end of Attila Street or Logodi Street. In such a furious barrage it is most advisable to walk along Logodi because that street at least has apartment buildings on each side. But since the Russians are firing into the side of Castle Hill from Hűvösvölgy, the shrapnel lands in the vicinity of Logodi Street. I have to jump into a gateway or crouch behind a stone wall, which is not easy with a lot of luggage and a heavy knapsack. All this happens on December 26, in the early afternoon with the sun shining. In the street, police are herding civilian men, pushing the unwilling with the butts of their guns. They are not interested in seeing any documents and take everybody without exception away to dig trenches.

At last, I reach the Kramolins, who no longer have any windows or even window frames. The family has moved into its one and only unscathed room, the maid's room facing the courtyard, where five of them are lying low. I drop my things with them and walk across to Pauler Street, where I show my caregiver ID with my photo and explain that I can no longer reach Sztehlo. I had been on Christmas leave just before the transfer. It's no longer possible to go back to Kelenhegyi Road and would they be prepared to let me stay with them? I also point out that to my knowledge the Reverend had wanted to transfer me to this home.

They receive me very kindly. There is an Aryan director who doesn't live in the home but in her apartment next to it on Attila Street in a building whose garden borders on the garden of the home. The rest are all Jews, the caregivers as well as the children, but all have forged papers. I discover that they survived the Arrow Cross raid a good while before Christmas. Some boys of fourteen and fifteen were undressed, but luckily the ones they had chosen did not present any problems.[10] I collect my things from the Kramolins and now I really heave a sigh of relief because the gunfire is becoming more and more

---

10 Boys were checked to see if they were circumcised, which would indicate their Jewish identity.

violent and anybody can see the serious siege has really started.

A dentist called Dr. Kapolyi lives with the Kramolins. His own apartment is next to theirs and that is where his wife, who is an Aryan, lives with his family and he, being of Jewish origin, has been sought several times by the Arrow Cross. Everyone in the building thinks he is away on forced labour, but he is really hiding next door, in the apartment of the Kramolins, where his wife comes to see him daily. He can never see his children, who might give away the secret. I became very fond of this Dr. Kapolyi. He was nice, intelligent and very good to me right to the end. I could turn to him with any problem, as you will hear later. Dr. Kapolyi and I agreed that the affair would be finished in a few days because the Germans could only hold the city for another week with the Russians attacking from a different direction than they had expected.

On December 26, there is a festive dinner at the home on Pauler Street. One of the caregivers donates some Russian tea, which we drink with brandy, eight types of sandwiches and *bájgli*.[11] All this happens in the pleasant, centrally heated dining room, in which a sofa has been prepared for me to sleep on. That night, almost everybody in the building sleeps in the cellar. I stay up here — like the other beginners in the game of being besieged — but fully dressed. By now I only feel bad because I don't know if the old couple are cold and if they have anything to eat, while I am eating lavish sandwiches. Next day I am dispatched to help in the kitchen and allocated two children to assist me, so that I am fully absorbed by the home on Pauler Street. The Aryan director tries to phone Sztehlo a few times about me, but by now the phone has stopped working.

Before I start the chapter called "Siege," I'll give you an impression of the appearance and the mood of your native city on the days before the siege.

Everybody is terribly nervous because all the bridges are visibly

11 A walnut or poppy seed roll, a traditional Hungarian Christmas pastry.

mined. Ever since Margit Bridge was blown up, many people are too afraid to step on any of the bridges, with the result that both the ferry and the "propeller" boat are overcrowded. My friend Juci, for example, doesn't have the nerve to cross to Pest at all. She asks me to do her errands in Pest for her because she is afraid she might not get back to her children. I point out to her that this phobia of crossing the river started as long as ten weeks before the bridge was actually blown up.

The whole city is full of tank traps, barbed-wire entanglements and concrete bunkers. The entire length of the Buda side of the Danube embankment is dug up for clusters of machine guns, dug-in cannons everywhere on the Buda side of the bridges, their barrels facing the bridgeheads, frightening instruments directed against Pest. (The analysts will be pleased to see people dreaming of such things for decades after the war.)

Above the iron railing running the whole length of the Buda Promenade, forced labourers took several weeks to fix dried corn leaves in a net opposite the bridgehead to camouflage the machine guns dug in behind the railings. The huge sweetcorn fence is ready and called the "Catlantic Wall" by some jokers, but this is, so to speak, the only manifestation of the famous Budapest humour in this period, a period most aptly characterized by the fact that even the people of Budapest are losing their appetite for humour.

In the beginning was The Armed German Soldier, who guarded the entrance to the bridges. By the end of November, he was already carrying bayonets on his rifle. By the beginning of December, he was wearing a belt of hand grenades. By the middle of December, ditto, but always carrying the rifle with the bayonet ready to fire. I was curiously awaiting the next stage.

The image of the city is bleak and frightening. Hardly any shops are open when I walk around the centre on errands for Juci just before Christmas. I buy toys in the Lopos[12] improvised premises (the

---

12 A department store owned by Gyula Lopos.

old ones have been shot to pieces), where I have to line up and fight. For Nünüke, I search the whole city for knitting needles but can't get any anywhere. Most of the famous handicraft shops no longer exist, but it isn't possible, for example, to get any lemon substitute either. The city was sentenced to death a long time ago but now there is a genuine morgue atmosphere everywhere. In the week before Christmas, the market halls are almost empty. Apples have also disappeared from the market by the middle of December, potatoes haven't been available for a long time. For bread you have to line up for hours, but I don't remember the prices. On the day before Christmas, I step into a news cinema in the city centre while running errands and watch the whole program (I haven't been in a cinema since March) but find it very dull: nothing but German victories, and I am sick and tired of them. I am also cold because buildings, cinemas, cafés and the like are no longer heated. I enter the bistro opposite (where you and I have often gone together) and can't believe my eyes: they are serving freshly cooked piglets' ears, and I blow all the cash I have with me on pork.

It's no good. I can't render the terribly depressing image and mood of the city adequately.

Once I had an interesting meeting, also during the pre-Christmas errands. Somewhere in darkest Krisztinaváros behind the back of beyond I stepped into a small bazaar crammed full of other shoppers as such places always are before Christmas. Facing the door and leaning against the counter stood a bored young girl I had known by sight from the No. 72 streetcar for years. She has been wearing an Arrow Cross badge on her coat from the beginning, and I had often heard her on the streetcar talking politics, cursing the Jews, prophesying the victory of Germany over the world, etc. When I walk into the shop, we stare at each other for a moment. I didn't even have time to get frightened before she turned on her heels and started to study something on the opposite shelf. Her posture seemed to say: *Don't worry, I didn't recognize you*. To be on the safe side, I beat a hasty retreat from the shop.

There are constant raids. By now they are no longer searching so much for Jews but rather for deserters from the army. You hear fantastic figures quoted in connection with military deserters, there are so many of them. This reminds me of a conversation I once overheard on a ferry after the Margit Bridge explosion. A high-ranking policeman standing next to me was telling somebody that after the destruction of the bridge a vast number of mothers, fathers, wives, etc., reported their military relatives killed in the explosion. The man from the police remarked with a sneer: "You wouldn't believe that there were about five thousand soldiers on the bridge at that precise moment."

I also know of cases where an Aryan soldier with forged Jewish papers hid with his Jewish fiancée in a starred house while his protection was being arranged. On another occasion, while I was looking for a job, I was offered an apartment with forged documents in exchange for Dénes's papers and Swiss or Swedish protection. This didn't come to anything.

But the sweetest advertisement appeared in the streets during the week before Christmas: It had come to the attention of the Minister of the Interior that certain black-hearted Jews were defying his orders not only by refusing to meet his deadline for moving into the ghetto but also by hiding without a star and with forged documents. He therefore appeals to these naughty Jews to examine their consciences and move into the ghetto by December 31, which they would still be able to do with impunity, but they'll regret it if they don't. (I don't remember what the punishment was, but I think it was kneeling in the corner or something of the kind.) The only unpleasant part of this advertisement was that it threatened the superintendent or house commander (not to mention the owner of the building) with whom such a naughty Jew was found.

Luckily Juci's family are clearly not interested in the poster, but it is nevertheless one of the factors that make me decide to leave, as I think that it would be better for the Red Cross to be made to kneel in a corner than for Juci and her family.

Everybody everywhere is in a bad mood. Suspicion prevails. The hairdresser, the policeman, the streetcar driver, the superintendent — nobody is as garrulous as they were before. Medicines and food aren't available anywhere. Very rarely some goods turn up in one shop or another, where if word gets around long lines form, and order is kept by the Arrow Cross "brothers" and the police.

As I said, everybody believed for a long time that Pest was the better place because the Germans would abandon Pest sooner and defend Buda. Therefore, I hesitated a little whether I shouldn't ask to be moved to the children's home in Pest. Everybody, possibly even the Germans, is surprised when the Russians forge ahead from Buda. You have to laugh at the Germans for digging their artillery in with their backsides facing the enemy and the whole defence apparatus turning its back on the attackers. It is not before the middle of January that Pest begins once more to be the safer place, but by the time we discover this it is too late. For a while, it also looked as if the Russians would come up the Danube from Csepel in assault boats.

By now, Hungarian army special units with Arrow Cross armbands and Arrow Cross men in formal black suits and green shirts constantly wore egg grenades in their belts and walked with gloomy faces in the streets. Around the middle of January, you could still see Arrow Cross uniforms in the streets but no Arrow Cross armbands. Then the green shirts began to disappear and the black suit with civilian shirt and without an armband served as a uniform. And gradually the Arrow Cross men disappeared from THE COMPLETELY SURROUNDED CITY, in other words they also shed the black suits, and I was very sorry that I hadn't memorized the face of one or the other even though I would have had many opportunities to do so because Pauler Street was situated in a decidedly Arrow Cross district.

Siege Dress

When I left Juci and her family on December 26, it was clear that the worst was still to come. I put on the clothes I had long since selected for this purpose, leaving the rest with Juci and Béla. It was lucky that your unit in Bereck returned the parcel that had been sent the year before, so that I was properly equipped and these goods could not be stolen from you either. Throughout the siege, I was wearing ski boots, thick socks and woollen stockings, a pair of warm loden ski pants, a blouse, two jumpers — one with and one without sleeves — an apron, four to five pairs of warm underwear, a nurse's headscarf, wrist warmers and two thick goatskin mittens, and make no mistake, all of these at the same time, because I dreaded catching cold and being ill. In the street, I wore over my beautiful black winter coat my incredibly grubby raincoat and on my hip, hanging on a strap, my checkered ski bag standing in for a handbag. I had brought three changes of knitted underwear, two blouses including the one on me, and a number of jumpers, which stood me in very good stead toward the end of the siege when I had to change from top to toe.

I also had the huge knapsack with me that I used to use for air defence. In the knapsack were a tracksuit, a dressing gown, ski slippers, warm blankets, towels, etc. Later, my colleagues very much envied my clothing because of course every decent garment rotted in the cellar, not to mention the civilian shoes, which stood up badly to the first Age of Shattered Window Glass and even worse to what came after, in the way of clambering over the rubble and wading through muck up to the ankles. My once beautiful bright-coloured raincoat served well as camouflage, because it was a less visible target in the snow than a black winter coat.

As well as the knapsack, I carried a woven hemp bag, which was my pantry and held my private sugar and lard supplies while they lasted, and my red checkered waterproof beach bag, which also proved very useful. I also had a mess tin, but this wasn't used at all at first and very rarely later. Let me boast of my foresight. I also had a lice-comb, which was in great demand in late January. Eau de cologne and cotton wool played a great part in allowing me to clean myself perfectly even without water. I also had medicines, among others Sedyletta, but I no longer needed this after the first serious gun battle. I also had masses of matches and a few candles, which I hoarded jealously because I was always afraid that we might suddenly be left in the dark. My wristwatch also worked well at the time. It died later, so I gave it to Béla to be repaired. Finally, I had a vast amount of money, which I spent recklessly because I was sure that it wouldn't be worth anything after the siege, and I also encouraged the old couple to spend. At that time the soldiers used to light their pipes with ten-pengő notes instead of spills.[13] Money was worth nothing.

13 A twist of paper used for lighting cigarettes or pipes before matches were invented.

The Siege

According to the world's press, the siege of Budapest officially started at some point during the first days of November. I say that it was on the morning of December 24 when the guns around us began to roar from all directions. Until then they had only delivered a few solitary shells from time to time (and we beamed with pleasure when a distant explosion made our doors and windows rattle, or, going to bed on Gellért Hill, we opened our balcony doors wide and told each other to be quiet so that we could hear the guns stationed in Kelenföld better), but now they fire continuously and one explosion merges with the next, sounding like thunder. People are running all over in the streets and I'm struck for the first time by how much more nervous the men are than the women. I go down into the street to try to find somebody who could climb up Gellért Hill with me and help me bring down the old folks' things. But this looks quite hopeless. Everybody is running, nobody cares for money. At every distant explosion they dive into gateways. The wildest rumours circulate, and since nobody knows where the Russians really are, everybody says something different, it's impossible to guess the direction of the firing. This alone could be the reason one can't get up Gellért Hill.

As I take up residence in the home on Pauler Street, I am certain this isn't the best place to be, not even if Buda falls before Pest. We are right at the foot of the castle and very close to Vérmező Park.

Since the great shelling started, I've felt very very relieved, although I still have a small fear of hunger left in me. The first time I eat lunch on Pauler Street and make the children say grace before the meal, I secretly burst into tears.

We eat sitting at tables in the dining room of the Hornyánszkys' ground-floor apartment. After Christmas, everybody sleeps in the basement, except me because I hate the dark and the overcrowding, so I stay on the dining room sofa as long as possible, that is, until January 2, when all the windows together with their frames fly out into the next street.

But first I'll give you a rough description of the other people in the building, because from now on I have to live in close proximity to them.

Mrs. Hornyánszky junior is about forty, very beautiful, intelligent and kind. I have already written about her elsewhere.

Mr. Hornyánszky looks like the hero of a novel. He is fortysomething, obnoxious, selfish, greedy, cold and strikes poses. The staff hate him. It's rumoured that his soldiers wanted to shoot him in the back during World War I. He is mean and personally keeps watch in the kitchen to make sure that the maid doesn't spend too much on cooking. He preaches thrift to everybody, but in the afternoons he sneaks out to the kitchen and looks for choice morsels to eat. One day half the content of a demijohn of brandy disappears. He openly suspects the Red Cross nurses and goes around dropping loud and unmistakable remarks. His wife is embarrassed by all this and tries to gloss over the affair.

Mrs. Hornyánszky senior is a scatterbrained older woman, who is also mean and a little resentful of the world because of the siege and the discomforts attached to it, but otherwise not much trouble.

Then there are the guests marooned in the Hornyánszky boarding house: The landowner Baron Kapry and his family are refugees from Transylvania. The husband resembles a retired general. He is a bit feeble-minded, speaks bad Hungarian and is only interested in his dog, Sunny. His wife, Baroness Erzsébet, is a nice, intelligent, good-humoured, elegant woman. She tells our fortunes from cards. She knew from the first moment who we were, but she never let on. Their daughter, Baroness Valéria, is an attractive young woman but moody and strange; I hear later that she is on morphine, and woe to the household if she happens to be in a bad mood. Mr. Schober, the house commander, is a quiet, stupid, minor civil-servant type. Major Vilmos Sáromberki Ziegler, Foreign Ministry councillor (in due course simply the Major), later automatically takes command of the building with the approval of all of us because he is sober, calm, energetic and knows how to do everything better than Mr. Schober. Vera Platt is an intelligent, pleasant woman of the world, who lived in Berlin until recently when her apartment was bombed.

It's typical of all the people I have so far described that their behaviour is really impeccable even at the most critical times. I have never seen any of the women unkempt or slovenly or neglected. They are always well turned out. Their hair is tidy, as is their makeup, and above all — with the exception of Baroness Valéria — they are always calm. They never lose their head and don't argue with each other — at least not in front of us. There are also many boarding house guests, with whom we hardly ever talk, mostly young married Aryan couples, not of the petty bourgeois type I know and am used to, but from some kind of gentry. One young woman, from a noble family from the Bácska region, literally loses control of her bowels each time there is a major bombing, while her husband stands ready to bring a bucket and brush after each raid.

The staff: bácsi Nyirsy,[1] the superintendent, is deaf. Both he and his wife are terribly dirty and they steal like magpies. The cook of the boarding house, Bözsi from Nagykőrös, is a big woman with a

1 The editors have corrected the misspelling (Nirschy) in Margit's original typescript.

big mouth, but well meaning and decent. The chambermaid of the boarding house is Mici, a middle-aged Viennese. The Hornyánszkys' maid for all general work is Juci. There is a further individual, called Jóska, also from Nagykőrös and related to a member of the staff. He has a car (in peacetime he is a deliveryman by trade) and appears either in uniform or in ordinary clothes, whichever promises to be more profitable at any given moment.

And then there are of course the caregivers. Actually, I'm sorry I started to describe the characters because it hasn't gone very well. The descriptions are bad and it bores me to analyze one person after the other. But I'll go on because it will perhaps help me to immerse myself once more in the atmosphere of Pauler Street and I'll do a little better with the others.

You already know Vera Nyilas, so I won't go into detail about her. This time I've got to like her. She has turned out much more asocial than I would have believed, but you can't be too cross with her because when push comes to shove you can always rely on her. You also forgive her because she is constantly making fun of her asocial personality and is even a little ashamed of it.

Dr. Kata Wald Pintér: She is a physiotherapist and massage therapist, married to a well-known radiologist. She is extremely *tüchtig*,[2] quick, dextrous, intelligent. She is the most conscientious among us and takes her calling most seriously. She keeps her five-year-old daughter here with us, feeding and caring for her brilliantly in the most difficult hygienic conditions. Her aggressive manner of addressing the children takes them aback. They all hate but also respect her. To me, Kata would start off very nice, doing me every favour, but then she suddenly changes face and would make my life hell, if I let her. We have never worked out exactly why she behaves like that. I think I have an idea, but it isn't interesting enough to be written down here.

---

2 German: efficient, capable.

Vera Nyilas believes it's because you can't have two pipers performing in the same inn and Kata suspects me of an inclination to be the only one. Kata also has a boy of six, who took refuge with his father in a Swedish protected house in Pest, but she hasn't heard from them for a long time.

Ilus (I don't know her full name) qualified as a physician in Brno. Here she works as a teacher. Her husband is in a labour camp. She hasn't heard from him for a long time. She is intelligent but not appealing, and brilliant at shirking any work or inconvenience. Otherwise, she's pleasant as long as you don't put the smallest obstacle in her way. If you do, God help you.

Ica's real name is Grünhut, but she's here with some divorced woman's papers. She's an attractive young woman, and we have discovered that we are distant relatives, but I mustn't talk about that because she wants the staff and others in the building to think she is an Aryan and is convinced that while people may not believe that I am an Aryan they certainly believe she is. She cooks for the whole company and has all my respect because she makes excellent dishes even though she has never cooked before for so many people (which is a science of its own) and because she stays faithfully by the side of her kitchen range even during the most exciting fun and games, of which she is very afraid.

Edit is a loud-mouthed, pushy, greedy, aggressive Jewish girl. She grinds on from morning until night, criticizing, correcting and lecturing in a monotonous voice. She knows everything better and gives any work a wide berth, but always manages to look as if she were the hardest worker because she is so good at advertising herself as such.

Bözsi Szilágyi is here with her two children. She is an embittered widow, fairly young and not unattractive. Of us all she is most afraid of the bombs and hides in the deepest recess of the shelter throughout the ordeal. She is rude and boastful, but I think she must be a good soul because the other children are fond of her even though she doesn't take much notice of them. She is bringing her children up terribly. It's almost unbearable to watch how they torment and plague her as a result of their bad training. But God save me from interfering.

Dr. Lili Révész is a pediatrician of about forty. She is tiny, very neat, terribly helpless and extremely neurotic. She attempted suicide when the persecution of the Jews began, but she was saved and brought here. She makes the most of her helplessness by getting people to pity her and then using them. She is incredibly clumsy even when she is doing medical work, and it hurts me to watch her. People are always laughing at her because she can never find her belongings (she has neither her own room nor her own wardrobe in the cellar), and whenever we come across any object in an improbable place we know at once that it belongs to Lili. She treats the children entrusted to her terribly, but she is offended if we point out any mistake she makes. She harbours some primeval hatred for Kata Wald Pintér. Lying in bed at night in the shelter I listen to their passionate arguments about, say, some problem to do with the education of children. But I wouldn't dream of joining in, no matter how much I am interested in the subject, because I feel that the argument is not really about what they are saying but about something completely different that I can't know and that is only an excuse for hurting each other. Mrs. Wald became my enemy about the time I told her I didn't think it very nice of her to be constantly upsetting and shaming a person in such a distraught state (because Lili was precisely that) in front of others, not to mention the fun the children were having as they listened to the adults quarrelling. But I came to like Lili in the process.

Now for the children.

The Hornyánszkys' little girl, Antónia, is incredibly pretty, spoiled and displays affectations. Her parents always speak to her formally. She often comes in to play with our children, whom she treats very nicely.

Andris is a handsome, agreeable and intelligent lad of sixteen.[3] We have to look after him specially because his brother died of tuberculosis at seventeen last year, and Andris is also too thin and tall for his age. We discover later that his father is my colleague in the bank.

Bandi Steiner, fourteen, is the son of a jeweller's apprentice in the district of Józsefváros. He is intelligent, streetwise, handsome and daring. There is something deceitful about him, but you respect him against your own better judgment because he is such a clever swindler. His father went missing in Ukraine. His mother has just been deported. He was first taken in by a woman in the building in which his family had lived, but then she changed her mind and thought it wiser to hand him over to the Red Cross. He is an excellent drifter, who gets hold of the best of everything, be it food or work, and who can make the most of every situation. Nor is his manual skill to be sneezed at. If anything in the building breaks, he knows how to mend it.

Zsuzsi, Bandi's ten-year-old sister, is not as gifted as her brother, but she can also look after herself. She knows how to make herself popular with the Hornyánszky family and is often invited by them to play with little Antónia.

I was the one who called Péter Szilágyi an eleven-year-old bachelor. Because that's what he is: ugly, dim, shy. He looks fifteen. Before he came to the home, his mother had his red hair dyed brown and his circumcision surgically restored. I'll talk about all this in detail later. He desperately tries to make friends with the other children but can't. They hate him, and I must admit they have a point. I try to make him more sociable, but in the few weeks I spend with him it can't be done.

Endre Kun is fourteen, intelligent, serious and very Jewish looking. Actually, he is a devout Lutheran. He is bright and obliging, but there is something repulsively hypocritical about the way he patronizes the other children, and he resembles a pompous priest.

---

3 Later Margit states that Andris is fifteen.

Lacika Kun is four and Endre's little brother. He is clever, antisocial and very wild.

János Forró is the only child of a physician. He is uncommonly intelligent, sleepy and slow-spoken. He performs poems by Attila József and songs by Kodály for the other children.

Péter Halmos, a.k.a. Sutyi, is the cousin of János and about the same age. He is quite good-looking and has fair hair. He is bright and would read all the time, which we could let him do upstairs in the apartment, but naturally no longer after Christmas by candlelight in the cellar. Now he constantly wants to play barkochba.[4]

Évi Szemere is a sweet, rather musical child aged eight. She is cross-eyed and wears glasses. We have a lot of trouble with her because she is very untidy. Gyurka is the younger brother of Évi. He is four and a half years old, and I must say an ungainly little boy. He lisps like a two-year-old and his intellectual level at most corresponds to a three-year-old's, but his physical development equals that of a five-and-a-half-year-old. He soils his pants every day, which is unpleasant enough for us now, but which will later become catastrophic given the unhygienic conditions. Of course he is a patient of Emmi Pikler.[5]

(The Szemere children's mother, Józsa Bródy, knew you and Jóska Dach well. I have heard recently that the children's father had been dragged out of a "protected" house to the Danube at sunrise one winter morning — Bódi Szerb was another — stripped naked, driven into the water and gunned down. Józsa, who was pregnant to boot, watched all this — as did Mrs. Szerb! Then they sent the women home, and it's not clear why.)

---

4 A guessing game similar to twenty questions named after Simon bar Kochba, the leader of a Jewish revolt against the Roman Empire starting in 132 CE. The game references a story of Kochba receiving information from a man even after his tongue was cut out.

5 Emmi Pikler (1902–1984), a Jewish Hungarian pediatrician known for her controversial theories of early childhood development and infant education.

Évike Szilágyi is a pretty and sweet little girl of seven. She has an excellent ear and a captivating little singing voice. I let her sing all kinds of things against my principles because she's so pleasant to listen to.

Imi Szilágyi, three, is the original cheeky little brat. He often wakes at night and sings uproariously in the dark for a while. He is so funny that nobody tells him off.

Dedi, as we discovered later, spent the second year of his life with us, and all that time we didn't even know his real name. He was brought to the institution by a superintendent and couldn't tell us his name but only called himself Dedi. He is an interesting child. You can't say that he is pleasant, because he is a lot of trouble, but I am fond of him and he entertained me a lot. Every night about midnight he would wake up and start howling angrily and resentfully, sometimes without stopping for hours. You could tell that he was getting tired, but he only stopped for a moment to collect new strength. The adults were furious and tried one thing after another. They shouted and smacked him. They stroked him, they hushed him, but every method failed.

Our fourteenth child was Panni, the five-month-old daughter of Kata Wald Pintér. She didn't cry once during the whole time, which is an admirable achievement for a baby who didn't leave the shelter for sixty days.

It wasn't a very good idea to describe the children one after the other, but now that I have started I'll continue. I didn't like these children as much as I had Palkó or those from Kelenhegyi Road. Perhaps I was too numb when I arrived at Pauler Street or perhaps I was unable to treat them like the earlier ones because we were unspeakably crammed. We had more caregivers than the number of patients justified, and every caregiver wanted to prove — no, not that she knew exactly how to bring up children but — that the others didn't. So when we hadn't been able to sleep for the third night in a row because of Dedi's ear-splitting howling, I, having kept quiet about the spanking, yelling and coaxing methods of the others, finally suggested that we try my methods: if we responded to the screaming with dead silence he would believe he was in the room alone because the persistent howling was clearly intended to punish or torture the adults. Naturally, I'm unable to get the method to be applied faultlessly, because the adults can't stop themselves swearing or at least heaving an angry sigh when the child screams loudly enough to jolt them out of their own dreams. I give a farewell lecture to the effect that they can't expect any discipline from a two-year-old child if they themselves lack all self-control. And having said that, I abandon the education of Dedi, with my seven colleagues' triumphant "You see, you couldn't do it either!" ringing in my ears.

As a new arrival and, as it were, a guest who can't refuse, I was immediately saddled with the two most unpleasant children: Gyurka, the pants soiler, and Péter Szilágyi, the eleven-year-old bachelor. The bachelor doesn't soil himself. On the contrary, he is very clean and tidy. Every day we have to wash something, sew on a loose button, darn the beginning of a tiny hole the size of a pinhead in his stocking (all this by candlelight), and we can't get rid of him until we have complied with his demands.

At this point I'm still ambitious enough to embark on the training of Gyurka. So far, the others have smacked him. If he soiled himself, they locked him in the toilet (where the poo the child spread all over the walls to freak out the adults had to be scraped off later), then they withheld his lunch, which was a harsh punishment because he loved his stomach. They also tried to promise him all kinds of things if he didn't poo himself, but none of this produced anything positive. I try to be so kind to him that he doesn't miss his mother. This works brilliantly for a while (apart from the fact that I sit him on the potty at the same hour every day and don't let him get up until he has produced something), but then there are more accidents and I no longer have the strength to investigate why.

On Pauler Street, we operate a "little mama system," where each caregiver is allocated a certain number of children to look after, for instance to wash or mend their things or to wash and feed them. With the bachelor I have no problems in this respect, because everything about him is nice and tidy. He is tidy, looks after his possessions and doesn't need to be supervised when he is washing, because he does it thoroughly, but I always have to referee because he is constantly at war with the other children.

My job with Gyurka is much harder. The clothes he has brought from home are very poor, even though his parents are well off. Everything is torn, neglected, untidy, incomplete, and that at a time when it isn't possible to buy any hooks, buttons, ribbons, etc., to mend his things a little. The other children call him "half-strap," because one strap of his trousers is always missing. Poor Gyurka is very lonely. The other children find him repellent because he is always smelly even though I wash him twice a day. The smell of his frequent accidents has penetrated his clothes so deeply that there's nothing we can do about it.

Outside, the fireworks have been going strongly since Christmas. Every minute the windows rattle and the building shakes with shells detonating nearby. We all gradually move down either into the cellar or into the basement: the Hornyánszky family and a small inner circle of boarding house guests into the boiler house, other boarding house guests into the superintendent's kitchen, others still into the so-called ironing room, and the Red Cross into the laundry, which is supposed to be the safest place in the building. This isn't deep either, but it looks out on the garden rather than the street and has a VAULTED CEILING. However, it isn't even as large as our dining room was on Kecske Street, and even of this small space a huge part is occupied by the washing boiler and a wash tub. We put the beds (wooden bunks with mattresses) close together to allow three of us to share two beds, with only an L-shaped passage left between the beds, but it's very tight. Next to the washing boiler there are two mattresses on the floor, which we always pick up and lean against the wall during the day, creating a space for the children to play. We cover the tub with a board and a sheet and use it as a table. The iron-barred window is being barricaded with rocks, so that fresh air can only come in through the small landing, which is full of suitcases and from which the door opens to the pantry. We also sit the smaller children on the potty on the landing. From the landing you get straight to the stairs leading up to the iron-barred garden door, and closest to the landing is the door to the kitchen, also locked with bolts. The kitchen is large. It has two huge windows looking onto the street, which we blocked with a brick wall when things began to turn serious. In one corner of the kitchen were our things, including our suitcases, and in my case a knapsack and a beach basket. In the other corner there is a huge sofa on which we pile up the bedding and mattresses during the day, because some of us would sleep out here in the kitchen due to the lack of space. I had slept on the Hornyánszkys' ground-floor dining room couch as long as possible (i.e., until the new year, when all the doors and windows were blown in). When I had to move downstairs, I would have liked to get a spot in the kitchen, but at that time the kitchen was in great demand, and as a guest I had to accept what I got. They made a space for me on the mattresses on the floor of the shelter, but since these mattresses were designed for children I couldn't stretch my legs or shift my position. I woke up several times in the night with every bit of me numb and the hair of the colleague snoring next to me stuffed in my mouth and tickling.

In the morning, I woke up shattered and decided to sleep on a chair in the kitchen rather than spending another night like that. When I did so, sleeping on a chair seemed no more restful, but luckily on the next morning THE FIRST SERIOUS BOMB landed in the middle of the yard in front of the building about ten steps from our kitchen window, as a direct result of which I was able to choose on that same day between all the beds in the kitchen because the privileged caregivers had raced to sleep in the shelter.

This is how the First Serious Bomb was dropped:

On the morning of January 2, a sunny Sunday,[6] some fighter aircraft are on the rampage above us. We are not particularly interested in the planes. Rather, we are trying to guess whether the explosions mean outgoing or incoming shells (a topic of permanent argument). I'm helping with the cooking in the kitchen. Someone breezes in to report that Mrs. Boronkay (our nominal leader, who lives in the building next door and no longer leaves her home to communicate with us but simply climbs the stone wall shared between our gardens by means of a ladder) is shouting from the top of the stone wall for one of us to come out to discuss the chores of the day with her. Ica, the cook-nurse, who has dough on her hand, asks me to run out to the yard and report to Mrs. Boronkay. I ask her quickly what to say and start up the stairs toward the garden. Halfway there I remember that I'm hot and Mrs. Boronkay is bound to keep me gabbing for at least half an hour in the cold. I suddenly decide to slip into the Hornyánszkys' apartment, where my winter coat hangs on a hook in the lobby and, what is more, in the corner that is the safest part of the whole apartment without even a window nearby. I'm just about to take the coat off the hook when I hear a whistling sound approaching and becoming louder above my head. A huge explosion follows immediately, making the whole building shake. There's a terrible racket and a cloud of white dust. I stick my nose out from behind my coat on the hook, where I seem to have hidden instinctively, but I quickly pull it back because the crescendo whistling signals an even bigger explosion than before. Then for a while the sound of debris and falling plaster. Another silence. I stick my head out again. By now I know that they never drop more than two bombs in the same place.

I'm not afraid. Rather, my knees are trembling a little under the physical impact of the explosion. Now Hornyánszky, the head of the building, saunters across the lobby, white with plaster dust, but at the

6 January 2, 1945, was a Tuesday.

speed he would have used walking, say, on the Danube Promenade in 1937. We stare at each other, a little surprised, before he gestures behind him with his thumb toward the apartment, slightly disgusted, and says: "Smashed to smithereens!" I run to the basement to see how the others are. They are all right, except that Ilus (the physician from Brno) fainted when the shock reached her, and our lovely, tasty lunch was ruined. The mushroom soup is thick with plaster dust and the ground hazelnut to be sprinkled on the hazelnut noodles twinkles with broken glass. We discover that one of the bombs landed in the middle of the road directly next to the building and the other in the garden. Mrs. Boronkay had fallen off the ladder and her husband had dragged her into their building before the second bomb hit the ground. The driveway has a deep hole. Water comes out of the taps in thin trickles and by the afternoon dries up completely — I can't stop myself guessing which wall I would have had to be scraped off with a spoon if I hadn't gone back by chance to get my coat. Later I gave up such speculations.

So the popularity of the kitchen on the street side as a place to sleep is greatly reduced. Consequently, I can happily spread out on the kitchen sofa all by myself. Among the boarding room guests there is a gentleman of about forty-eight to fifty. His name is Dr. Endre Schulhof, but everybody calls him bácsi Bandi. He is a legal adviser of Beszkárt,[7] but he hasn't been going to his office since Christmas, and as the restaurants are also out of action we feed him, which he acknowledges with small favours. He clearly has a soft spot for Mrs. Szilágyi and her children, and he is supposed to be a relative of her late husband. The woman treats him coldly and rudely, but he doesn't mind that a bit and looks after them with fanatical adoration. This bácsi Bandi is also squeezed out of the shelter and so he borrows Vera

7 Budapest's public transport company, Budapest Székesfővárosi Közlekedesi Részvénytársaság, which operated from 1922 to 1949.

Nyilas's folding camp bed on which he sleeps on the far side of the kitchen table. When Vera also wants to sleep out here, he puts mattresses on the floor. So from now on they are my sleeping companions.

We haven't had any water since January 2. The power supply broke down a few days earlier. Initially, we get water from a hole made by a bomb at the corner of Pauler and Roham Streets. Later, we manage to get some water from the taps in the buildings on the even-numbered side of Pauler Street. Naturally, we have only drunk boiled water, that is, tea, since. We use primitive petrol lamps constructed by the owner of the building for lighting. They are dark, smelly and sooty, and their light is only enough to prevent us bumping into each other in the dark. There is also a hurricane lantern in the building, but that is used by the staff. We must be very economical with water for washing ourselves, and suddenly washing our underwear also becomes a large problem. I have been on strike[8] since October, like most of the women in Budapest, but of course I break the strike as soon as the water stops running, which is extremely embarrassing in the circumstances, even though luckily this is only a pale imitation of the real strikebreaking before the war with regard to both intensity and the general discomfort attendant on it.

So this is how we exist, between monotonous gunfire and shelling. We have got quite used to it, but what irritates me more and more is the dark and the dirt. I can't get used to that. (Today it's still my darkest memory of the whole siege, and if you hear me say that it was terrible, that's what I always mean!) Still, I could manage well enough if I weren't tormented, for example, by the thought of what Nünüke might be eating, because I know that restaurants have been closed everywhere. So on a relatively "quiet" day I get on my feet and visit them. I must say it's quite an exciting excursion. I walk the length of Logodi Street because Attila Street is by now out of the question, but

---

8 Margit's euphemism for lack of menstruation.

Logodi is also under heavy fire. The least agreeable parts of the excursion are Vérmező Street and Széna Square, which I can't avoid and which, as you know, are completely undefended on one side, which is exactly where they are firing from. I cross this part at a run although I would love to stop and take a good look at the streetcar station in Széll Kálmán Square, which is an interesting sight. The Stühmer pavilion is burned out. The No. 81 and No. 83 streetcars stand inside, riddled with bullet holes, the track is torn up in many places and the streetcar rails are twisted up toward the sky. On Vérmező Street, near the corner of Ostrom Street, there is a chemist's shop, probably Jewish because it's sealed and the window is full of things we haven't been able to get for six months. For instance, toothpaste. In the home, the worst arguments are about toothpaste and tooth powder, and I'm also running out.

When I go to Nünüke for the first time, the window of the pharmacy is smashed and the finest toothpastes are lying in front of me. I stop and pluck up my courage three times to lift them out of the window, telling myself that if I don't take them somebody else will. By now many shops with such bomb damage have been looted by the public, but I can't make up my mind to do it, even though the area is completely empty because of all the firing from Olasz Avenue in that direction. I walk on without any toothpaste, because when I at last dare to lift up a glass shard to reach the toothpaste underneath, I set another shard in motion, which has unbalanced a third. A few more drop inside the window with a loud clatter. They give me a huge fright, and I run away as fast as I can.

I see the first dead body in Széna Square. A man of about fifty, who looks like a worker, is lying on his back on a pedestrian island with his arms spread out, showing no wounds. At every step I come across a dead horse. I'm very sorry for the dead horses: what has all this to do with them? Margit Boulevard is in awful condition. I make a short detour to Béla and his family's apartment, since they live near Széna Square, but I only find Irén at home. She tells me that Béla will not come home for a few days because he is hiding from the police, who are picking up men from every building and taking them away to dig trenches whether or not they have exemption documents. (I have already explained to you how this is done.)

From here I go on to Juci Lénárd's. I locate Juci in the cellar and take her up to the apartment (which naturally also has no windows left and is covered by a thick layer of plaster dust and glass fragments). I collect all the food we have hidden with them: tin cans, flour, lard, jam and other treasures of the kind, and loaded with these I climb up to the Gül Baba Boarding House, where Mother receives me in tears. She thought that I was dead, because of the rumours in the city about how heavily the castle and its neighbourhood had been shelled. She is delighted with the food, because even though the Bem Apóhoz restaurant on Margit Boulevard is still cooking, the guests have to line up at the kitchen in the back to collect the food. Old regulars like Nünüke can always get stuffed cabbage, but traversing the street is becoming more and more difficult even for such a short distance. At the bend of Margit Boulevard, from the Admirál Cinema to the other side, there is a deep tank trap and in front of it a huge steep barricade that poor Nünüke and family have to climb every time. I'll get each of them another warm quilt from Juci's sister-in-law and for Nünüke borrow a sweater and some women's underwear from Lívia. Juci has a Transylvanian refugee working for her as a maid, who has some flour of her own. I'll sell her my Tyrolean sweater with the many small flowers for a few kilos of flour, which I'll also take to my parents.

Of course, Nünüke is very popular in the boarding house, where she cooks pancakes instead of bread for the whole company. They have been living in the "shelter" of the boarding house for a long time. I don't know why they call the area a shelter, perhaps because it's just as dark, damp and airless as the shelters, but it is not even in the basement, so you have to climb a few steps UP from the garden to this structure, whose main wall faces Pest and is totally undefended. The higher parts of the boarding house have been shot to pieces by now.

A maid called Teri, who had been stealing everything combustible from the beginning to keep the old folk warm, was killed by the first shell and buried in the garden. Poor Nünüke doesn't dare to ask me to come again because she knows how dangerous it is. In the afternoon, I get back to Pauler Street, where people have been worrying about me and strongly disapprove of such dangerous excursions. But they stop disapproving when the next day promises to be quieter and I go up with Vera to the store at 16 Úri Street in the Castle District to collect some food.

The Castle District can't exactly be called safe either, so Vera and I run up the shortest and steepest stairs. Apart from me, Vera alone is prepared to go out into the streets at any time to fetch water, bread, etc.

The head of the stores in the Castle District is Mr. Mayer, who doesn't want to give us any food because it hasn't been long since we were last there. We have to explain to him at length that we no longer wait until our supplies have completely run out before we ask him for more. We have to carry the items now while we can still walk in the street, and nobody can know how things will be in a week. Very reluctantly, he gives us ten kilos of bacon, tinned meat and sugar cubes, although he still has plenty of everything. We are annoyed that he is so unwilling to hand out the food even though he also holds the rations intended for the other homes and knows as well as we do that they can't come ask for them until after the siege, if at all.

Vera and I have a lot of fun on the way. We like the fact that walking from Pauler Street to Úri Street has become such an exciting adventure. At home the fodder is received with an ovation, and Vera and I are allocated a special ration of the day's dinner. Emboldened by having returned alive, I suggest to Vera the next day that we should take a walk to Kelenhegyi Road to get some candles, and she agrees at once. This goes back a while. When Béla wrapped up the entire candle supply of the Kassai family and sent it from the pantry on Miksa Steet to the home on Casino Street, I deposited four bunches of wax candles in the pantry of Casino Street, and when we had to make our express move the candles ended up in the pantry of the home on Kelenhegyi Road. Of course, you can't imagine what a candle means at such a time: you can even get bread in exchange for it. So we set out to look for the Kassais' candles in the pantry of the home on Kelenhegyi Road. But on that day, Vera and I only get as far as the bottom half of Szent János Square because our dear Germans — God knows why — have been blowing up the hydro poles all along the line, so that after a short hesitation we turn around and postpone the matter until the following day. I loved hanging around with Vera. We had plenty of good fun together. We laughed a lot, not only at others, but also at ourselves, and what idiots we were to be walking in the street when we didn't have to. At that time, Vera was not yet afraid of anything except the biggest bangs, and of those not as danger to life but as noise.

I think it was January 4 — and a quieter day — when we decided to go to Gellért Hill again and at last get those candles. It was a very interesting excursion. From the start we came across very few civilians, and between Döbrentei Square and Gellért Baths we didn't see any at all. However, there were many more soldiers. We hadn't even reached Döbrentei Square when some dreadful gunfire started, although with the loud echoes everywhere we couldn't work out where it was happening or whether it was moving closer or farther away. As we walked on, we stopped a number of soldiers, some Hungarian, others German, to ask where the firing was happening and whether it was possible to walk toward the Gellért Baths, but they only shrugged: NOT A SINGLE ONE OF THEM KNEW WHERE THE FIRING WAS. When we asked some Hungarian officers coming toward us how far we could walk, they answered: as far as Horthy Circus, but there were already some Russians there. At Erzsébet Bridge on the streetcar rails below the St. Gellért statue a TRAIN ENGINE with a PULLMAN COACH attached to it sits with its windows missing. Along the whole Danube embankment from Erzsébet Bridge to Ferenc József Bridge,

German cars were parked close together at a right angle to the river to save space. There were cannons everywhere, as well as German soldiers who were grumpy and nervous, their answers to our questions gruff and unfriendly. We try to get bread, cigarettes, matches off them, but they refuse to give us anything. They haven't got anything either, they say. By now the Gellért Baths and Hotel are beautifully decorated by artillery action. The children's home is behind the bath. To reach it, you have to take Kemenes Street from Horthy Miklós Road. In front of the home's garden there is a huge tank trap. In the garden of each villa there are cannons. We turn into the garden, where my favourite Biedermeier wardrobe still stands leaning against a wall, underneath a balcony, unscathed.

The director is no longer Daisy Ullmann but Mrs. Klára Kellner (perhaps you remember her as the wife of Pali Kellner, who was with Dénes in Ukraine and came home last year). She is barely twenty-three, very bright, nice and *tüchtig*, and she embraces me warmly without any ceremony. She runs the home brilliantly. She gets twelve kilos of military bread a day from the German soldiers, which she toasts and squeezes into our bags, and she also gives us some German night lights. Unfortunately, we can't find the candles of the Kassais, which those who moved to Vilma Királynő Road seem to have taken with them. Klári would like me to move in here, but Daisy Ullmann doesn't hide the fact that she is against it, and to cut the argument short I say quickly that I want to stay at Pauler Street, even though I already know this will make me last to be occupied by the Russians. Kelenhegyi Road is also well provided with water. Someone has installed a rubber pipe leading from a reservoir into the apartment building through the cellar window, so that the residents don't have to step outside if they need water. Nor have they stepped outside since one of the young breastfeeding mothers was hit in the shoulder by shrapnel while she was shopping and is still in bed with fever caused by the infection in her wounds. Without any candles but loaded with toast, we start our return journey, which proves to be much harder than the journey out. At Döbrentei Square we find ourselves in the middle of such a furious barrage that all we can do is head home as quickly as possible. There is no *Deckung*[9] anywhere, the terrain is open on two sides, and we don't even know where the firing comes from thanks to the deceptiveness of the acoustics. We arrive home gasping for air. The toast is a roaring success.

Now I'm going to sit still for a few days on the bottom of my ski pants (as I have hardly any bottom of my own left). I remember Kosana (Lívia's sister-in-law in Belgrade) telling us what a siege would look like: The Russians would surround the city on all sides, sit down calmly

and fire,
and fire,
and fire,
and fire again,
and fire still more,
and when everybody has long since gone to hell,
they still fire.

Well, that was exactly how they did it. In front of our eyes the whole of Krisztinaváros was slowly shot to smithereens. To begin with, we could only see the Castle District from below, from a frog's perspective, as it were, and even so the destruction was noticeable. But the bombing was something else. If I went out in the street after a bombing raid, I always thought that it wasn't possible to destroy a street more thoroughly. But the next day I saw that it was indeed possible, and the third day even more so, and so on. Sometimes I would step out of the gate at sunset to have a look around the buildings and wouldn't recognize Pauler Street because even its geographical footprint had completely changed. Initially, Pauler Street had been a quiet, deserted little Buda street. Then the Hungarian soldiers arrived

---

9 German: cover.

and set up an anti-aircraft battery at the Vérmező end of the street, and every time they came to do some anti-aircrafting we got such a fright that we dropped our spoons. Luckily, we soon realized that it was not until a Russian plane had come, dropped its bombs and was leaving for home that the Hungarians began to anti-aircraft it from behind like the not-so-brave guard dog who only barks at a stranger with a stick if there is a safe distance between them.

Later the Hungarian soldiers and their battery disappeared and only Germans were to be seen in the open, but then all the Germans moved onto Pauler Street, letting their supply wagons pile up to bring almost all movement to a halt and forcing local people in search of water to squeeze themselves and their jugs through the narrowest gaps between trucks and building walls. One reason why traffic had become extremely complicated even between neighbouring streets was that by then many buildings had been destroyed. On the corner of Pauler and Roham Streets, for example, a bomb had hit a four-storey apartment block, with the loss not only of its shelter but also of the majority of the people in it. The building itself had collapsed into a mountain of rubble in the middle of the street. Vera and I stand for a long time one evening staring at the first building that we see from up close in such a condition. An elegant modern armchair covered in pink plush peeps through the debris, next to it two or three old issues of *Új Idők*[10] and on top a black bowler hat, a little dented and stained with mortar.

Since the first great bombing, we have been collecting our daily firewood as well as fragments of shutters and remains of window frames in the streets. We find many other things in the process. I often think of Andersen's fairy tales when I see the shards of a beautiful antique teapot in the street or shreds of a lovely rug or a piece of a picture frame or a painting in tatters. On every "quiet" day, when we

---

10 A Hungarian literary magazine published from 1894 to 1949.

have finished carrying water we go gather wood. This is not a pleasant task because by now it's cold and my hands freeze, even though I have warm gloves made of goatskin.

The best kindling comes from the church in Krisztina Square, that is, from the neighbourhood of the Auguszt pastry shop, and yet this is where the smallest number of people collect things. That is perhaps because this area is full of dead horses and people are still squeamish. The Auguszt pastry shop has been demolished by gunshots, explosions and shock waves. I can't help remembering how we had wanted to travel to Lake Balaton, but the train was full, and to cheer ourselves up we stuffed ourselves in the Auguszt until we almost burst, do you remember, my Pipus? Though it seems to me that the next day or a few days later we did travel. I often remember things like this, but gradually I suspect that I get lost in demolished well-known streets. As time passes, street signs can't be relied on because they fly around. One fine morning I find a sign with "I Distr. IV Béla Road" written on it in our garden, meet one of Roham Street's signs in a broken shop window in Krisztina Boulevard, and someone returns one of the Pauler Street signs from the middle of Vérmező after the siege. On another fine morning, when I come up to the garden from the cellar, I discover a pay phone from a phone booth lying in the snow. Only an enamel sign can be seen sticking out of the snow, on which is written PAY ATTENTION TO THE SEQUENCE (first insert the coin, wait for the dial tone, then dial, etc.), although by then I don't feel like paying attention to anything, least of all to the sequence.

Later the children removed the twenty fillér pieces from the coin box, half-heartedly, for who would believe that you could ever buy anything with the money. One time a small drugstore on Szent János Square was open for half a day in the building where the Belcsák family used to live. I went in and bought up everything available: toilet paper, paper napkins, shoelaces, floor wax (for candles), and it only occurred to me when I got home how stupid it was of me not to have spent all the money I had on eau de cologne, after all what could

I do with money, while with eau de cologne I could at least clean myself. The next day I went back to the store, but fortunately it was already closed. Thanks to this, I still had some money after the siege, although I'd wanted to squander thousands on eau de cologne. Everyone was throwing money away, because apart from such exceptional events you couldn't buy anything for money.

As far as my health and strength are concerned, I continue to feel very well. I can achieve great physical *Leistungen*[11] with one hand and without batting an eye. I have a strange stomach complaint clearly caused by rapid weight loss, which first appeared before the siege toward the end of October when I used to stuff myself silly with scrumptious food at the Rapochs' even though I wasn't hungry but simply didn't notice in the middle of a heated conversation that I was eating. That afternoon I vomited all the way along Baross Street, with Béla supporting my head. Luckily the street was dark, but later, I continued being sick at the Lénárds'. This happened a few more times — though not too often — when I had eaten too much (say as much as at a Sunday lunch before the war). Within half an hour, the stomach cramps would begin and I would throw up, or the cramps would become so unbearable that I would force my finger down my throat to make myself sick. Conversely, if the food was particularly tasty and nourishing I didn't have the heart to give myself the finger in the throat treatment but struggled for long spells to get over the attacks without losing control, although I only managed that a few times. This was one of the complaints.

The other complaint was very common at that time and is still frequent: I often had to pee and was completely unable to hold it. The urge came suddenly, and I had to run to avoid being too late. This latter complaint upset me infinitely because it was very unpleasant to totter out of the shelter in complete darkness to the terrible toilet.

---

11 German: feats.

Yet another problem is so common that there is hardly a woman in Budapest — or indeed in Hungary — who was an exception to it, that is, that they completely stopped functioning as a woman. My last period arrived immediately after the famous October 23. This was followed by a long interval, before a pale imitation of the genuine pre-war article showed up, but of course precisely when there was absolutely no water to wash with, and since then really nothing as if I had been cut off.

What I never managed to do was to catch a cold. Not even the slightest sniffle. It looked as if no part of me had frozen, although it is now gradually becoming clear that everybody's hands or feet have chilblains. Cini, Lili, your mother and many others are in hospital with severe frostbite.

We have reached the first week of January. I would very much like to visit Nünüke and my father, but the bombing has become heavy again. Now the legends of the LIBERATING GERMAN ARMY are beginning to circulate. The German supply unit based on our street is visibly galvanized by such rumours. The German soldiers are generally in a better and more generous mood. A canteen truck distributes food. We all run out with containers, and I carry an additional one to grab extra for Nünü. I manage to collect a big plateful of semolina, a large bottle of tomato purée, oat flakes, malt, beans and peas and combine these to be taken to my parents next time I go to see them. Suddenly, I remember that Béla has taken our food supplies from Miksa Street to Szabó, the salesman in the Klauzál Square market hall, who is now living on Wesselényi Street. I think I should collect it, but the idea is so absurd that I reject it at once. It's risky enough to walk to the next street, let alone all the distance to Pest.

Nevertheless, I wake up one morning determined to go to Pest and to bring back whatever I can from Szabó. On January 10, 1945, this is such an impossible idea that I dare not mention it to anybody. I only say to the others that I've got a job to do and will be back by the afternoon. I don't reveal my plan to anybody except Vera because she is just as mad as I am. It is rumoured that Erzsébet Bridge is the only permitted crossing at this time. I set out at about 9:00 a.m. even though it is snowing heavily. I wear my Red Cross nurse's headscarf inside the hood of my raincoat and carry a knapsack, a shoulder bag and several baskets. This time even fewer people are walking in the streets than usual because of the snowfall. Practically the only other passersby I meet are soldiers, who dive into a gateway every time a crack or whistle is heard, although by then it is too late. People generally behave stupidly and most of them are deaf too.

At this juncture the "enemy" is firing from such a distance that incoming fire can be clearly distinguished from outgoing, but it's hard to find one soldier in a hundred who can make that distinction. The soldiers jump full of fear into gateways at the long-drawn-out whistle tone anticipating the approach of a missile from far away, but they can't tell this signal from the short and sharp bark that announces the imminent impact of a short-distance missile.

Strangely enough I do not instinctively jump into a gateway or drop onto my front and hardly ever hunch myself up or flatten myself against a wall. I usually just stroll along calmly and don't even want to hurry because I am convinced that nothing matters.

In the home, for all my secrecy, they knew where I was planning to go even before I left. They were naturally horrified and tried to stop me. I didn't know what to answer them. I couldn't tell them that I was going for a *ziher* and knew that I would come back unscathed. This strange certainty remains with me throughout the action. There are days when I am not prepared to go as far as the garden wall, even though there is no more shelling than at other times: I just have a feeling of Not Now! At other times I walk to the far side of Krisztina Boulevard extremely calmly (an unimaginable distance when they are firing from all sides!) in the middle of the most savage sounds of explosions to fetch some water and know that nothing will happen to me. Of course, I also wonder how many civilians may be lying on the edge of the pavement, having headed out with the same sense of security as I do.

When I chat with my fellow caregivers who have no idea where their husbands have been taken and how they are, I look at them with compassion: poor you, how unpleasant it must be to wait and hope here for the return of a husband who may be in mortal danger or even dead and of whom you have heard nothing. Sometimes I remind myself that you are not exactly on holiday in Miami either, but the possibility of something untoward happening to you goes beyond my imagination.

So I don't answer the horrified attempts to stop me because I can't tell them for sure that I will come back in one piece. The snow has softened the terrible picture shown by Krisztinaváros a few days ago. It covers the many nasty things, the rubble, the blood, the dead horses and whatnot. One is only really reminded that there is a siege going on by the crunching of broken glass under the snow one treads on, and you could even say that it's a grand siege. And of course there are the masses of soldiers, mainly Germans. The women who venture outside at such times are regarded with disgust even by soldiers. I couldn't help observing how much more nervously and feebly men react to permanent mortal danger than women. But they are ashamed of this and therefore they hate the braver women.

The men in my building would gladly wring my neck because, however involuntarily, I steal their thunder. Imagine how unpleasant it must be for a retired major, who has invaded a neighbouring street, to plan on his way back under heavy shelling his presentation of that heroic deed to the women at home, where he finds that nobody is interested in his story because I get back at the very same moment from shopping for food in the Castle District. (The additional reason I didn't feel like getting injured was that it would have given the men an opportunity to make snide comments, such as: Was it worth it to play the hero? Because of course they would have considered it playing the hero that I didn't agree to being hungry and thirsty as long as there was a chance to fight against it, even if it meant danger.)

So I march in the heavy snowfall fighting the elements and defying a thousand perils like a film heroine. In the park at Döbrentei

Square, dead German soldiers are lying next to each other revealing the true German love of order. I can't see their faces because they are covered by snow and it is their feet that are bare. There are quite a lot of them, I guess at least fifty. My first thought is that they look like a truckload of merchandise waiting to be removed. Then it strikes me that somebody is waiting somewhere for every single boy lying here dead as we are waiting for you and Dénes. If we came across such an association of ideas in a film, we would be bored and call it corny. But I can tell you that my associations led to very painful ideas even though — as I have told you a lot of times — I never imagined that you or Dénes could come to any harm.

I turn toward Erzsébet Bridge (Firing!!), which is guarded by German soldiers with bayonets fixed, holding rifles and hand grenades ready to attack and carrying all kinds of explosives around their waists. The footpaths on the bridge are closed to pedestrians, who are only allowed to walk on the central road where the snow has already built up to calf height, which makes walking exhausting. Single individuals are not allowed to cross. When ten or fifteen people wishing to get to the other side have collected (which takes nearly a quarter of an hour) a soldier with a bayonet escorts them as far as the Pest bridgehead (Firing!!). The snow blows into my eyes, and I can't see things as clearly as I would like (Firing!!). The snowfall is so dense that I can't see the next bridges. And they are firing, firing, firing.

I have reached Pest. Eskü Street and Kossuth Lajos Street are relatively undamaged. I see an open Meinl shop,[12] where I get some sweetened coffee substitute and quickly buy as much as I can. I also find a half-destroyed pharmacy (at the corner of Semmelweis Street and Kossuth Lajos Street) where I buy some Darmol tablets for Nünü and am very proud of this acquisition because it has been impossible to

12 A delicatessen chain owned by Julius Meinl.

get anything like it for months. I even find an open pharmacy somewhere on Wesselényi Street, where the grumpy owner serves me in a very bad mood, and I am lucky that he is only willing to sell restricted amounts to me, otherwise — as I have said elsewhere — I would have spent all my money. This is how I get all the lanolin cream, the toothpaste, the toilet paper, the paper napkins, the talcum powder, etc., I need for months ahead. Then I wander to 60 Wesselényi Street, where Szabó, the market hall salesman, lives with his family near the Hungarian Theatre. And the firing continues all the time, with impacts nearby every minute.

By now everybody has vacated the apartments. Szabó and his family are also living in the cellar, but he is out and has taken the key for the section in which our things are hidden. I leave my shopping here and set out to visit Gyula Kővády, who lives with his family beyond the Ring, at 46 Wesselényi Street. Their apartment was also destroyed, but they don't live in the cellar but rather in the kitchen of a ground-floor apartment and are very pleased to see me. The reason I had gone to see them was that I wanted to ask for some of Mrs. Kővády's late mother's underwear for Nünüke, but they were unable to give me any.

As I step out of the Kővárys' gate, I see a long procession of people being herded into the ghetto. The hoarding surrounding the ghetto begins a few steps from the Kővárys' gate, and one of the entrances is exactly on the corner between Akácfa Street and Wesselényi Street. I walk toward it and stop on the edge of the pavement, watching what is going on. I see long rows of relatively well-dressed and fairly healthy-looking individuals with and without stars, carrying their possessions partly on their backs and partly in laundry baskets they drag behind them with the help of a rope. Since the Jews had to move into the ghetto by a certain deadline in December, I calculate that these can only be "protected people" from the Swiss or Swedish houses. I think of Cini, of whom I haven't heard anything since October; I wasn't the only one who hadn't heard from her, because Dóri, the engineer Teil and many others who are even more desperate for some news from her haven't heard anything either.

I watch the procession for a while, wondering if I will see anyone I know. Next to me on the edge of the pavement stands a patriot with an Arrow Cross armband. He looks me up and down out of the corner of his eye. I ask him innocently who these people are and where they are being taken. The hero glares at me. Instead of answering, he turns his back on me. I decide to leave discreetly and quickly. By the time I get back to the Szabós, feeling guilty about our many "protected" friends, they had already prepared my possessions. We had stored a fair amount of food with them — tinned meat, jars of jam, beans, peas, etc. I simply put all these into my knapsack. It's terribly heavy. The Szabós tell me not to carry it all at once because it's just too heavy, but I know I will not be able to come back and accordingly must take everything now. When I pick up the knapsack, I almost fall on my back. It's so heavy that I can only carry it if I double over. Pipus, if only you had seen me, hunched and staggering along the Ring!

I knew from the first moment that I couldn't carry that load as far as Krisztina or even a much shorter distance. But I was also sure that something would happen. During the whole drama it seemed as if the spielbergerism were being peeled off me. I didn't even ask myself what would happen. When I turned onto Rákóczi Street my tongue was hanging out. I waved down one or two vehicles (naturally only German vehicles were running), and the third allowed me to put my luggage on it and stagger along behind. The motor traffic was so closely packed on the single bridge that vehicles could only proceed at a snail's pace. This could have been the beginning of the retreat to Buda, because in the opposite direction there was no motor traffic at all. The reason I couldn't put my luggage on one of the previous vehicles was not because their drivers wouldn't let me but because we could only have shared a short stretch of the way. As my vehicle was going toward the Castle District from Krisztina, we would have had to separate at the Artillery Monument, but from there it was a child's game to carry the load as far as Pauler Street. All that time, the firing continued unabated, but I was less bothered partly because my ears had become used to it and partly I had become absorbed in a lively conversation with the soldier who accompanied the vehicle.

By the time I had reached Pauler Street, I had become such a celebrity that people in Krisztinaváros were pointing their fingers at me. Strangers from the neighbouring buildings were also dropping in when they heard that somebody had come from Pest. They stormed me with questions about how things were in Pest. I dare not tell Mrs. Wald that even "protected" people are being dragged into the ghetto, because her husband and her little boy are in the Swedish house in Pest. I don't mention this to anybody except Vera, since Mrs. Wald, who by the way is breastfeeding, is very restless because she is not getting any messages from her husband and keeps asking herself whether her little boy wouldn't be better off here in the home. Finally, we bring bácsi Bandi into the debate and decide not to say anything to Kata because now she wouldn't be able to bring the child across anyway and the stress would only make her milk dry up, in which case the baby would die.

Yesterday I couldn't take any food to the old folks partly because it was too late (we are only allowed to walk in the street until four o'clock) and partly because, to put it that way, I am a little on the tired side. But the next morning I set out with a heavy load immediately after fetching the water. As I pass the Bélas' lodging, I note that they are alive. Margit Boulevard is getting nastier and nastier, more and more ruined. When I visit my parents at the Gül Baba Boarding House on Mecset Street, I usually walk up the side with the odd-numbered buildings and only turn to cross over at the garden gate. Today I can't go all the way on the odd side because a building that has collapsed onto the street is blocking the pavement. The moment I notice this some people I know as my parents' fellow-guests in the boarding house approach me. I call out that this (I mean the collapsed building) was different the last time I was here and ask when it had happened.

One gentleman glances at his wristwatch and says casually: "About eight minutes ago." You see, Pipus, I'm just saying — this followed me around throughout the whole game, this mad and incomprehensible series of lucky coincidences. This is how bombs, missiles, Arrow Cross raids, police raids, etc., always hit the ground five minutes before me or eight minutes after me, two metres to the right of me or five metres behind me, not to mention the eight different sweet tools that dropped into the Hornyánszky house in the shape of a bomb, a big and a small shell and an incendiary bomb, and NOT ONE OF THEM EXPLODED while on the right was Sabbath, on the left was Sabbath,[13] but then everything around us collapsed. When you get back, I'll take you to Pauler Street and show you.

In brief, I arrive safely at Nünüke and my father's lodging. NÜNÜKE IS NOT AT HOME, because of course she wouldn't be sitting indoors in such good walking weather in which a bang nearby can make one go deaf in an instant. I am told that she has popped out to Zárda Street to see some friends who had promised her some lard in exchange for something else. She is already on her way back, beaming with pride, with the lard in her basket. It has been demonstrated once again that there is no need to worry about Nünüke. I cried every night wondering what my parents might be eating, while Nünüke was knitting stockings for the owner's wife in exchange for food, and they are doing quite well under the circumstances. Nevertheless, they are pleased with the food. There is no bread to be had anywhere by now. (Imagine my father!) My mother never lets anything get her down, but my father visibly shrinks and lets himself go.

---

13 An allusion to a then well-known Yiddish joke about a rabbi who declared that the Sabbath was not occurring wherever he was, even though it was definitely the Sabbath all around him, just as the war and the violence and suffering is happening all around Margit — just not wherever she is.

It's strange that my father no longer ventures out in the street even on a calm day, but I find it reassuring to see how well Nünüke copes with every situation. I decide to tell them that having supplied them with food for some time I won't be able to come again for quite a while because the route is becoming nastier and nastier, more and more dangerous. They accept this and I say goodbye to them.

Nünüke walks with me all the way to the garden gate amid the violent firing and shows me how she has unpicked an old forgotten yellow jumper of mine to make a pair of stockings for me for my birthday. She tells me that Papa is pressing her daily to commit suicide with him, using sleeping pills of which he has a vast amount. Nünü refuses angrily: "Certainly not, I want to see our children again!" (By the way, she believes no more than you or me that he is serious.) But at such times she cooks him a special *lángos*,[14] which to some extent reconciles him with living, although for no longer than half an hour, after which the sighs and laments recommence. Nünü looks much better than my father. This time I don't see them again for more than a month, that is, at the end of the siege.

Before I go home, I visit the Lénárds and then Lívia, who has moved with the Tedesco family into the shelter of 2 Török Street. I note with satisfaction that everybody is still alive and then I amble home through moderate grenade fire. This was my last major excursion. It was followed only by smaller excursions dictated by necessity, such as fetching water, food, etc., involving shorter distances but much more adventurous than the long-distance ones described above. But more about this later. In brief, the last time I saw Nünüke and Papa was January 11.

It was around this time that the Great Dance really began. Every blessed morning at about 10:30 a.m., the Russian planes come to bomb and fire their machine guns at us. Pauler Street, Roham Street,

---

14 A savoury, deep-fried dough.

Krisztina Boulevard and Attila Street are so full of German supply vehicles that we can hardly move, as I have already written to you somewhere. It's becoming more and more difficult to squeeze in between the walls of the buildings and the tires of the vehicles, one horse here, another horse there, and a mass of horses milling in the yard of the building facing Attila Street. Consequently, we can't blame the Russian pilots for firing at us ceaselessly.

Initially, when we needed water we could cross over to the even-numbered side of Pauler Street, but eventually there too the conduits were damaged, and by mid-January the water was only running on the other side of Krisztina Boulevard, and even there only in the cellars. We generally used to go to the so-called mission house, where there was a laundry room in which we could still draw water from two taps. This building was roughly the second or third building from the corner of Krisztina Boulevard and Karácsony Street. It may not be more than fifty steps from us as the crow flies, but at first there is no question of taking such a direct route. We had to skirt Vérmező Park or cross Roham Street to get to the other side, and either walk could be described as an adventurous undertaking.

But luckily enough the block opposite is soon hit by a shell and the firewalls separating the two buildings collapse, so that from now on we have to go in through the gate of 12 Pauler Street and come out through the gate of a building on Krisztina Boulevard, run a little askew along the road of Krisztina Boulevard and we are already in the mission house.

But such a journey can be terribly long when there is shooting. Initially, we would fetch water in two containers, with a capacity of fifteen litres and two handles, each of which had to be carried by two people, one on either side, but in this way it wasn't possible either to run into a gateway, and then we would have spilled half the water by the time we got home. So we picked up two ten-litre demijohns and some buckets (which bácsi Bandi had begged from German soldiers) and from then on we went to fetch water with these. For a siege, the giant demijohn is a practical invention, but it has the disadvantage that only one man — or do I mean one woman? — can carry it and it is very heavy. There were some days when nobody except me and the neurotic woman doctor ventured out. On such days, I ran the course with a ten-litre demijohn in each hand. By now so many things had happened that I am finding it very difficult to report, but it would have been even more difficult if I hadn't started to make notes in the evenings.

I must say a few words about the horses because I am so sorry for them. They get more than their fair share of the war and yet what do they care for the war? We live in an uncommonly close community, the horses and I, because as I say the streets and their surroundings are stuffed full of supply vehicles. The horses are very thin, there is no fodder and they are so hungry that they are eating the most unlikely objects. I saw a desperate supply horse sticking its head through the window of a telephone box on Pauler Street — naturally with the glass long gone — and chewing the pages of the directories.

In the garden adjoining ours, German military horses live with all kinds of furniture for which the Germans currently have no use and have thrown out, for example, polished dining room furniture. I myself saw the horses chewing the veneer off a dresser. The most terrible thing was that they were also eating each other's carcasses. I had refused to believe this until I saw it with my own eyes because I believed like everybody that the horse is the most fastidious animal in the world. Baron Kapry, a great animal lover, equestrian and horse expert, also refused to accept it until he went out specially to see what they were doing and came back very upset. You can't imagine what a depressing spectacle this is. I did not question at the time why amid so many horrors this particular one left such an impression on me and others. If a horse descends to such a thing, people must have been wondering what it would be like if one day humans began to starve. By now there are horses living in every ground-floor apartment in the area and they look extremely funny when they stretch their heads out of the glassless windows.

There are also horses in the former Philadelphia Café, in restaurants and in garages. A Hungarian soldier coming from Pest reported seeing horses in Café Gerbeaud confectionery in Vörösmarty Square, where people pulled the drawers out of the walls and fed them sweets. On January 10 in Pest, I saw some cafés with their display windows intact but with horses living in them, which was an even more grotesque sight. So much for the living horses.

The dead horses were also in great demand. After every attack people appeared and cut the meat for their daily lunch off the horses with huge kitchen knives. By now nobody is fussy, not even me, especially because our excellent cook can prepare unforgettable goulash soups from the horses, which the children have christened pony soup. Horse burgers are not bad either. I don't think I ever had such an opportunity to eat so much fresh meat, because the animal is still warm when they cut it to pieces. I often saw a steaming carcass with eight to ten men hacking into it.

One day we are lining up for water in front of a laundry, with the back of the line standing in front of a building that looked like a shed that could have been a garage before it was ruined. Now there are soldiers in it and of course horses. The soldiers drag in a freshly killed horse from the yard and one of them — obviously a butcher in civilian life — ties a large leather apron around himself and expertly starts to skin the horse. Several other soldiers stand around him and are joined by an officer with a round beard like Count Széchenyi in his youthful pictures. Of course, we in the line are watching the event, if only because we are bored. When the horse's stomach is cut open, a huge whitish-grey shiny object resembling a sac slips out of it. The butcher-sergeant steps back somewhat startled, the soldiers exchange confused glances, and as silence descends one of them says, "She was pregnant," to which another adds: "She would have had a beautiful filly."

They do not open the sac and after a while continue the butchery. My partner and I exchange a glance as if we were saying that after what we have just seen horsemeat will not go down our throats for a long time. But next evening, when pony soup with dumplings and vegetables is served again, none of us still thinks of the dead equine hero, because we are so hungry we wolf down the hot food.

I have to devote a separate chapter to the toilet misery and declare that in this respect we were treated royally in comparison with those in other shelters. Since we were not in real cellars but only in a basement, we had a genuine toilet at our disposal, from which only one thing was missing: water. Into this toilet, we were only allowed to pass fluids, but for more serious fecal material a chair with a hole and a bucket under it were placed next to the toilet, followed by another bucket holding ashes and a shovel, with which we could sprinkle a token of our grief for what we were leaving behind. The joke is that apart from the laundry, which served the children's home as a shelter, the toilet was the only vaulted and therefore relatively bomb-proof place, but during the bombings hardly anybody dared to go out there, possibly because it had a little vent opening onto the garden, which was permanently open, so the firing sounded terribly loud.

As if this wasn't embarrassing enough, the guests of the boarding house included a young wife from Bácska who was so afraid of the attacks that it would have been more practical for her not to get off the bucket during the entire raid, but unfortunately she preferred our vaulted shelter, which proved to be a painfully impractical solution. The funniest thing was that she performed all this with a rosary in her hand, praying incessantly. Her husband had the dustpan and brush in readiness, and after the raid swept up after his wife as one does with circus horses.

There was a lot of traffic in the only toilet, although several of us held back our more serious output until sunset, when we could climb up to a secluded corner of the garden (sometimes wading through snow up to our necks) and take up our "watering stations," a name inspired by the German "firing stations" directly across from us. It seems that I am a genuine upper-class girl because I didn't catch cold even though I was granted many opportunities to do so (politely). God forgive me, but I don't think I ever laughed as much as I did with Vera Nyilas on such occasions. Once when we went on a health excursion into the garden, we both started laughing like mad in the dark, and it transpired that we were both thinking at the same time and in the middle of the same activity of how we would tell the other guests of the Gresham Café about peeing in duet in one of the gardens of Krisztinaváros in powder snow and infantry gunfire and beside muzzle flashes. Otherwise, as already mentioned, peeing generally presented problems insofar as almost all of us displayed the — in the given circumstances rather unpleasant — phenomenon of having to go out frequently when the urge came and could not be held back. With most of us — including me — the complaint persisted for a long time after the siege and for some until now. Physicians say that this is one of the symptoms of being generally run down. I am not even talking about how in January even the strongest woman was no longer menstruating. Admittedly, one had to be very determined to allow oneself such a luxury because by now we had to be so economical with water that there was only a quarter of a wash basin for washing and cleaning one's teeth. Laundry washing in the second half of January was only permitted for the children who wet their pants.

I mentioned several times that a German supply unit was stationed on our street and a German kitchen vehicle in front of our building. Bácsi Bandi, whom I have also mentioned a few times, had made friends with the chef of this kitchen vehicle, a Sudeten German miner called Anton in civilian life who had learned to cook during his five years in the German army before he obtained a one-year

Erholungsurlaub[15] as a result of contracting dysentery somewhere in Upper Hungary and being sent to his hometown, where he had two beautiful children whom he had not seen for a year because of the war. He told us all this in our kitchen where he showed up every evening freshly washed and shaved, neatly dressed and carefully combed, sat down in the seat of honour (a basket chair from the garden) and gathered the children around him. The caregivers did not need to be expressly called to him because they were sucking up to him so wildly that it made me feel sick to watch it even though I sympathized with him.

Anton is fond of children. The way he sets them on his knee and plays with them, he would be a perfect illustration for a festival edition of *Die Gartenlaube*.[16] You wouldn't believe it. (The reason I talk like this is that I have long since become bored with barkochba and am now playing "Mr. Kovács" with Vera Nyilas; the game consists of trying to say the most banal thing that a Mr. Kovács would say in any situation or saying the most banal thing that can be said in any situation we can think of. Vera is an expert at this game, which is great fun to play.)

The only upright character among us is Dedi, not a very friendly child at the best of times, but when Anton tries to lift him on his knee he becomes a child who protests with angry and indignant screams, stamping feet, furious and determined refusals and — what is most interesting — without the slightest sign of fear. He is not afraid of Anton but detests him. Anton is actually a kind, intelligent man, with whom we get on very well. On some evenings, if he sees that we are all depressed, he tries to cheer us up by explaining that the liberating

---

15 German: convalescent leave.

16 The first popular mass-circulation German magazine, published from 1853 to 1944.

German army is very close — somewhere near Esztergom — and could be here in a few hours to free us from the encirclement (of course he has no idea who we are). You can imagine how this puts our minds at rest. When Anton leaves, lethargy returns and I fight it desperately because I see its spreading as a great danger. I don't believe in the liberating army or, better, in the possibility of a breakout, and I am afraid that a German counteroffensive could extend the siege into infinity. I therefore swear at everyone who falls for such a stupid story. My determined opponent is Vera Nyilas, who never stops telling me that NOBODY CAN GET THROUGH THIS ALIVE, but who is not just playing "Mr. Kovács" but says what every Mr. Kovács said at that time. I am seriously supported by bácsi Bandi, although we never know whether or not he meant what he was saying.

In any case, at the mere report of a relieving army, the German soldiers, who had been rather unkind to us, began to distribute gifts. When things quiet down, all the tenants in the building set out on expeditions, and they arrive back with quite a bit of loot. Once we received a whole case of soap. It is also a great help that since we have made friends with Anton we no longer have to cook our own breakfast, because he includes us among the soldiers for whom he makes first-class sweetened black coffee, from the Treasury.[17] In the morning, two of us simply get hold of a fifteen-litre container and step out in front of our building, whereupon Anton adds the breakfast for the twenty-two of us to it. In that way we are not only spared the discomforts of early rising, the efforts of lighting the stove, the hardships of economizing on firewood and sugar, but also the bitter struggle for WATER. Anton further budgets the soldiers' lunch to cover the dinner of the children's home in the evening. In addition, he cooks interesting things that I like a lot. One of his dishes was oat flakes accompanied by an onion and paprika sauce or a sweet item sprinkled

17 Supplies distributed by the state.

with cinnamon and sugar. At other times, we had split peas cooked with dried potatoes, which was excellent because the potatoes neutralized the flavour of the pulses, and we did not notice that we were eating peas. Admittedly, we often found fragments of glass and nails in the vegetables, but who cared about such things at such times?

We gradually developed a custom whereby after lunch we waited for a relatively quiet moment, when bácsi Bandi and one of the women grasped the fifteen-litre containers and set out for Anton's kitchen. The woman who reached out for the other handle of the container from the far side was usually me, because that was the best way to avoid the washing up work. (I never enjoyed washing up but least of all when I had to be economical with the water.)

One mid-January about lunchtime, God knows why, bácsi Bandi went off with the container on his own without saying a word to anyone. That morning there was a major air raid. We had lunch late, and after lunch I went looking for bácsi Bandi on my way to Anton but couldn't find him anywhere. In the afternoon, a German soldier whom I didn't know came to report that the gentleman with glasses who used to visit the kitchen vehicle with the containers was lying in front of the apartment buildings, obviously wounded because a time bomb had exploded nearby. The home is gripped by frenzied activity. The first aid box is dragged out, the neatly folded laundry pulled off the couch, a stretcher is improvised and the neurotic doctor goes out into the street to examine the wounded. She comes back as white as a sheet: bácsi Bandi is dead. He is lying in front of the next building, the container with the two handles has rolled to the middle of the street and is splattered with blood. Some soldiers tell us that Anton was also hit by a blast of air pressure and taken to hospital.

We spend the rest of the day in a terrible mood. I am seriously afraid for the sanity of the children. We don't tell them exactly what happened, which I think idiotic because even the youngest could sense that something had. Vera declares once again that nobody could get through this alive, while I decide precisely at that moment that I do want to survive. The Major and another man in the building are preparing to bring the body in on the stretcher, but at that moment the Russian Ratas[18] appear over the Castle District and THE NEIGHBOURING AREA for hours. THE NEIGHBOURING AREA is basically us. The mood in the bomb shelter is terrible. The children are sitting in deathly silence, afraid to move a muscle, while the caregivers sob and throw suspicious sideways glances at Vera, Mrs. Kata Wald and me because we are not crying. It's not until sunrise that the Dance ends. We need to collect the bread we had prepared ourselves and had delivered in the early morning to the Turkish bakery on Attila Street. Nurse Ica and I volunteer. If I thought yesterday that it was not possible to destroy Pauler Street more completely, I now have the opportunity to see with my own eyes that it is only too possible. In front of the neighbouring buildings, German soldiers shout at us to take away a large heap of indefinable garbage, which after some careful examination I clearly recognize as poor bácsi Bandi's cold, if not frozen, body.

We try to put the Germans' minds at rest by telling them that things have been sorted out inside the building and we are on our way, but as soon as we turn onto Roham Street we see that the bakery has been completely destroyed and discover that not only has our bread disappeared under the ruins but also the whole staff. Determined people scrape half burned bread out of the rubble to take home. Nurse Ica is among the mourners, but I would like to get some bread out of the ruins to replace our lost bread; however, the sooty beams hanging close to my head suggest otherwise and I decide to do without, albeit with a heavy heart.

By this time BREAD is such a valuable commodity that I can only write about it in capital letters. We in the Red Cross home have enough food to eat every day, although not much. We regard with

---

18 Nickname for the Polikarpov I–16 Russian fighter aircraft.

a superstitious awe Nurse Ica, who knows how to make excellent homemade bread. Kneading the bread is truly a divine service. We all stand there and devotedly watch the process wondering whether it will rise properly. From the beginning we have very little flour and must be very economical with it. We eke it out right to the end and have just one very thin slice of bread for breakfast, spread with such delicacies as margarine or Szitmaltin,[19] which believe it or not is very good. Sometimes we cover it with liquid malt extract and the whole shelter is sticky.

To return to bácsi Bandi: by the evening he is finally brought to the apartment building. Naturally, they do not bring him to the shelter, but place him in the children's ground-floor room in the Hornyánszky apartment, which looks out on the garden. It looks as if his pockets have been searched and that his wallet and valuable gold watch have been taken into protective custody by the German soldiers. His private documents are still on him. The stretcher and the floor are full of blood where his frozen body thawed and started to bleed.

The whole building has been taken over by a deadly mood of mourning. I myself somehow feel that I am hardening and do not allow myself to get sentimentally close to the events. The following day, another hellish concert with crazy bombing. At the corner of Attila Street and Roham Street, a massive four-storey block of apartments has taken a direct hit, and forty people are buried in the ruins. This does not improve the mood of the company on Pauler Street. Meanwhile, we do not pass a single day without receiving a grenade or an incendiary bomb in the building or garden. And NOT ONE OF THEM BLOWS UP. I get used to this and would be surprised if one exploded, because such things cannot happen to Pipis. Once, I go up into the garden and my nose is hit by a penetrating smell of

---

19 A brand of powdered malt extract with added cocoa powder, powdered milk and dried eggs.

ammonia and at the same time I see a dirty yellow kind of smoke creeping just above ground level. I run down, call the Major from the boiler house and tell him. He comes running up with another man, and they smother the cause of the yellow smoke and stench, an incendiary. By now the Germans' munitions bombs (I'm not sure if you have seen anything like them) are falling thickly. They resemble a missile of about 100–120 centimetres in height and about 25–30 centimetres in diameter or a similarly lavishly executed container holding chocolates, cigarettes, tin cans or other ammunition. Every evening between six and seven o'clock, the JUs[20] arrive with their slow sleepy hum, which even Dedi is able to distinguish from the Russian fighters with their aggressive racket, and dropped these munition containers on parachutes. The parachutes are made of beautiful, deep orange or red silk, attached to the bomb with thick, white silk ropes. The bright orange-coloured capes on the snow of Vérmező Park are a beautiful sight in the morning. One such munition bomb tears through the mansard ceiling and lands in our top floor bathroom. We would love to open it, but that is punishable with death. Everybody is obliged to report such a bomb to the nearest German sentry. It is forbidden to touch them, and accordingly we report the bomb, and immediately German soldiers come running and carry away even the white silk of the parachute leaving nothing apart from a thick piece of white artificial rope behind. Such munition bombs are mainly dropped on Vérmező Park, where the other bombs dropped on the neighbourhood are also frequently collected. Particularly clever are those that contain missiles, lined with leather and packed with wood shavings, handles, levers, sliding valves, pistons, rotors. The whole thing is so beautiful, and you could play with it for hours. One time I address a German soldier and ask him what there is in such a munition bomb. He answers proudly, but scratching his head, "Alles, was ein

20 German bombers manufactured by Junker.

deutscher Soldat nur braucht."[21] By this time, a German soldier's most elementary needs include insect powder. By now there is less and less talk about the relieving army as there is about being uncared for, unwashed, dirty, untidy and bad tempered.

Nevertheless, poor bácsi Bandi still needs burying. This leads to a huge amount of fuss in the home. The house commander strides up and down issuing inane orders but not knowing what to do. According to instructions posted earlier in the streets, the home's air defence commander is to appoint some residents to dig a grave in the nearest promenade or public park and have the body interred there after the details had been recorded. Fair enough, the house commander also knows this, but the instructions don't say how to dig graves under constant fire.

It is decided that six men should march out to the inner edge of Vérmező Park at daybreak and bury poor bácsi Bandi there. In this context the Major informs us caregivers that it is now our duty to clean up the dead man, that is, wash him a little, etc. It still rankles me to remember how all the women present turned toward me, looking as if they expected me to do all their dirty work, but I managed to declare calmly and firmly that I was not prepared to volunteer for such a task, and to drop a hint that there were — *unberufen*[22] — two women doctors in the group, who were perfectly able to do so.

They are still a little cross with me for my rebellion, but the two physicians can't find any legitimate excuse for a rapid avoidance of the unpleasant obligation, and ultimately it is the two physicians or, more correctly, Dr. Lili who takes care of the job, while Dr. Ilus has a fit at the decisive moment and stands by the body sobbing until Dr. Lili has done all that has to be done. This includes pulling the deceased man's smart shoes off his feet and giving them to one of the

---

21 German: Everything a German soldier needs.

22 German: uncalled upon, unbidden.

physicians' oldest boys who hasn't any. The funeral is at 6:30 in the morning. I don't sign up to go, even though attending such functions is part of my job and not going could cost my life. By some instinctive reaction, I push the whole bácsi Bandi history away from myself.

Meanwhile, we are constantly being bombed, shelled and machine-gunned, but the nights are relatively quiet, at which time we talk about what a bad place we have landed in, actually the worst in the whole of Budapest, from every point of view. I keep saying that surely people in every shelter believe they are in the worst place and we don't know if somewhere else isn't even worse. Vera tortures me by reiterating that we should sneak over to Pest before it's too late. She would be able to go to Penke on Nagymező Street. I tell her that I have nowhere to go because I haven't got anything to eat and can't expect anybody to feed me when they haven't anything themselves.

More and more Hungarian soldiers and military trains come across from Pest. They report that the line of hotels on the Danube Promenade is burning and so is Vörösmarty Square. We don't enquire about the ghetto because it would make us too conspicuous, but we are prepared for the worst and also know that the least they might do is set fire to the ghetto before retreating. On the evening of January 19, I walk out into the street with Vera to inspect the latest damage. We meet two policemen and ask them if civilians are still allowed to cross to Pest. The policemen ask in surprise how we want to do that. We say: for example, by Erzsébet Bridge, whereupon they tell us that since yesterday there haven't been any bridges because the Germans blew all of them up before they evacuated Pest.

Poor Vera, I thought she would have a stroke there and then. I quickly drag her away because she has started to jump up and down and swear like a sailor. Strangely enough I was also very upset even though we had known for months that this would be the end: no bridge left intact but humanity still hoping for miracles. When we tell the story at home, our relations are equally beside themselves, although they too had foreseen it. Vera was still blaming herself violently for not crossing while there was time. Now we were really sitting up to our necks in the mire. We had thought the Germans would themselves occupy the castle and its district and had expected them to defend us to the "last bullet," as was their custom when a whole city had fallen to the enemy. We were all in a bad mood. Here and now, it had become very difficult to be a child caregiver if you really wanted to take care of children.

We invented all kinds of clever things to entertain ourselves, each other, and the children. We played endless games of barkochba. Vera is a grandmaster at this game, but Andris Surányi, our fifteen-year-old charge, is also an excellent player. The other children breathlessly watched the game, even the youngest who didn't understand but wouldn't miss one word of it. Almost every day I have to organize an evening of arias and songs for the children. The children's songs are very successful, but the "Two Grenadiers" is even more so, and as for "La Marseillaise," I have to sing, recite and translate the words separately. We cannot play with the children because of the lack of space and adult overcrowding.

Here is how I spend my days: I get up at about 7:30 a.m. (if I am not responsible for fetching water), light the stove (if I am), contribute to preparing the children's breakfast, help with making the "beds," feed and dress the children and help in the kitchen. I then walk out to the home's garden gate, where it is already light but one still has to jump out of the way quickly if a vehicle approaches, and I mend the children's torn clothing. If there is any water, I wash clothes. From time to time I peep into the shelter and suggest some songs or games to the children. Then I prepare our lunch. After lunch, we caregivers wash the dishes, and after washing up I sit down in the darkest corner of the kitchen, thinking for hours about food. Later I look in again on the children if nobody else does. Then I play or chat with Vera to kill time until dinner. (Dinner is usually at half past six, and we try to make the day shorter by getting up late and going to bed early). Then we prepare supper, feed the children and in the kitchen wash the children down one by one with warm water beside the reserve cooker.

As the water miseries worsened, keeping ourselves clean became a great problem but keeping the children clean an even greater one. We had an ingenious system whereby we were able to nominally clean fourteen children with half a basinful of water. We even decided to patent this after the siege. For each caregiver in the tighter times there was half a glass of water for cleaning purposes but sometimes not even that much. You can't imagine how brilliantly I could clean my hands and teeth with that amount of water, but that was simply all there was. I washed the rest with cologne-soaked cotton wool. We washed our underwear at least twice a week with repeatedly recycled water, but I could never once be called neglected or unkempt. I got the water from the underground in the strictest sense of the word, that is, from melting snow, which makes the clothes extremely ugly and apparently even dirtier than before, but what matters is that they have been washed. We often also use snow water to wash the dishes and even ourselves.

Meanwhile, the Great Dance is becoming more and more colourful with hardly an unscathed building around us. Carrying water is also becoming a less attractive task. Vera and I are the most determined water carriers. On one outing we notice that the two of us are already at Krisztina Boulevard when I see that we have brought one container more than we could carry when full. So I run back with the surplus while Vera goes ahead into the so-called Áldásy house, and stands in the line until I return. But I hardly reach home with the jug when the Russian fighters arrive and tune up for their habitual jokes, so that I can't leave again. We are all worried about Vera being out. The raid is still going strong when she arrives home. She is pale and nervous. We asked her if she had gone crazy walking up and down in the street during a raid. She says that in the Áldásy house soldiers cooked and lit fires and there was a lot of smoke and smell. She was bored by it all and came home. Then she casually remarked that something had hit her, possibly a piece of shrapnel. When she removes the thick woollen scarf, which she always wore, we could see a piece of material hanging freely at the back and inside it a piece of shrapnel that had torn a hole but also got stuck in the scarf and further also torn a hole at the neck of her coat's thick woollen material. Vera puts the shrapnel away as a souvenir, but we could not lure her out again until the siege ended.

But the siege lasts as if it never wanted to end. My secret suspicion is that it was not the shrapnel that taught Vera that *Krieg ist Krieg*,[23] but that time on our way home from water carrying when on the inner edge of the park we saw a German soldier firing his machine gun at a dog in the presence of two civilians. The dog had sunk up to its knees yowling pitifully each time the soldier fired off another volley. I couldn't understand how that was possible, because the soldier was aiming from a very short distance. Vera almost had a fit. She slammed the water buckets to the ground and rushed, with her fingers in her ears, toward the apartment building. I could barely keep up with her, but all the way home we heard the machine gun and the dreadful yowling of the dog. After that day, Vera jumped every time she heard shots, although I tried to persuade her not to worry because nowadays only human beings were being shot and not dogs.

The Grand Dance was slowly approaching its climax, but funny things happen all the same. Jóska, the guest soldier from Nagykőrös, always parked his car in front of our building, although it resembled more and more the scrap metal into which the cars of the German supply unit were turning, but one morning Jóska can't find it. He goes outside, looks here and there and finally does find it exactly where it had been, but flattened to a pancake during the night. We had heard a tank rumbling through Pauler Street in the night. That tank had reduced the remains of all the vehicles in the street into one dimension.

---

23 German: War is war.

The buildings, like the cars, had gradually begun to be unrecognizable. In a quieter moment, I decided to make the Great Excursion to peep across at the Kramolins, who lived on the street corner, to discover what had happened to them and to Dr. Kapolyi, but I can hardly recognize Attila Street.

One afternoon a huge grenade bursts in on us in the Hornyánszky apartment, sideways through the gateway and drops onto the floor in the third room BUT IT DOES NOT EXPLODE! It crushes the German soldier skulking on a wall underneath it, where he remains lying for a whole day covered by his grey soldier's cape with only his terribly muddy boots showing. On the wall there is a huge bloodstain, and the staircase leading to the apartment is also bloody.

There are times when we are unable to cook our lunch because we must stay in the shelter without a break. But we have to give the children lunch. Fortunately, we still have a little bacon and malt extract, and so we can give them a picnic. That is good because it does not need any water and bad because a lot of bread is consumed despite the fact that everybody gets, at the most, one and a half thin slices. But again the vanishing supply would need to be replenished. As I have already mentioned, the central food store of the Red Cross is in the Castle District, quite high at 25 Úri Street, which is the property of the Hüvös family. To climb up there at this time is such an enterprise that nobody would dare to advise it even to buy food. But one day I wake up again knowing that today I will climb up into the Castle District and also know that I will come back. This day promises to be calm, and I ask the neurotic physician if she would enjoy coming with me. In this case I think enjoyment is going too far, but Dr. Lili is immediately won over. I empty my knapsack and place the things I take out of it in another hiding place in the Hornyánszky apartment, which is a rather complicated operation. With one basket in each of our respective hands, we set out despite our colleagues' pale attempts to dissuade us. At the last moment, Vera also suddenly decides to come with us because she knows how much food we will have to carry, perhaps so much that it would be too heavy for the two of us and who knows when we will be able to buy food again. By the time we reach the edge of Vérmező Park, the shells are already crackling, so German soldiers drag us into a former restaurant cellar and tell us off for gallivanting around in the streets at such a time. We are down there with them for about a quarter of an hour while a young German soldier with an attractive, intelligent face cautiously but disapprovingly talks about the continuation of the war. Indeed, he doesn't even like war as an institution anymore. A soldier's life is beautiful, he says, but a bath from time to time isn't bad either. The poor boy is really extraordinarily dirty. The detonations turn slightly quieter, but Vera declares that it would be the most idiotic thing to start out and she goes home. But if we turned back now and if I had to repeat the packing and unpacking, I would have unpacked all the stuff for nothing and purely out of laziness, now that I have started, I am going up. Physician Lili is prepared to come with me, and we start climbing the snow-covered Logodi staircase. The sunlight is blinding, everything sparkles. We can hardly bear to keep our eyes open. Meanwhile the firing continues. When the more serious whistles come closer, we sometimes bend down but without any conviction because by now neither one of us believes that such a small gesture makes any difference. On a bend in Lovas Street, I suddenly find myself facing a colleague from the Credit Bank, one of the institution's most well-known Arrow Cross pillars. A month or two ago, I would almost certainly have had a heart attack, but now I don't think anything like "what is going to happen now, will he betray me to a policeman?" Nothing of the kind happens now. He is pleased to see me (I haven't been in the bank since Christmas), and having been only on a nodding acquaintance we stop for a short, but all the more friendly, conversation inspired by the shells.

Neither Lili nor I were too excited by the adventurous excursion, but we still heaved a sigh of relief when we turned off the bends exposed to the Buda Hills and reached Szent György Square and the relatively sheltered Úri Street. By then the Castle District was in a quite spectacular condition. My heart ached for the many beautiful old buildings and their Biedermeier furnishings. Walls two metres thick have been pulverized, but so far only in the way that the knight jumps, that is, every fifth building. At 25 Úri Street where the food store is, Mr. Mayer, the warehouse keeper, gives us a somewhat unpleasant welcome. They hadn't counted on anybody coming to buy food and thought that they would be able to eat the whole supply themselves or do whatever else they wanted with it. I am angry but try to talk to him kindly because I want to squeeze as much as possible out of him. He is a shady character with whom I have to fight for every single item. He doesn't want to give us any bacon at all, with the excuse that it was in the attic, making it dangerous to retrieve because the roof is threatening to collapse and he can't instruct people to go up there. Luckily his "man" is present and volunteers to bring down a ten-kilogram bag, to the anger of Mr. Mayer. Mr. Mayer shouts after him that a smaller one would be all right, but I shout that he might as well bring the larger one if so many of us put our lives at risk for it. I liberated two big boxes of malt, sugar cubes, beans, peas, tinned meat, tomato purée, etc. The servant brings a large slice of bacon down from the attic covered with lime and fragments of glass. We carefully pack everything. I sign the receipts for the food, and we turn toward home. As we step out of the gateway, I hear a suspicious distant hum. We stop and listen; the hum is coming nearer and becomes more and more familiar: the unmistakable music of Russian fighters approaching.

We go back to Mayer's cellar. It has two storeys and many steps with the stairs making two turns. The residents of the building live in the lowest part, a huge, vaulted building that could have been built as a wine cellar hundreds of years ago. Now it is almost designed to be comfortable with thirty people living here, including young children and even infants. They invite us to wait there, and we have hardly sat down when the raid begins and the whole cellar rocks with us. The woman of the house has a large glass of brandy sent over to each of us.

We drink it on empty stomachs. I am wrapped in a kind of pink haze and I talk non-stop. I don't know what I am talking about but I think I am telling my life story to Lili, who doesn't listen because she has become sleepy and is nodding off thanks to the brandy. I understand what is happening outside and also the very slight possibility of my ever meeting you again, but in this funny way I see that as something humorous and I chat to you as follows: Hello, Pipus, and there will be no little Kiskas. Who are you going to shout at now? I also nod off.

We are offered lunch, of course split peas and delicious *lángos*. The air pressure repeatedly blows the flames out in the cooker and extinguishes some lamps. The cellar rocks. I either chatter or nod. Most of the residents kneel in front of the altar in the deepest recess of the cellar and pray. A small baby howls. The time passes. It already gets dark at five o'clock these days, and at the risk of being shot no civilian is allowed to walk in the streets after dark. I agree with Dr. Lili that we shall celebrate all future January 25ths — whatever may be — together, if possible, in a cake shop and next to a glass of brandy. The residents watch us suspiciously because they don't like us not being afraid. At last, the concert outside calms down, and we decide to leave for home because darkness is falling fast. We thank the locals for their hospitality and wish them good luck as we leave.

We hardly recognize Úri Street. Every other building is falling out into the street, some are burning, others smoking, and we must avoid many of them. There are policemen on the street. They throw rubble on the flames to extinguish the fires. We reach Dísz Square. Everywhere dead horses' bodies, torn to pieces. The winding road cannot be recognized. In the morning it was blinding white, now it is dark brown, completely churned up. Instead of snow-covered asphalt, clay everywhere. The staircase we walked up in the morning is in pieces. We run past the stair's landings with the soldiers constantly shouting to us to hurry up because the Russians are shooting right here. We can't hurry because Lili's knapsack is too heavy (she is tiny and thin). At every step, fallen trees block the way, and it annoys me that we are not walking but crawling and it is possible that we will have to turn around and look for another way because either the road was destroyed that morning or debris completely blocks the way. We have to turn back and look for another way several times as darkness is falling. We are tired and the mass of food is heavy.

Further down, we meet people coming toward us; one man lugging an old woman on his back asks us how far it is to the Hospital in the Rock of the Castle District. The people are pale and frightened. The situation looks dreadful. I keep reassuring Lili that we will get home because after all it is my birthday. Looking at this from our brandy haze, it seems very logical and Lili accepts it. We have already reached the lowest portion of the staircase, which is blown to bits, so we must balance ourselves across huge rocks. There are men coming right toward us when we try to climb across the blocks balancing our knapsacks and baskets across them. I secretly hope they will help us over, but one of the men is in such a hurry that instead of helping me he GIVES ME A BIG PUSH, and I fall out of his path. A siege here or there but this is too much, and in my anger I call after him and what I shout is, I am afraid, not too flattering.

The lower we get, the more frightening the image that awaits us. Attila Street is in such a condition that Lili and I stop and look at each other. We dare not continue because we are afraid that our building will no longer be there and that our friends are dead. We pull ourselves together and turn onto Pauler Street, which can now hardly be called a street. Another big building has collapsed, but we can see from the corner that it is not ours. Just as we approach, a man is pulled out of the ruins crying and madly repeating "they have both left me." We discover that his wife and daughter were underneath the ruins. It is 11 Pauler Street that has been hit and sliced in two from the fourth floor to the cellar. Our people are running toward us in the street and embracing us, crying. They believed that we died in the Castle District. The mood is indescribable. This is the first attack on such a scale, and it is not difficult to guess what will happen to us if it is repeated.

We head into the Red Cross's separate shelter and open what we have brought with us there, and not in a kitchen where the other residents would also be present. By now nobody dares show their food to other people. The bacon and cube sugar receive huge ovations. The bigger children stick their heads together whispering and then walk out from the shelter to the hall in front of it. When I leave the shelter, they produce ear-splitting cheers. We are the heroes of the day. The residents later gather, and we have to tell them about our experiences. On that day, Lili and I are given a special portion of supper. Whenever Dr. Lili and I look at each other, we must laugh loudly at the fact that we have survived, however bad our case seemed to be.

Toward the end of January, the Great Dance seems to acquire serious dimensions. We mark every day that we get through alive as a battle won, but we water carriers in particular go to bed conscious that another even harder battle follows. But now there are more and more days when it is not at all possible to go out, even to fetch water. So we limit our water use even more. Naturally, the women also behave impossibly in this respect, turning it into a matter of status when one doesn't get more water to wash in than another. By now the water is under lock and key in the pantry, and Ica, the nurse in charge of cooking, allocates some water to each of us separately. To wash in the morning, a caregiver was due half a glass of water, which she could use as she wished. I usually used half of it for cleaning my teeth and half for washing my hands. The maximum drinking water left was one glass per head. I drank my portion (boiled of course) either as cold tea or flavoured with crushed lemon substitute tablets because it quenched my thirst better, and we were always thirsty due to the pulses and the soy products.

Every evening, we held a great war council about what to cook the next day to use less water. We boiled beans in the water in which we soaked them, but the beans were not a good idea because they made you thirsty. The same goes for peas. Millet did not use a lot of water but it had to be soaked twice before cooking, so this wasn't a good solution either. We preferred to cook spaghetti. It is true that this also used a lot of water, but we turned the leftover water into soup the next day. Frequently for breakfast we had just one slice of bread covered in jam or lard, because we did not have enough water to make coffee substitute or Szitmaltin. We then gave the sugar cubes to the children separately. When the water situation had got even nastier and the women were constantly falling out over water rations, I was landed with the honour of being appointed the watchdog with the power to approve or refuse water portions outside the norm. I can say that this is a thankless task. One of the most unpleasant aspects of the lack of water was the washing misery. There were twenty-two of us. Twice every day, twenty-two plates and spoons as well as a lot of glasses and a huge pot had to be washed in a palmful of water. Among the children were two brothers and two cousins. One fine day somebody got the idea that brothers and cousins could really eat from one plate, whether simultaneously or successively. Later we extended this to everybody, and each of the caregivers also chose a plate cousin.

I shall be proud as long as I live that Vera Nyilas, who is famous for her painful fastidiousness, chose me for her plate-cousin after lengthy reflection. I had by then abandoned all refinement and sophistication and could laughingly have eaten from a chamber pot. Indeed, I had the opportunity so to speak, because I often had to eat my lunch or supper after cleaning a filthy Gyurka and rinsing my hand with a quarter glass of water or even less. As I have said before, we were only able to wash the children thanks to some clever tricks. Every evening, we carried half (on worse days a quarter) a basin full of water with a flannel and half a jug of water. We washed the bigger children down to the waist and the smaller ones from top to toe with the wet flannel, which we always squeezed out in the basin and then sprinkled with a little clean water from the jug before washing the next child. In this way — however incredible it sounds — we were able to clean fourteen children with half a basinful of water.

Gyurka had a favourite gimmick of soiling himself at least twice on such days when there wasn't even enough water to drink and we had to wash not only him but also his clothes. This meant that at sunrise the next day we had to cross Krisztina Boulevard to its far side to collect enough water to cook with. I tried all the tricks in the world on Gyurka, but I am still convinced that not only is Emmi Pikler at fault but also that the child is not normal. Gyurka lives and dies for food, which is where I wanted to trap him. On the one hand, if he soiled himself he did not get any lunch or supper (to which he reacted with frightening rage, although I tried to ensure that he didn't see what the others were eating, kept him out of the kitchen and punished any children who wound him up by talking about lunch). On the other hand, if I managed to get him to do his job in the toilet, he was given an extra ration in solemn circumstances when he not only enjoyed the food but was also proud of eating his special ration in front of the others. Every day after lunch I would sit him on the pot and ask him politely to do his job and state that he will not be allowed to get up until he has finished, and sometimes he sits for hours, even falls asleep, without doing anything. I finally have to let him get up, and half an hour later the accident happens. When I ask him why he didn't say anything, he gives the same answer with the same stupid face: "Next time I will tell you." Once I am woken in the night with the message that Gyurka has had an accident. I have to get up and wash the child's backside in a basin of cold water. I am also a little worried that he will now surely catch cold, but there is no question of that. He is as fit as a fiddle, although a moment ago his teeth were chattering with the cold water.

All our lives revolve around the question of water. We all envy Dr. Lili, who receives a gift of a whole jug of water from the residents as a physician's fee for washing and dressing a small wound of the building owner. But the scandal is that while there are two or three women prepared to venture out for water, this does not mean that I would have to go much less, because two people are needed for carrying water and nobody is prepared to step out into the street without me. When I ask them why, they can't tell me, but each of them says that if they are with me they are not afraid. I must say that I didn't mention to any of them the strange certainty that nothing untoward could happen to me, but clearly something of the kind happened on Miksa Street: they sense that I am not afraid and that is why they cling to me.

Luckily, when we were in the greatest need of water the thaw began and the melting snow trickling from the gutters proved usable. We placed all the wash basins from our apartment building in the garden to let them drip full. In the afternoon, I needed a basin and took one back, ignoring the residents' disapproval of the reduction in the amount of water collected. But bringing it back was also lucky because that was how at least one of our basins was preserved. That afternoon, the building next door was hit by a shell, and all the basins left outside turned into sieves. And this not only happened to the Red Cross's papier mâché and Nurse Ica's enamelled Lampart basins but Baroness Kapry's heavy red copper basin also developed holes so large that the children could stick their fingers through them. That was the end of our first snow-water collection, but it also complicated cleaning ourselves using the one remaining basin.

Not long after the Úri Street expedition, I found the FIRST LOUSE on me. I will never forget that day. I was rather jaded by then but still believed that now the end of the world had come. I had been relatively cheerful and lively all day, but in the afternoon I suddenly felt something crawling around my waist. I stepped discreetly out in search of privacy, which was only available in the toilet, though that was dark. Even in the dark I caught something and unobtrusively carried it to a candle flame to give it a careful examination. It was light grey, round and flat, with a black spot in the middle and violently wriggling legs. I tottered over to the toilet, where I threw it into the bowl before I fell into such a lethargic condition that everybody noticed it, especially because half an hour earlier I had been enthusiastically playing barkochba with the children. I was already so hardened that nothing moved, startled or frightened me. I now slipped into the darkest corner of the shelter and took up my good old defensive position: sitting low with my elbows resting on my knees and indulging in a long secret cry. I didn't say anything, not even to Vera because I would have been excommunicated at once. But I decided that if a quiet ten minutes were to offer themselves I would nip across to Dr. Kapolyi to ask him for advice.

Actually, whenever I was in trouble I thought of Kapolyi first and as far as I know I wasn't the only one. On one occasion in the early days of January when the porcelain part of my crown had come off my tooth I went to him, and he mended it in five minutes, by candlelight, using the most primitive tools and refusing any money, which was just as well because money wasn't worth anything.

Although he was a dentist, he worked as the physician of the district surgery, dressing wounds, operating, acting as a midwife and doing everything in the most awfully unimaginable conditions.

A young married woman of my acquaintance in our building found herself in the throes of labour on the morning of the most critical day. She was laid down on the kitchen floor. When the baby was already halfway out, a grenade landed in the courtyard and blew in the door. Kapolyi bent over her and luckily his back protected her from the flying splinters (the birth was otherwise smooth, and mother and child are alive and well). So I immediately thought of Kapolyi in connection with the louse business, but I still had to wait two days before I could claim the quiet ten minutes when I was allowed to walk across to him. That is a very long time, when people are firing and something is crawling up and down one's back.

I managed to see him. He was in the first aid station with two army doctors. I walked up to him and told him that I would like to speak to him privately. He came out to the passage with me and when he heard what I wanted he started to laugh loudly, saying: "Thank

God it's only a louse. I thought you meant a greater problem when you came to me whispering and secretive as you did." And he was just about to ask when and how and especially from whom I managed to acquire this greater problem. I described the external appearance of the creature, and he told me kindly that it was probably a crab louse. He advised me to examine everybody in our shelter, because if somebody as fastidious as me was infested by lice, others were likely to be as well (!!!). He gave me some sublimate and vinegar solution and ordered me to wash twice a day those parts of me most popular with crab lice. Then he explained to me that in the cellars of Buda everybody had been infested with lice by now and anyone who claimed to be free of them was lying or had not yet discovered any. This put me into a more positive mood, and the next day I suggested to my colleagues that we examine the children, as a few of them seemed to be scratching themselves. I was concerned, having noticed some of them scratching their heads.

In January, on one of the quieter days when it was possible to walk in the streets, two little boys, Endre and Lacika, had come to us from the Red Cross home on Bogár Street, which the Germans had burned down as they were retreating. This was also a hospital, where the boys had stayed for a week among wounded soldiers and civilians who had taken refuge there. On the evening of their arrival, we undressed and bathed them as well as we could and washed their underwear, but we had no opportunity to examine the rest of their clothes (we never even thought of it) because the dim light of a single candle in the cellar barely prevented us from bumping into each other. Some children were scratching themselves, and the younger boy from Bogár Street scratched his head more often than the others. I had enough to worry about (see Gyurka), so I only warned the other helpers that we should look at the heads and clothes of the children. Everybody agreed with me that we "should" look at them.

Actually, everything was like that. There was always somebody who demanded that we should do this or that and the others sang in a chorus that "we should really do something" and the others sang after them that "one should really do something" as everyone waited for everyone else to do it. I called it in private the "William Tell game." If you remember the opera of that name, the chorus first sings for hours that the Count has been drowned and "we must, we must, we must… save him" for hours, but everybody is only singing, is only singing, is only singing. The caregivers on Pauler Street were doing the same, but this time I picked up the children one by one and carried them to the top of the iron staircase leading to the garden, where there was enough light to examine the heads and clothes of the children. I went through their hair with my own fine-toothed comb. Naturally, I found lice on four or five children. This caused great alarm among the caregivers, who started combing their own hair and then each other's and only after that the children's. Next we examined their outer clothes and found masses of lice in the clothes of the boys from Bogár Street. We carried the bedding up into the yard, where we dusted, swept and aired it.

To avoid further infestation, we used my system in the battle even though that system needs a minimum of two sets of clothes. I myself rolled up the items taken off, spread them all over the front yard and put on a new set of clothes which I had shaken, brushed, and aired in readiness. I must note that we all, even the children, slept fully dressed at the command of the Major, because we had to be prepared for the Germans' retreating further and as was their habit setting fire to the whole row of buildings. (This is what happened to Jancsi Máté's family!) We prepared our things like this every evening so that we could gather the most important items within a few minutes. I could do this easily because I arrived with just a single knapsack, but the others had brought masses of possessions in suitcases, etc., so everybody selected the most important possessions and repacked them into an easily portable suitcase or knapsack. Vera Nyilas suffered terribly when she had to decide which of her things were absolutely essential. I will never forget her kneeling in front of her knapsack and agonizing whether or not to save her pessary.

Apart from the dirt and the lice, I am depressed by THE

DARKNESS. It is not possible to write or read or sew by the candlelight or even to find a lost object. I was obliged to get accustomed to order during the siege because if one put anything out of one's reach for a minute one would never find it again. Not because one person would have stolen the property of another, but because in the cramped and dark conditions anything that was not put safely away was immediately lost. This cost me one towel that I couldn't hang among any other things because it was sopping wet, which immediately disappeared. Nor was there any point in trying to separate outer wear or bedding because this was simply impossible. One always had to be on one's guard against somebody hunting for something they had lost.

When word went around that we had lice — which is difficult to keep secret in any case — the people from the boiler house demonstratively avoided us. When, at the threshold of the iron gate, I was searching my own and the children's clothes for hours in the mornings, they always told me not to do that there but to move further out in the garden. I explained to them meekly that I had no intention of doing this elsewhere because I couldn't jump from the middle of the garden straight into the shelter when a shell was approaching.

It was very cold. Upstairs my fingers froze in spite of my gloves. On such occasions, I had to stop hunting lice and run downstairs to warm up a little.

Later we had a great deal of fun in the boiler house when we noticed that they too were scratching themselves, although they claimed that they had started to imagine things once they knew there were lice in the building. But I put a bug in their ears by telling them what I heard from Kapolyi, i.e., that in Buda everyone is covered in lice in all the bomb shelters. They would bring their clothes up from the boiler house and declare in loud voices that they hadn't found anything. However, I once saw the Major's shirt full of the characteristic traces. Looking at the tiny spots of blood, I couldn't stop myself saying to him that he shouldn't be misled by their absence because even if the louse is hiding its unmissable traces have been left behind.

It was also the louse story that made us finally introduce the practice of cutting the boys' hair. Pipus, I became a perfect gentleman's barber. I can cut men's hair so beautifully that I could have made a career of it, if only I had had number zero clippers. We shaved the little boys' heads bald and trimmed the hair of the bigger ones. If a girl had longer hair than usual, we gave them a bob cut and even trimmed the caregivers' hair.

I learned a lot about myself. For example, everybody hated soy flour and we didn't know what to do with it. We tried to bake some kind of biscuit, but even with large amounts of sugar and cinnamon we were unable to take away the characteristic soy flavour so hated by us. Later on when the bread shortage was biting, we tried on one occasion, accompanied by disapproval, dark laments and mocking laughter, to mix the soy flour with paprika and caraway seed, and it turned out to be an EXCELLENT SUCCESS. After that we baked it as a substitute for bread, which the children loved when it was spread with lard or canned liver paté. For me, it had the special advantage that I could nibble from it while I was baking, and the soy has a pleasant characteristic of being extremely satisfying as well as making one terribly thirsty.

The next step was the soy *lángos*, which we were eating instead of meat with vegetables. We tried once to mix it with bread, but it didn't work. At this time, around the end of January and the beginning of February, our stomachs were very much in command of us. Everybody was primarily and exclusively interested in food. I observed that the children also talked about eating and food all the time. I also observed with Vera that in normal circumstances all the gossip revolved around our sex lives, in other words who was having it with whom, when, how and where, but now the happy sex life has been replaced with all the gossip and intrigue in the cellars by who was eating what, how much, when, how and why.

When the family had withdrawn to the boiler house, Mr. Hornyánszky, who preached parsimony but enjoyed huge meals, reappeared and discreetly opened the kitchen cupboard, which he kept under seven seals, and turning his back on us politely ate himself to the edge of the grave with all the good things of this world. Although in our case one could not talk about starvation, I did notice, looking at myself, how far hunger demoralizes a person. I had a hard time stopping myself from cutting a slice of bread from the landlord's loaf. Sometimes when someone was in the pantry, for one reason or another, it was difficult not to steal the odd sugar cube. We had such seasoned thieves among us that to this day I don't know who was doing it. At other times when the director cut exactly as many slices of bread as we were and tried to keep an eagle eye on it, by the evening one or two slices were missing, so that the director needed to compensate for the missing pieces. Whoever stole the bread had to be especially crafty since all of us were around the table the whole time and all our attention was focused on the distribution. In January, we were still baking pastries and had exactly as many pieces left for dinner as we were, but by the evening some were missing. We still had some almonds, hazelnuts and raisins, which we couldn't use for baking because of the lack of flour. From these the director shared out tiny portions, and of course we made sure that on solemn occasions there was no shortage of these. For instance, we celebrated the day when nothing bad happened except the grenade that burst into the pantry (IT DID NOT EXPLODE!). The grenade solved the problem of airing the room by carefully placing a hole next to the original window.

The blocked window takes my mind back to when we first had the bright idea of shielding the windows by piling bricks in front of them. That was why, on a quieter morning (by quieter I mean that there was no bombing, only shooting!), the Major ordered all the residents outside to build protective barriers in front of the windows of the bomb shelter and the kitchen using bricks from the collapsed building next door. We formed a "chain" and passed the bricks from person to person for a whole hour, but when the shelling became too much we had to stop until the evening. I am writing you this because what follows is closely connected to a story I read as a child, entitled SECRETS OF A CHILD'S HEART.[24]

We were talking to the children one day about the Russian custom of making students vote on which teachers they liked and which ones they didn't. Mrs. Kata Wald thought that if the children here were made to vote, she would get very bad marks. Andris and Bandi, the two oldest boys, looked at each other and started laughing because néni Kata would certainly have failed. So we asked them if they could elect only one of the caregivers, who would it be? They shared another laugh and answered promptly that it would be either néni Margit (me) or néni Bözsi Szilágyi (the mother of the two Szilágyi children). Asked why us two, they answered that they would elect me because I know how to treat them well, better than the others, and mainly — they stressed this heavily — because I wasn't playing favourites with the children assigned to me. They would vote for néni Bözsi because she is kind-hearted and good to the children.

I ask them how they could both give the same answer so quickly, is it because they've already discussed this? They look at each other and laugh again. Then they proceed to tell me that when all the adults were outside carrying bricks (see above), they played a game of pretend about what would happen if a bomb fell at that moment and all the adults were to die outside on the street while the children were left all alone inside. Then they changed the game by having either néni Bözsi or me surviving because we had returned to the building to collect something. They continued the game, showing how they would furnish the building and how they would stay alive by dividing up the contents of the Red Cross and the Hornyánszkys' pantries (the Hornyánszkys' legendary ham would have featured prominently), and deciding who would be doing the cooking, the cleaning, who

---

24 The popular young adult book *Misunderstood* by Florence Montgomery was published in 1869 in English and later published in Hungary with the title *A gyermekszív rejtelmei* (Secrets of a child's heart).

would be caring for the smallest children. They discovered that neither of them would know what to do with Mrs. Wald's baby, and so they changed the script and had the baby stay with the adults so that it would be outside in front of the building when the bomb dropped. Mrs. Wald was beside herself and scolded the children and us too for getting engaged in such conversations, but it was a truly instructive discussion because it not only let us gain insight into the secrets of these children's hearts but also showed us an interesting caricature of ourselves and revealed that these children formed an opinion about each of us individually and about all of us as a group. This is small wonder since my colleagues would always quarrel in front of the children and made no secret of what they thought of each other.

By now we have gotten used to the Great Dance; however, we have new problems to worry about: Sutyi, an uncommonly nice and intelligent boy of nine, is dizzy, vomiting, has a headache, a high fever and is lying in bed all day in total apathy. Everyone finds this really depressing. We don't dare to talk about it but are all convinced that at the very least Sutyi has meningitis. Later it turned out that the more pessimistic ones among us, including one female physician, thought that it was typhus. Of course, we have no way to isolate him, so he lies in the corner of the shelter during the day. At night, I personally carry him out to the camp bed set up in the kitchen, to avoid laying him down among the others. I sleep next to him and over the course of the night frequently get up to check on him. This boy is Vera's "child," but Vera no longer dares to sleep outside the shelter. In exchange, she has to take Dedi out to pee every night. A few days later when Sutyi gets better, we all heave a sigh of relief and agree that we'd rather put up with a million lice than with an illness.

Delousing has now become an item on our list of everyday chores. Nobody finds it disgusting anymore. We comb through the little girls' hair every other day. We are used to the darkness and the dampness (the only way we can use the matches is by first drying them in the oven for at least half an hour), and we quarrel less about the overcrowding. Each day we grow more fearful about the prospect of the Russians occupying the far side of Krisztina Boulevard, which would no doubt lead to our deaths from starvation and thirst.

As it is, water carrying is becoming more and more of a pain. Unfortunately, I'm not any good at comparing degrees of intensity or else I would describe in detail how difficult this task was at the beginning of January, how much more difficult by the middle of the month, and how much more difficult still it became in the early days of February, and I could go on like this forever. I had the same problem when trying to describe the images of destruction. If on the day that bácsi Bandi died I thought that a street could not be more destroyed than this, on the following day I saw that it could, and on the third day even more so and then even more still. On January 25, I thought that we had reached the pinnacle of destruction, but what came after I won't even try to describe. Of the early days of February, I remember only how depressing it was to continually worry about water and that it was about the same time that Sutyi's illness occurred.

Without exception, we all enthusiastically receive the joyful news that at last we are being put into "the front line," which means we would no longer be bombed but only shot at, albeit with all the weaponry at their disposal. Memorable date: February 4, brilliant clear sunlit weather in which they launch a mad, concentrated attack against the castle, but it looks as if it was only the castle and not the surroundings. On hearing the hellish racket, the Major climbs up to the garden gate and comes back reporting that there seems to be a musical changing of the guard in progress. I can say that it is an eerie concert. (For a moment I wonder whether I will ever again listen to music in a concert hall.) All imaginable weapons join in, from those of the infantry all the way up to the heavy artillery. On the next street over, submachine guns and cannons rattle, further up the hill, a machine gun and bombs (I have become an expert at recognizing every instrument by its sound!). Everything is happening so close by that I can no longer distinguish between incoming and outgoing fire.

We hear from a reliable source that up in the Castle District the situation has been terrible for days. They no longer have any water, they get their supply from filthy water tanks, the Rock Cellar and the Hospital in the Rock are crowded beyond imagination, everywhere lice and more lice, dirt, darkness, nowhere any food, the wounded are lying in the corridors of the Hospital in the Rock, in the best-case scenario their wounds are being dressed every five days, but even so they are running out of dressings and medication. The two major entrances to the Hospital in the Rock have collapsed, and the ventilation system has failed so that the heat and stench are unbearable. We hear all this from a Swiss woman who is working with Born[25] and who came to visit us on one of the "quieter" evenings. She tells us that in the Castle District there is no way of hauling away the dead, they are just thrown out into the street, because the attacks go on practically day and night with only short interruptions, not long enough to remove the corpses. The Germans have moved into the castle cellars, and it's rumoured that they have every intention of defending themselves until the last bullet.

On Pauler Street, the uniformed Arrow Cross men had long since disappeared, followed by the Hungarian soldiers, and finally one could only see the occasional vehicle, once part of a German supply convoy.

To me, February 9 is also a memorable day. By this time, we are so badly off in terms of water that we have to go out to get some even though we are under heavy fire. At dusk things calm down a little, and after a brief discussion, three of us — the Major, on behalf of the boiler house staff, and Nurse Ica and I, representing the Red Cross — set out. We get to the mission house on Krisztina Boulevard without any problems. We then need to cross a courtyard with a laundry room at the back where we have to draw the water from a tap. So

---

25 Friedrich Born, the Hungarian representative of the International Red Cross.

many people are already lined up that the end of the line stretches out into the courtyard. We stop to discuss whether we should join it because night is falling rapidly and, as I have already mentioned, we will have to walk through the cellars of collapsed buildings on our way back. We decide to go home and manage with our remaining supply and come back the next day. No sooner do we start out and reach the gate than a grenade hits the building and debris from the rooftop lands on the people standing in the courtyard, causing screaming and chaos. We hurl ourselves into the shelter in the middle of the yard, but we've hardly reached the staircase when the next grenade explodes. The pressure from the blast makes me fall forward down the stairs but luckily not all the way because there are a lot of us, so I only tumble onto the person in front of me in the dark. Then we all go into the beautiful, vaulted cellar where the missionary sisters are performing their evening devotions. One of them is standing in front of the altar reciting a prayer or something, and after each line the others repeat in a monotonous tone the refrain, "Have mercy on us!" This goes on for a long time. There are fifteen to twenty candles illuminating the praying faces from below. It is a beautiful scene, but it adds to the unreality of the whole thing. If only the blast wave hadn't given me such a hellish headache, I would think that I am merely imagining it all. But I have cold shivers running up and down my spine and the strong feeling that I'd almost met my end, even though I've experienced life-threatening situations before. We sit with the sisters for hours. Meanwhile, it has grown dark, and the shelling has quieted down, so we set out for home in almost total darkness, feeling our way along the ruins. By this time none of us is thinking of the curfew, because there is nobody around to shoot us down for contravening the orders, at least not with army rifles. In the last few days, we have hardly seen any German soldiers. But the worst thing is that after all the fuss we are heading home WITHOUT ANY WATER.

At home our friends, who are waiting anxiously for our return, politely try to hide their disappointment. Early the next morning, we still manage to fetch some water, but however much we bring it is never enough for twenty-two people. We announce that from now on drinking water will also be reduced to half a glass per person. Unfortunately, this does not take Gyurka into account. In the afternoon, after sitting on the chamber pot for hours, without any warning he soils himself while playing, whereupon I suspend my pedagogical method and, against my better judgment, give him a spanking before washing him and his soiled clothes. Nevertheless, after supper that same evening when we've already put the children to bed, out comes Évi, Gyurka's eight-year-old sister, reporting that Gyurka is doing something very suspicious: he is lying in his bed grunting, straining and smelling awful. My premonitions did not deceive me: Gyurka has tricked me one more time this day, sparing no effort to punish me for spanking him. This time I have to wash not only him but his pyjamas and even his bedding, with fresh water from a wash basin because I'd already thrown out the old. I'm ashamed to admit that I give the child such a walloping that I end up in tears myself because I'm so upset that I wasn't able to cope with him.

On February 10, a new shell bursts into our courtyard AND DOES NOT EXPLODE! I am sorry that I didn't count them all, but the older boys did, and they can tell you exactly how many missiles spared us by failing to explode. There are times when the mood of the company sinks one degree lower, say for instance when we hear that the primary school on Attila Street is again in German hands or that the Russians have withdrawn from Szent János Square to Döbrentei Square. Otherwise, we know nothing of the outside world. There are rumours of a red flag flying on the roof of the Parliament building, people walking along the Danube embankment, electric lights functioning in Pest and the cinemas showing films again. Of course, later it turned out that of all the stories only the one about the red flag was true.

Here ends what I call the "posthumous diary," and now I hand the floor over to the real one:

The Death of Buda

Sunday, February 11

I get up at half past five to go and fetch water with two of my colleagues and the Major. Bullets are whizzing by, but they don't faze us. We stand in line in the laundry room of the school beside the church. It's only a small crowd, since few people dare to leave the cellars. We need to wait for a long time because the water is only flowing from the faucet in a small trickle. This is when we usually learn the latest news about the outside world. A Hungarian sergeant is standing next to me in line. I ask him: "Where are the Russians?" He answers grumpily that he doesn't know but wishes they were here already! He says all this in a loud voice in the presence of several Hungarian and German soldiers.

We spend the afternoon huddling in the shelter again. By now we are quite bored of the barkochba game. Vera makes up a new game, strictly for adults, saying that by now we are quite bored with ourselves and with each other, so let's have a game where we tell each other about our lives, a bit every day. Only three of us participate: Vera, Lili (the neurotic physician) and me. We draw lots, and it's decided that I'll go first. I talk about my parents and my childhood. Later, at the children's urging, I sing some Schubert lieder with classical lyrics, which I translate into Hungarian for them word by word.

Along with the Schubert lieder, the "Two Grenadiers" and "La Marseillaise" remain the top hits.

In the evening, there's a huge fire somewhere nearby, the whole sky is lit up. We are trying to guess where it might be. By all indications it's probably somewhere around Szent János Square. I write in awful darkness by the annoyingly flickering flame of a candle, and unfortunately it's impossible to sew by such light, even though I really need to do some mending, all my clothes are torn. The last time I read was on October 22, almost four months ago.

We get word today that a corn-fed horse has fallen in the defence of his country in the garden of the building across from us. The animal was so fat that the residents of our building could make crackling from it. We don't dare to go outside to cut a slice from the horse, besides, we wouldn't know how to. It doesn't occur to the residents to help us.

Tonight, I go to bed in despair again, although it's not certain that the news is true about the Russians being pushed back to the new Szent János Hospital. German tanks are rumbling one after the other in the direction of Vérmező Park. Are they perhaps still capable of a counteroffensive? That's hard to believe.

Monday, February 12

After a rather miserable night (Dedi subjected me to his special brand of torture, meaning that every half hour, just as I'd fallen asleep, he would start bawling right into my ear), I wake up to find out that the Major and the sisters who'd been assigned to fetch water have returned. They recount that the neighbourhood is completely quiet and deserted, no one knows anything about the Russians or the Germans, and there's not a soldier in sight. Half asleep, I can still hear them as they discuss our provisions, which they say would last another three weeks only if we immediately introduced the one meal a day rule. And even that will only work if we have enough water for cooking.

Angry at myself for my lethargy, I hide under the duvet and go back to sleep.

What awakens me suddenly is the door swinging open and Andris bursting in, shouting with his cracking voice: "THE RUSSIANS ARE HERE!" Of course, it's impossible to describe the impact of this announcement, everyone goes crazy, they randomly shout things like: "That's not true!" "How can it be?" "How do you know?" The younger kids are wide-eyed with fear. Andris swears he saw the Russians with his own eyes, the street is full of them, they are confiscating weapons from the Hungarian soldiers, who throw away their guns in a happy frenzy and keep hugging the Russians. We start to believe it at last. The kids are jumping up and down on the beds like savages, screaming, and for some minutes I'm not able to see or hear anything because about half a dozen children hurl themselves at me and kiss me all over. In the meantime, I am bawling because it starts to sink in that I seem to have survived the worst of it. Then we jump into our clothes at lightning speed and rush out to the gate. Ukrainian prisoners in German uniforms are being led out of the building across the way, these are the same Ukrainians Vera had gotten acquainted with to practise her Russian. They are lined up against the wall, and all we see is that someone aims a handgun at the first one, a big, good-looking blond giant with a bushy beard, who falls on his knees and implores with folded hands, at which point we run inside, and to this day I don't know whether they were shot or not.

At first, we got the news that Buda had fallen, but it seems it's not true. The castle is still being held and there's heavy shelling from up there. Our shelter is in a precarious position in relation to the shelling from the castle. The residents, especially the staff, clearly in a lousy mood and walking around with long faces, are rude to us, which surprises me. We spend the morning under sporadic machine-gun fire, with a few hits here and there. Around noon, we hear shouting in Russian from the yard, and when we look outside all we see is old Baron Kapry at the door, both arms in the air, jabbering excitedly in

Slovak. It turns out that two drunk Russian soldiers came looking for liquor and aimed their guns at the old guy, but the Major talked them out of shooting him and somehow tricked them into going away. We don't dare to keep the front door locked, because we heard that whenever the Russian soldiers encounter locked doors, they use hand grenades to open them.

After the noon meal, we continue with our *Decameron* game. First Vera talks about her childhood, then Lili, the physician, follows. In the afternoon, the three of us want to go fetch water, but we need to wait because Russian planes are bombing the side of the castle that faces Pest. At last, we can leave. On Pauler Street — or at least in the middle of the dirt and rubble that used to be called by that name — Russian soldiers are chasing horses. The state of the street is simply indescribable. Yesterday, when I was last outside, I naively thought that a street could not look any more horrible. And — voila! — here is a further escalation. This is because in the meantime the thaw has begun in full force, the sidewalk has disappeared, telephone poles have toppled to the ground, we need to jump over downed phone and power lines, the snow that covered the bodies of dead horses has melted, and it seems that debris has blocked the sewer grates, the whole street is a sea of mud. We climb across two collapsed buildings, springing from one brick to the next through the rubble.

Reaching Krisztina Boulevard, we can barely make it across the street due to Russian supply trucks and countless blown-up vehicles and the dangling wires. Because of the car wrecks blocking the street, it's impossible to enter the building where we usually get water, so we go to the school beside the church, where there's a long lineup for water, and everyone is ranting against the Germans (as if they'd always held that opinion), that they are responsible for all of this, they are the ones who ruined the country. A few people call the Tatar-looking soldier "tovarish"[1] in a jovial tone. He shoves them aside and gets water for his horse out of turn.

---

1 Russian: comrade.

As we leave, at the street corner we come across a group of disarmed German and Hungarian soldiers, pale and exhausted. They ask us for water. We stop hesitantly. Vera wants to give them some, but a Russian soldier rushes up and yells at us in Russian not to give them any because they're German. Although Vera says that this man happens to be Hungarian and not German, the Russian drives us away. While we were standing around waiting for water, a Hungarian gendarme, who, as a prisoner of war, was carrying water for Russian horses, told us that the castle had almost completely fallen, there were only a couple of insignificant pockets of resistance. He was captured inside the Ministry of the Interior and was brought here with captured German soldiers. He reports that they haven't treated him badly, except they forgot to give him food and are "housing" him in the street. He relates that for the whole duration of the siege in the castle, they read *Kitartás*,[2] in which, as its name signifies, the Arrow Cross leaders, who fled to the west in time, preach perseverance to those who stayed behind, and the paper goes on and on about the relief army that is on its way and is now very close to Buda.

That evening at the children's home, we have a celebratory meal, and everyone gets two servings of spaghetti with tomato sauce. Afterwards, a celebratory wash: everyone can wash in their own personal CUP AND A HALF of water.

Tuesday, February 13

As I am delousing our clothes in the yard in the morning, the mother of one of our clients bursts through the gate and falls on my neck, sobbing. She had been hiding on Rózsadomb in a villa that had fallen into Russian hands about three weeks ago and had been watching to see when Pauler Street would be free so that she could come to

---

2 A Hungarian publication of which only a few issues were published in January and February 1945, whose title means "perseverance," the unofficial Arrow Cross motto.

collect her child. She is having such a crying spell that we can hardly calm her down. She says that looking across from Vérmező — and even more so from up close — she didn't dare enter Pauler Street and she couldn't believe that there could be anybody still alive there. This woman knows all the latest news. We drag her into the shelter, where everybody stops the delousing, and we listen to her with our mouths wide open. She tells us that not long ago it had still been possible to walk from Pest to Buda on the frozen Danube; that most of Buda had fallen long before our part of it; that human losses hadn't been great (at least among the civilian population of the city); that most of the ghetto had survived the affair;[3] that people had generally been able to return home; that some areas of Budapest already had electric lighting and some NEWSPAPERS WERE APPEARING; and the cinemas, while not yet showing films, were advertising in the papers.

I'm very excited, swallow my tears and decide to go to Nünü at once. I try to find out what time it is in order to calculate when I'll be back, but it's impossible, because nobody has a watch. If someone's watch hadn't been stolen by a Russian soldier, then the owner had hidden it in the ground or a wall. I set out in full siege uniform, with the Red Cross nurse's scarf on my head. I always used to dismiss proverbs, popular sayings and the like as empty clichés, but on this occasion the idiom "to wallow in blood" describes, not figuratively but quite literally, what I found myself doing in the ruins of Buda for the next hour. I confess that I was afraid of what I might find there even before I reached the Southern Railway Station, and the only reason why I didn't turn back was my spielbergerism. The street looks like what is normally called indescribable, but I'll try to describe it.

Tacking between countless car wrecks, kicked to the side by

---

3 At least 38,000 Budapest civilians died during the siege of the city. In that short period between December 1944 and the end of January 1945, about 20,000 Jews were taken by members of the Arrow Cross from the ghetto in Budapest and murdered on the banks of the Danube River.

drunken Russians making their horses jump, I arrive at Vérmező Park. To get to Széna Square, I can walk either along Attila Street or Krisztina Boulevard. The apartments on Attila Street overhang the street at such extreme angles that I choose Krisztina Boulevard without any hesitation. I wade in a mushy russet liquid, jumping over torn electricity and telephone wires. Only a strip in the middle of the road is usable, because both sides are blocked by walls of rubble and car wrecks. For the same reason, Russian cars also use the middle strip, at full speed, splashing me up to my neck with mud (though if I call the disgusting stuff they spill over me "mud" I'm really being refined!). They don't go in for honking or braking, so I have to jump into a deep puddle every minute or so to avoid being hit.

But only as far as Széll Kálmán Square. Afterwards there aren't any puddles. The hollows are all full of dead bodies. If I step to the side, I end up stepping on a hand or foot. I must have grown callous because I'm not horrified, or is the whole thing too unlikely to be believed? The bodies are fresh, no older than twenty-four hours by my estimate. Later I hear some gossip that on February 12 the Germans tried to break out of the Castle District in two different directions: toward Olasz Avenue and toward Óbuda on February 12, but that was exactly what the Russians had been waiting for. They were encircled and ground down.

How often had I read the cliché "They were encircled and ground down" in war reports, but I must say that actually seeing these twenty-year-old kids encircled and ground down is a very ugly experience. I take a stealthy look at each face although I'd like to look away. I feel an embarrassing confusion as if I were doing something indecent or watching something forbidden. I also look at their hands, each greyish yellow and grubby. The head of one of them is completely shattered, a bloody lump of mush with only the teeth peeping out white and crushed like bread crumbs. The expression on all their faces is roughly similar, not at peace but not suffering or distorted. Only one has an angry expression, with his eyebrows drawn close together and an angry grin on his face. The hand of another was paralyzed in the middle of a strangely twisted movement, a gesture I had only seen before in primitive paintings of saints.

You can tell that the most savage fighting took place here in Széna Square near Ostrom Street, where there are huge heaps of dead bodies. (I don't discover until later that what I took for a huge mass was in fact only a fraction of the victims of that battle: these were only German corpses, because the Russians collected their dead immediately.) In front of the old Szent János Hospital in Széna Square near an ambulance shot full of holes, a half-overturned stretcher lies on the ground, on it a naked male corpse half covered by a sheet, his arm half bandaged, the roll of gauze hanging down to the ground: they seem to have both fallen while he was being bandaged. He was probably a very young boy with an extraordinarily beautiful body, yellow like wax. A little further in the middle of the road, with arms stretched out like the letter T, another is lying on his back. He looks as if he has been run over by a tank or two and so flattened that I can't resist thinking of the coloured and embossed pictures Dini and I used to collect passionately when we were children.

At last the bodies begin to thin out, and once I'm roughly level with the end of Statisztika Park, I don't see any more for a while. From here again I only need to avoid dead horses, car wrecks and soldiers on horseback. Russian soldiers on horseback buzz around like Hollywood extras in films about Russians. The building of the Regent Café is completely razed to the ground. I had never seen a building so destroyed, even around Pauler Street, which is saying something. As I turn into the ruins of Margit Boulevard and see the equally ruined Admirál Cinema and its even more ruined surroundings, I'm suddenly overcome by tears, sobbing even though I know that Nünü and my father can't be dead because no such thing can happen to Kiskas and her loved ones.

Nor did it happen. Both burst into streams of tears when they see me. They have been in Russian hands since January 30 and know that the Castle District and its neighbourhood are bombed, shelled, deprived of food and water. Add to all this that they hadn't seen or heard from me for a month. They both look ill, particularly my father, who has turned into a depressed, irritable, doddering old man. My mother is also in bad shape, but the worse things get, the more active and alert she becomes. In one way or another, she always managed to get some food for both of them. They still have three meals a day, with two courses for lunch, which is a great luxury because you have to prepare two sauces instead of one. But I haven't the heart to tell them so, because they'll manage somehow.

They tell me that on January 15, the Arrow Cross had taken them away from the cellar of the boarding house with all the other guests but had let them go free after some questions, to which Nünüke had stood up fabulously. One of the Arrow Cross henchmen had asked them sternly where they had lived in Debrecen. Nünüke answered without any hesitation that they had lived on Péterfia Street, which was the address I had looked up for them a long time ago in the inter-urban telephone directory.

Arrow Cross man: "I must warn you that I come from Debrecen!"

Nünüke (bursting with delight): "So you're a fellow countryman, my boy? My God! At last. It's been so long since I last saw someone from Debrecen" (falls on Arrow Cross man's neck). It could have ended badly, because they started questioning Nünü as to why she had been a kindergarten nurse in Budapest if she came from Debrecen, and if she lived in Óbuda how she had got back to Debrecen, whereupon another Arrow Cross warrior stepped forward and said: "Leave her alone. I've known the Kassais for a long time. They really lived in Óbuda for a long time." After this, they were released. The second Arrow Cross man had once worked as an odd-job man for the coal merchant from whom we used to buy fuel and had always been the one to deliver it to our home. Didn't he know that the Kassais were Jews, or did he know and did he want to help them? We'll never find out now. None of the boarding house guests the Arrow Cross detained on that occasion were seen again.

I don't have the strength to repeat that terrible walk today, so I decide to stay here for the night. Before dark, I cross the road to the Lénárds with Nünü, which isn't easy, because right in the bend of Margit Boulevard, precisely in front of the Admirál Cinema, stretching from the walls of the buildings on one side to those on the other, the wide and deep tank trap remains, with the huge barricade in front of it, except that now it's even more unmanageable than it was when I last saw it in the morning. At the bottom of the trap large amounts of water, freezing snow, etc., had built up. The only way to get through was to enter by the side (Török Street) door of the collapsed cinema and out through the main door, having left the barricade behind us.

Meanwhile, Nünü tells me that the front line was at the Admirál Cinema for about ten days. They were already in Russian hands, while Juci's family were still held by Germans. Juci and her children are well and their apartment is almost undamaged, which is all the more astonishing because — as I said — there had been savage fighting for weeks in that area and the outside of the building is very badly damaged. Nünü and my father fell into Russian hands on January 30, Juci and her children just two steps further away, on February 10. Juci is thin, her children look pale and grey, they all have lice and almost nothing to eat. They haven't heard from Ernő for weeks. (He was doing military service on the road to Fehérvár and was "thrown into battle" at the last moment.) Juci tries hard to persuade Nünüke to move in with her, explaining that she is afraid to be alone in the apartment with all those Russians coming and going. I also try to persuade Nünü, because I think it's a good solution from their point of view. Juci has two rooms opening onto the yard, the nursery and the maid's room, they are undamaged, even the window panes are unbroken, a stove is hidden in the cellar, and there is fuel, so it's immediately habitable.

We make our way back to the cellar of the boarding house and have supper in the pitch dark. I share Nünüke's bed. We whisper for a long time. She is very happy to have me there. She keeps squeezing my hand. I tell her about the children in Pauler Street.

Wednesday, February 14

It's my father's seventy-third birthday. I wish him all the best and leave early to find Reverend Sztehlo to discuss my parents' immediate future. On my way I drop in on Lívia-Mária. She is well. The Arrow Cross had taken her away and pestered her for hours but didn't get anywhere with her. After three hours' constant questioning, she had still not admitted that her documents were forged, and finally they let her go. So far she has even been spared by the Russians.

The stories one hears about Russian rapes are becoming more and more frequent and increasingly horrifying. From Nünü's building they took a few women away for a short time. From Lívia's also, and now she is on her way to her mother who had been hiding in Marczibányi Square. The two of us walk the full length of Keleti Károly Street, which in comparison with what we have seen on our way here looks almost as peaceful as it did before the war. I accompany Lívia to her mother's building because in front of the garden gate the bloody corpse of a middle-aged woman with a shopping basket in her hand and potatoes spilled all around her stops her in her tracks. She dares not go on because she is afraid that those in the building have been hurt. But then we find that nothing untoward has happened.

So I say goodbye to her and set out along Fillér Street toward Gábor Áron Road. There are more bodies of German soldiers in the gardens of these villas, so it seems to be true that they also tried to break out in this area. I had made a mistake by choosing the route across Rózsadomb so that I wouldn't have to pass by those bodies again, and I had jumped out of the frying pan into the fire.

After a long walk I arrive at Guyon Richárd Road. Apparently Sztehlo can be found there, but there are no numbers on the villas and no Red Cross anywhere, although there is shooting from an indeterminable direction. Street signs are also rare. It's just as well that I set out with a map, otherwise I wouldn't have got anywhere. In the garden of one villa, a Russian soldier is just sitting there. I call out to him: "Hi."

He looks around but doesn't bother to answer. Instead, he drops his trousers and with his back (to put it politely) turned toward me crouches to do the big one.

At last I find the building I'm looking for, but Sztehlo left a long time ago and only Mr. Gyürk, his business manager, is still there. We discover that I have known his wife for a long time but didn't know that she is now called Mrs. Gyürk. She used to be Sári Stohl, my colleague. They give me Sztehlo's new address, but it's so far out in Hűvösvölgy that I can't get there today. While I chat with the Gyürks, somebody fires a shot through the garden window. We can't tell who or why. To get back into the city I could take Olasz Avenue, but everyone I see walking advises me against it because I would have to climb the mountain of corpses at the Cogwheel Railway. So once more I have to cross Rózsadomb and pass the bloody lumps of mush held together by shreds of uniform.

A woman greets me from the garden of a villa and asks where I'm coming from and where I'm going (as people have been doing since the beginning of the siege). She tells me that about thirty German soldiers had broken into an abandoned villa on the previous day and defended themselves there as long as their ammunition lasted, but they were then shot by the Russians one by one. They were still lying in the villa on the spot where they had died.

On the roadside in the grass along the fence of one villa, a brand new Hermes Baby portable typewriter is getting soaked (it started to rain while we were talking). Next to it a bloodstained soldier's coat. My heart aches for the typewriter, and for a moment I consider taking it with me, but I naturally dismiss the idea at once, not because of any moral scruples but because of practical considerations. There are masses of other valuable objects in the streets that I could use:

cigarettes by the boxful but covered in mud, fur-lined jackets and lovely warm gloves, but they are so dirty that I would rather die than touch them. In every garden, on every roadside, in every ditch and every hidden corner of a yard, German and Hungarian military tunics, rifles broken in two, discarded cartridges, cartridge containers, revolver cases, caps. I get back to the home feeling miserable, tired and depressed, for the first time since the beginning of October. Along the whole way I had spoken only once to a Russian soldier, who had asked with a friendly grin what my Red Cross badge meant. I concentrated my entire knowledge of Russian into one complex sentence to tell him.

In the home, the children receive me with a great ovation, although they didn't think I had lost my way, since yesterday I had managed to get somebody to deliver a message when I was halfway through, so had assumed that I probably wouldn't get home that day. They almost tear me to pieces for news, which I supply copiously. Most successful is the four-days-old February 10 issue of the young people's daily called *Szabadság*,[4] which I borrowed from someone in Nünü's boarding house. None of us has read a newspaper since before the new year and certainly not one whose tone and standards are exactly the same as those of *Virradat*,[5] which only differs from it by its colour.

The women almost give me a beating when I offer them this observation. For them you can never be aggressive enough. While I was away, the *tovarishes* were there, going in and out of the building as they did in all the others. They have also taken Andris's watch. We are afraid that one night they could pay us a visit looking for women as they have done in every building on the street. But that's something I

---

4 Left-wing daily newspaper, published between January 19, 1945, and November 13, 1948, whose name means "freedom."

5 Far-right weekly publication, published between 1936 and 1944, whose name means "dawn."

somehow can't be seriously afraid of, just as with the bomb, not only because I am more repulsive and older (and so thin that by now it can really only be guessed by my primary sexual characteristics that I might once have been a woman) but because I still maintain that such things, like any misfortune, can only happen to others.

This night I have such a good sleep, better than I've had in a long time. This was despite the fact that the mood in general is really bad. Everybody is disappointed, and so am I a little, although I had not expected things to be much better after the siege than before. The women are particularly bitter because our Russians not only fail to respect the Red Cross but also the fact that someone is Jewish and — by her own account — has suffered a great deal.

Before I go to sleep, I reflect for a long time on what a marvellous person Nünüke is and how many terrible things the old couple had had to endure. I forgot to mention that the Russians walk day and night through their bunker as if it were a public passage. They took my father's watch, and they pointed a handgun at him when he implored them to give it back. Looking for arms, they forced him to unpack a pile of junk in a corner and when a rifle was found fired a bullet very close to his ear to give him a fright. My mother never loses her head. She already knows how to ask for bread in Russian and clearly doesn't take this war seriously. For my father's birthday, she found, God knows where, a loaf of bread two kilograms in weight and infinitely more in value, which the whole boarding house turned out to admire.

Thursday, February 15

In the morning, I set out to fetch water with the doctor and Bandi, one of the older boys. The latter is happy to be able to go outside and look around at last. (Our children haven't left our apartment building since Christmas.) There is no point in going to the water sources we were using before, because either there's no water there at all or the trickle of water is so small that the line is growing into the thousands. We search the whole neighbourhood, but there is no tap water anywhere, only well water, and we have neither the bucket nor the rope required for the job. There are dead horses lying five to ten steps away from the wells, completely taking away our appetite for the water, which is a suspicious colour to begin with. During our hunt for water, we make our way through the Southern Railway Station, amid the wreckage of railway cars. The Márvány Street bridge is blasted to bits. This neighbourhood too was the site of fierce fighting that lasted several days. The whole area is in a terrible state, although it's not as bad as our street. In Városmajor Street, there's a blown-up tank with its gun barrel pointing skywards, and thrown across the gun there's a dangling corpse, more precisely it's just a uniform with a lot of missing body parts; the head is there, it's hanging at the bottom, the hair is caked with blood and mud, the face is a dirty grey.

A few steps away, some well-dressed women are picking up boxes that are scattered on the sidewalk. I ask what's in them. It's some sort of hair oil that apparently has landed there from the storage room of the pharmacy, and they are taking it home to use as fuel in their lamps. I drop in at the Red Cross home on Csaba Street looking for my young colleague Évi Bolgár. They are all fine (although infested with lice), except for Sister Margit, the head deaconess, who'd been hit by a German partisan's bullet as she was carrying water; this happened after the Russian occupation began (they have been in Russian hands for three weeks now). Évike is fatter than ever, even though she has been through some awful things. I won't bother mentioning the Arrow Cross raid she had to endure, because that's already old news. To add to her misery, the poor girl got knocked up by Russian soldiers, which must have been quite a horrible experience considering that she was basically a virgin and engaged. She is a naive and silly little goose, because she is firmly convinced that nothing really happened to her and that she couldn't possibly have picked up a disease. I don't dare to enlighten her, that will be the job of her uncle, a doctor, whom she wants to go see in Pest about this matter. The other women delight in telling the story of how lucky another caregiver was (by the way, it turns out that she's an old friend of yours, Dr. Magda Szerényi, a chemist). A drunk Russian captain took a fancy to her, but he was so sloshed that for two whole hours he couldn't even manage to begin an assault on Magda's virtue. (Finally, the captain fell asleep, but Magda didn't dare to flee the room where they were locked in together, meanwhile the others thought that he had long since murdered her.) Still, at the end the captain threatened Magda that he'd come back and shoot her if he'd picked up a disease from her.

All this took place in the children's home in a room that had been emptied specifically for this purpose. From all I've heard, I can safely say that this is *gang und gäbe*.[6] There is not a street, not a building, where similar things haven't occurred. Up until now, we'd been spared in this respect, thanks in part to Vera's knowledge of Russian and in part to the sign on the entrance door that has "Children's Shelter" painted on it in Russian. Although they show up at our place several times a day under various pretexts, so far they have only come during the daytime and only to steal, and mostly just from the owners of the apartment. They did open our door, but once they saw the kids, they turned on their heels and left.

Getting back to our expedition in search of water: I am walking with the caregivers from Csaba Street and with one of the Russian soldiers billeted with them to the well in the garden of the building at 46 Városmajor Street, where the Russian pushes to the head of the line and fills his container and ours with dirty water. Some other interesting things:

1 A Russian soldier with the face of a Tatar coming toward us across the Southern Railway Station tracks carrying a beautiful photography spotlight. God knows where he was taking it and

6 German: an everyday occurrence, a common practice.

what he thought it was, but I would dearly have loved to claim it.

2 A puppy that tagged along with us, and we had a really hard time getting rid of it.

3 A civilian gentleman who came up to me and took one of the demijohns and helped me carry it almost all the way home, which was such a startlingly unusual act during a siege, that I slowly began to believe that the siege was over and that everything's going to get back to normal. In the meantime, the sun came out, which I have trouble enjoying not only because it's accompanied by a thaw, which means the muck will start flowing again and the corpses will decay faster. It seems that no one thinks of carting them away, and there will be typhoid fever sooner, but also because my eyes that had grown used to dim candlelight in the cellar are really sore and inflamed from the unaccustomed brightness.

When I get home, I collapse onto a kitchen chair without even taking my coat off, and I don't move for hours and don't talk to anyone. That's how the street, the scarcity of water, the terrible destruction and the hopelessness of the situation affected me. No matter how hard I try to use my famous imagination, I can't picture that there will be life in Buda again.

In the afternoon, a woman shows up, she'd been sent by the Reverend to the different homes to collect the children and bring them all together in Hűvösvölgy, in a beautiful villa located at 19 Völgy Street. This plan does not include the caregivers, because unfortunately he can no longer provide for us, given the meagre food supplies. I start to panic, because even if I can find other lodging after leaving here, nobody has food, and even if they do, they can't be expected to feed me. By now I've calmed down, having realized that things won't happen so rapidly, that the other women won't instantly be able to take care of themselves either. Perhaps I'll manage to get a job in the new children's home, but if not I won't starve to death right away, because when they liquidate our home they will most likely distribute some of the remaining provisions among the caregivers who are being let go.

Another big problem is how to move the children, because even if we manage to get a car from the Russian headquarters for this purpose (tomorrow Vera and I will go to the Buda Castle to see about it), it is still no simple matter. The two female physicians won't be coming with us, as they want to work in a recently finished hospital in a school building. I would also like to drift toward a new career, if I only knew, my Pippancs, where you are and what is happening to you, and we could discuss where we want to go and what we'd like to do after the war. Of course, if it were possible to cross over to the Pest side, there would be a lot more I could do toward finding employment. I figured out the reason today is the first time I'm feeling so utterly depressed and exhausted since the whole circus began: it's because up until now all I needed to do was ENDURE IT, and that, I can say, is something I did better than anyone else, but now it is time to act — and wisely and effectively to boot — and this plunges me back into the darkest blue funk. Furthermore, even in the most awful times during the siege, when huddling in filth and darkness, listening to the most horrible concert outside and waiting for the roof to collapse on my head, I had the impression that this can't be true, that this can't really be happening, and I've gone completely mad and am just imagining the whole thing. But this destroyed city, the squalor, the corpses decomposing in the bright spring sunshine, have the desolate ring of reality to them. I can no longer pretend that suddenly I'll hit my head on the nightstand and wake up.

This evening one of my colleagues brought out a bottle of Aszú from Tokaj, which we drank to prevent the Russians from finding it and to have one thing less to lug. Before lunch I GOT WASHED, in warm water to boot, in warmed up rainwater, that is, my share was almost HALF A BASIN FULL. In the dark kitchen you couldn't tell how filthy the rainwater was. I felt like an empress, and almost clean, perhaps one of these days I will even be able to brush my teeth, it's too bad that by then my neck will be dirty again. When it comes to underwear, for a long time "clean" has been a relative term, and as to my pillowcase, I bury my head in the sand like an ostrich, which is to say I never take it to the courtyard to air during the day, because if I saw it in daylight I'd never be willing to sleep on it anymore, no matter how unfussy I've become.

For the past few days, our evening fun has consisted of putting on makeup: that's the time when all the young women make themselves look ugly, they sprinkle talcum powder on their hair so it appears grey, they paint wrinkles on their faces with an eyebrow pencil, they put on glasses, tie on black kerchiefs, cover half their face with a compress as if they had a toothache, aiming to look as old and ugly as possible with the hope of being less appealing to the Russian troops. For the last couple of days, two teenage girls have been sleeping at our place, hidden among the children. They live in the building across the street, from which several women have been abducted, but they've managed to escape that fate so far. Fortunately, I don't need to put on makeup, since all I would need to do if some determined Russian should pick me is take off my clothes and let him see that I'm no longer a woman. These days I sleep on the floor in the kitchen, we place mattresses on top of rugs spread out over the stone tiles. I share a mattress with Edit Kozma. Altogether, there are nine of us sleeping in the kitchen.

Friday, February 16

I wasn't the one who went to the castle with Vera after all, but rather the director, Mrs. Kata Wald. It was a brilliant sunny day with mild spring breezes and the pungent smell of corpses. I am in the courtyard cleaning my clothes. Someone somewhere managed to get hold of a printed copy of the detailed conditions of the armistice.[7] We make him read it aloud, and we discuss it. It leaves a bad taste in

---

7 The armistice of January 20, 1945, was signed in Moscow by representatives of the interim Hungarian government led by acting Prime Minister Béla Miklós de Dálnok.

our mouths. Every night we're afraid the Russians will come for the women, they've scoured the whole neighbourhood already, ceaselessly plundering anything they can get their hands on. Afterwards, they sort out their loot on the street and throw everything they don't need in the mud. Starting yesterday, we keep the entrance door locked even during the day, and this clever trick works; it seems the Russians (the *tovarishes* are such *Drehkopfs*) think that the people who dare to lock their doors even in the daytime have nothing to guard, so there's no point in entering.

Vera and her companion have returned: the city headquarters don't exist anymore, all that remains is a smouldering Royal Castle that's mostly in ruins. Everyone is preparing to get out, but all you hear everywhere is that the regular occupying forces are coming, along with the Hungarian troops led by Veress.[8] And so there won't be a car available for our move. The two physicians, Lili and Ilus, leave for Hűvösvölgy to have a look around and take Andris along, whose mother is currently the cook there. I talk Vera into coming to Attila Street with me to see Dr. Kapolyi. Attila Street is almost as ugly as Pauler Street, or rather, it's hard to say which is worse because Attila is not as destroyed as Pauler but it contains more corpses. We don't find Kapolyi at "home" (by home, we mean the laundry room of the building, which was later turned into a bomb shelter, then a first aid station). The wounded are carried in and out. I can't figure out whether they are civilians or not, because they are covered up to their chins, but they are all men with long beards. Mrs. Gizi Kramolin approaches us and is very dejected: when her husband was carrying water yesterday, he was detained by a Russian patrol and taken to the Russian secret police to have his papers checked, and they didn't

8 This likely refers to General Lajos Veres, an anti-German general active in Horthy's failed attempt to withdraw from the war and consequently arrested by the Arrow Cross.

allow him to come back because he was deemed suspicious on account of his profession, namely royal attorney. While we are standing there consoling the woman, her husband shows up, they had let him go home after checking his papers, and he can't stop talking about how politely and decently they behaved toward him, except that they forgot to give him anything to eat or drink for more than twenty-four hours.

I forgot to recount that Vera and her colleague went to see all sorts of officials in an attempt to get protection for the children's homes, to save them from looting and other atrocities, but the answer they got everywhere was: "Oh, well, it's wartime," and "there's no need to worry, the soldiers won't hurt anyone, and besides they are moving on to go to the front because their business is not here but in Berlin." Vera explains to one of the top officials that they need to give special consideration to this home because it provides shelter for the children of victims of the Nazis, Jews for example. Playing innocent, the top official asks if the German army had taken this into consideration as well. Vera replies, "Yes, perhaps not exactly, but they did show consideration for the children." To which the Russian remarks sarcastically, "Oh, yes, the Germans have always been a very humane people."

The cellar of the building across from us, at 10 Pauler Street, caught fire, with smoke billowing out through the cracks in the windows. The men from the neighbourhood, including the ones from our building, grab their shovels, spades and buckets and rush over to put it out, but they quickly return, saying they were shot at by drunken Russian soldiers, who as it turns out had set the cellar on fire because they didn't find any booze in it. Of course, the cellar in question, like every other cellar, is occupied by people, not only by the building's tenants but also by families who'd escaped from nearby shelters that had been destroyed. Later the fire is extinguished somehow, I don't know how. At the same time, a mine that had landed a while ago in the adjacent garden exploded. By describing all this, I just wanted to give you a cursory sketch of a weekday morning in Pauler Street.

I found out Busi's most recent address from Mrs. Kramolin (they've been bombed out of several places); at present they're living on Mészáros Street, in the same building as the Association of Psychoanalysts. We stroll over there. We pass by Horváth Gardens, which is no easy feat. The last time I walked this way (about two or three weeks ago) it was a cemetery with makeshift crosses and the statue of the actress Mrs. Déry in the middle. At this point, the square and the whole neighbourhood looks like a scene from a newsreel about Stalingrad. Mrs. Déry looks extremely comical, standing on tippy toes and making a charming gesture amid pieces of blown-up tanks, but the poor thing no longer has a head.

In front of the Philadelphia Café (remember, Pippancs, we once explored this neighbourhood), a Russian officer of some sort is taking pictures of the ruins of the Krisztina Square church and its surroundings. No doubt it's an interesting picture, except it would look better in colour. The orange-red silk of a parachute from a German bomber lies draped over the roof of the church, if it can even still be called a roof. Chunks are broken off the steeple, the face of the tower clock decided to have an independent life, hanging down, separated from the steeple like a stranger. The Russian fellow puts his small Zeiss Ikon on the tripod and views this truly poetic theme through it. We stop and watch. He gives us a friendly grin, displaying quite a few gold teeth. I look at his camera while Vera explains to him that I'm also knowledgeable and a good photographer. He asks if I have a camera and materials. I answer in my broken Russian, "No, the Germans made off with them." He explains that he'd be willing to barter anything for cameras and photo supplies: bread, sugar, meat. We tell him that unfortunately we don't have anything to trade. We set off again. On the way, Vera manages to bum a cigarette off another officer and is very happy because it's a real Russian cigarette. I don't have the nerve to ask for one even though it would come in handy since I'd be able to swap it for flour to give my parents.

Mészáros Street is ugly. We find Busi's building, but for a while we only hang around the entrance because there's looting going on inside and it's better to keep out of the way. Russian soldiers are carrying bundles of those huge pieces of leather used for making soles and loading them onto a truck. Busi and her family have already moved from the cellar, and now the three of them — Busi, Muki and Emmerich (her brother, a former Austrian police chief, who'd been in Dachau) — are living in one of the rooms of their third-floor apartment. Busi is nothing but skin and bones. She is starving and has recently recovered from typhoid fever, but what shocks me more is how dirty she is. Seeing Busi with dirty ears and neck remains one of my most traumatic impressions from the siege, it almost has the same effect on me as the sight of the burning castle or the first blown-up bridge — even though by now everyone is very dirty. (Busi was always famous for her almost obsessive cleanliness.) Muki is dirty too, but he has a nice grey beard; however, it doesn't conceal the fact that he's alarmingly thin, with sunken face and eyes, and they say that living in a cave damaged his lungs. Busi wants to reclaim her apartment in Óbuda, which is possible in principle, but the poor thing cannot go outside to make this happen because the Russians have made off with all the clothes she left in the apartment, and all she has to her name is the housecoat she was wearing in the cellar while her apartment was being plundered. All Muki had was a pair of pyjamas because he was lying in bed at the time. Busi invites my parents and me to live with her in the apartment in Óbuda if she manages to get it back. I would find this a good solution for my parents in all respects.

Vera and I make our way slowly home in a relatively good mood. The sunshine lifts my spirits, even though I didn't sleep well last night. For the third time in recent weeks, I had the same dream: that for some reason you're very angry with me and that most likely everything is over between us, and even though by now you've been back for quite a while, you only contact me by phone, and when you do, you treat me with indifference, or I'm waiting for your call but you don't phone even though I know you're nearby. This makes me feel hurt and anxious (sensations I'm not familiar with when I'm awake), and I stay under the spell of the dream for a long time, although there are plenty of new things happening.

At home, I go to the courtyard and pick up my assault on lice where I left off this morning. All at once a tattered, slovenly older woman arrives, whom I recognize as the wife of my boss, Mr. Rapoch. This is yet another shocking siege experience, because half a year ago this woman was the most chic and elegant woman in Pest. She has come to see the Hornyánszkys and later also summons me, to save having to tell the story twice. Throughout the siege, they lived on Gugger Hill, which the Russians finally occupied on January 25, but before that it had changed hands several times, meaning that it was alternately under German or Russian occupation. Between Christmas and the day of final liberation, they couldn't even go to the outhouse in their garden because of all the shooting going on around their building. Two of the tenants died, but it was several days before they could take their bodies outside to bury them. I learn from Mrs. Rapoch that Jancsi Máté's apartment was burned to the ground, the Germans set it on fire and didn't allow them to try to put it out. That means I no longer have my Rolleiflex, my photo negatives, photo albums, pillowcases, quite a few dresses and shoes, some cloth, thread, bars of soap, etc., that they were hiding for me. For some time now, I've come to terms with not having anything left, but losing the photo negatives is a real blow.

In the afternoon, the two doctors come back dead tired from Hűvösvölgy (it's awfully far, they say). The Reverend assigned me to the home at 92 Pasaréti Road, which has mostly new mothers with babies. Vera, however, is being sent to mind older children on Völgy Street. I'm sorry that Vera and I will be separated. I have grown very fond of her. This change will be difficult for me, and I'm anxious about it. On the one hand, I would like to find some other means of supporting myself, and a location on Pasaréti is not convenient for this purpose (lack of transportation and free time), but on the other hand, what's the point of finding work if it's not possible to get hold of food? From what I hear, in the children's home there is just enough food to ward off starvation, and I'm also not able to provide for my parents from this distance at all. This is hard to bear, and it bothers me that all our family's bed linen is gone: some of it was left in the home on Kelenhegyi Road, the rest at Bérc Street, with my parents' other belongings. It's impossible to retrieve it or to have someone retrieve it, even if any of it is still there, which is highly unlikely. But it's still imperative that I leave this place, if for no other reason than the impending epidemic. There's no water here, mind you there's none at Hűvösvölgy either, but supposedly the wells are clean, and it's worth your while to carry water from quite a distance. In the evening, we discuss these matters for a long time. Meanwhile, two Russian soldiers barge in through the locked front door and start to look around, but upon seeing the children, they leave with friendly grins, taking only a nice flashlight with them as a souvenir.

That's where the original diary ends. From now on I will continue my story based on my daily jottings.

Saturday, February 17

Early in the morning, I head out to my parents' place. On the way there, I look in on everyone in geographical order; therefore, the first on the list is Béla and his family. Their apartment was levelled to the ground. They moved into the bomb shelter of a building that was under construction. That building is still standing, or at least its structure is undamaged, but there is debris everywhere, and no sign that it might be occupied. I stop the first passerby (I have to wait a long time for someone to walk past!) and ask what happened to the people who were staying in the bomb shelter. The person assures me they are still in the shelter, that I should just go around the collapsed front entrance and enter the building from the back. Indeed, the rear staircase is intact. There is no one in the bomb shelter, but I meet someone in the staircase who tells me that the family of "Mr. Nádas the Engineer" (Béla's name according to his false papers) moved to the third floor. I climb up using the completely intact rear staircase and indeed find them there, living in the kitchen of one of the destroyed apartments that's under construction. Béla put in windows using panes he found in the cellar, installed a lock on the door, set up a fine little iron stove for cooking and fitted up the adjacent room as a workshop. It's got everything from a lathe to a microscope. He spends his whole day making and repairing things. He's nervous about leaving the place because one time when he went outside he was caught and taken to the Russian secret police, where they confiscated his beautiful wristwatch and his slide rule, then let him go after checking his ID papers. These days he does shoe repair, watch repair and window installation in exchange for food and baby clothes, because Irén is in her last months of pregnancy. He also cleans up debris, but he's paid well for that service, and he removes corpses too. A young railway worker by the name of Jóska lives with them. Béla spent twenty miserable hours trying to dig him out from under the rubble of a building at 10/c Hattyú Street. When the building collapsed, there were nine people trapped in the bomb shelter who were banging and screaming for help. Béla joined a large group of men who were starting the rescue operation. They worked and worked, but the shelling got so heavy that gradually they all dispersed, except for Béla, who crawled through to the shelter on his belly. At that point, Jóska was the only one left of the nine, but Béla managed to drag him out. These days, Jóska procures food for Béla's family out of gratitude and has attached himself to them. Béla and I are overjoyed to see each other. He is also somewhat proud that I am alive, because in truth that is partially his doing. We're stunned at how skinny we all are.

I only stay for a little while, anxious to get to my parents because I need to be back at Pauler Street by the afternoon. It's another day of brilliant sunshine. There's a sea of mud everywhere. Ostrom Street and the Széna Square neighbourhood including Hattyú Street must be the ugliest area in the whole of Buda, or even in the whole of Budapest, I think. There are corpses all over the place, but by now they no longer resemble wax figures, because they are covered all over with sticky black mud. A corpse lies in the middle of the road at the entrance to Hattyú Street, so completely coated in mud that I only notice it when I've almost stepped on it. A vehicle must have rolled over it, pulling down the man's pants and exposing his mud-caked penis, which is upright and so grotesque and horrible that even though by now I'm quite inured to such sights, my stomach revolts and wants to spill its contents.

In front of the Apolló Theatre in Buda there's another shocking scene: the seats are all torn and broken, there are dead horses between the rows and the shattered ruins of a chandelier lie on top of one of them. My ski boots once again serve me well. Without them, I wouldn't be able to walk any further due to all the mud, rubble and debris. I stop by Grünberger's apartment on Margit Boulevard, though no one knows anything about him, he disappeared in October and hasn't shown up since. I also look in on the family of my colleague Piroska at the bomb shelter of the building on Bem József Street. They are all right, but their food supply is running low. These days the mood is such that even casual acquaintances embrace when they meet. People are practically drunk on the knowledge that it was possible to survive all this.

I just want to pop in at the shelter where Lívia and her family are staying, but she's not there, and now I start to sprint to my parents' place on Gül Baba Street. The boarding house, or rather its cellar, is almost completely empty, the building itself has been shelled to pieces. I find out from the remaining residents that my parents have moved to Juci's place, so I head over there. Juci hasn't heard from Ernő for weeks. She was afraid to be alone in the apartment (they moved back from the bomb shelter because two of their rooms overlooking the courtyard remained intact) and so asked my parents to move in with her. It was a good opportunity for my parents; they could leave the filthy cellar on Gül Baba Street. Juci's got fuel, room and bed linen, and her family can really use Nünüke's help in return. Juci's maid, a refugee from Transylvania, treats the old folks well.

That was the very day Juci got news about Ernő. A nurse came to tell her that Ernő was in the hospital on Gömbös Gyula Street because of a bullet wound in his leg. Juci's so petrified by the Russians that she doesn't dare leave the building to visit Ernő. Nünüke offers to accompany her. I don't like the idea of Nünü going along because the hospital is far on foot, the streets are in horrible shape and it's difficult to walk, especially in ordinary shoes, but there's no way Juci would have the courage to go on her own. They decide to leave early in the afternoon. But first the bread dough needs to be taken over to the baker's, and Juci doesn't even dare go by herself to the bakery in the adjacent building. We swaddle the dough in a thick kerchief and scramble into the half-collapsed Zimka Bakery, where they accept the dough for baking but with no guarantees, because as the baker mentions, yesterday the Russians made off with all the bread. Then the three of us set out, walking together all the way to the Southern Railway Station. En route, somewhere around Vérmező, we come across Boci, and from a distance she shouts that Ervin's cousin met you, my Pippancs, sometime in October and that you were okay. When I get home to Pauler Street, I am suddenly feeling miserable. It's hard on me that the others are excitedly making plans — Vera has a million ideas about what she ought to do — and I don't have a single one and can't even imagine what my next move should be. One after the other, people show up at the home to collect their family members. We are getting ready for the trip the next day: according to the Reverend's instructions, we need to move the remaining children in batches to Hűvösvölgy.

Sunday, February 18

A few of us set out for Hűvösvölgy early in the morning. We walk along Városmajor Street (for weeks this part of the city was the site of heavy fighting — and it looks it), avoiding the infamous Olasz Avenue, but we have to pass by the new Szent János Hospital. The corpses haven't been removed yet, but luckily by now they've all been piled in one spot in front of the hospital entrance. They are laid out one beside the other, or rather on top of each other, in an orderly fashion, the way firewood is stacked. Ragged, bloody pieces of clothing are scattered all over the place.

Beyond the hospital, things start to improve, and the weather is beautiful. For a while, we are still walking past damaged buildings with broken windows, but eventually we leave the bombed area and encounter a row of villas, where the windows are still intact, and if it wasn't for the presence of grim Russian soldiers everywhere a person could think that nothing had ever happened here.

We first stop by the nursery on Pasaréti Road, but it doesn't look promising. It's dirty and crowded, and for the time being there's no possibility of keeping it clean because they don't have any water either, and the wells are located far away and have been taken over by Russian soldiers. In any case, I leave my bag there and follow the others to Völgy Street, where I want to talk to the Reverend. It's quite far, almost as far as the streetcar terminal, but around here the snow hasn't melted yet, and we march on snow that sparkles in the sunshine, which I really enjoy after having lived in a cave for so long. I gulp in the fresh air with gusto. I need to squeeze my eyes almost shut because they are sore and inflamed.

Sztehlo gives us a warm welcome and immediately agrees that I should go there and not to the nursery, although he warns me that it'll be very hard work because the caregivers are expected to do everything in and around the residence, from scrubbing floors to chopping wood. They offer us a meal consisting of some sort of dumpling made of crumbs from coarse bread, served with an oniony paprika sauce. It tastes great to us, we are terribly hungry. There is no bread. There are plenty of lice, however, and the residents warn us not to sit on any upholstered furniture.

The villa at 19 Völgy Street belongs to Count Zsigmond Széchenyi.[9] It has a gorgeous location, the likes of which I've only seen in movies, and it's beautifully furnished, with old-time elegance. It's enormous. All around there are huge picture windows, each with a view of a different Buda hill, opulent chandeliers, paintings, engravings and antique Biedermeier furniture. Only half of the villa is allocated to the children. Hungarian Dálnoki soldiers[10] are quartered in the other half (that's how they call the Hungarian soldiers who swore allegiance to the new government, you can recognize them by — and Pippancs, don't laugh — their WHITE ARMBANDS).[11] These soldiers, like all the others who've endured the siege, are lice infested. Previously, the villa was inhabited by Russians, and when they left, the caregivers gave the place a thorough cleaning, dusted, brushed and shook out everything, scrubbed the floors with hot water and lye soap, and no sooner had they finished than the Dálnoki soldiers arrived bringing fresh lice. The children have shaved heads, and they're all scratching like crazy. There are not enough beds, most of the kids sleep on the floor, and the caregivers have it even worse. The indoor sanitation doesn't work, and the fancy looking porcelain toilets are filled to the brim with crud, which the caregivers must empty.

---

9 Count Zsigmond Széchenyi (1898–1967), scion of one of the leading aristocratic families of Hungary, famous for his African travels, hunts and travel books.

10 Dálnoki soldiers was the name given to the eight Hungarian army divisions Béla Miklós de Dálnok agreed to establish to participate in the offensive against Germany in the armistice of January 20, 1945.

11 Although Margit's husband had converted to the Lutheran faith, he was still considered Jewish and was forced to wear a white armband, which signified Jews who had converted to Christianity.

Currently, seventy children are living in the home. With only three wash basins at their disposal, we need special permission from the Reverend to wash any clothes. You can imagine the rest. Some other interesting things: A life-sized portrait of Count Széchenyi by a famous artist with both eyes vandalized by puncture holes, green silk wallpaper covered in reddish brown stains, which I later learn is the handiwork of Russians who smashed jars of tomato preserves against the wall just for kicks, the tomato sauce dripped down the wall onto the beautiful English etchings. And some of the furniture didn't fare any better: the Russians brought huge pots of soup hot off the stove and set them without any kind of padding directly on top of the most beautiful Biedermeier trumeau commode, the dirty dishes and cutlery ended up in the same place. Speaking of cutlery, we take turns eating since there isn't even half as much cutlery as we need. As guests, we are served first, of course. We eat standing up because there are hardly any chairs and the long wooden benches set up in the dining area are occupied by the children. I help to serve the food, carrying it to the children one plate at a time. I am not too keen on this task, and my only consolation is that the affable young caregiver called Hedda is here as well, and I think if she can put up with it, so can I. Hedda not only puts up with it, but she's cheerful, round and rosy-cheeked. She recounts that during the siege she worked in the children's home on Bogár Street (in Rózsadomb), which was on the battlefront right from the beginning, so they had to flee in the night with the help of German soldiers, making a huge detour to reach the home on Gábor Áron Road. They were led by a German SS officer with a machine gun slung over his shoulder, carrying little Tomika Weisz on his arm and holding the hand of Pistike Krausz. Their bundles were carried by SS soldiers, who would most likely turn in their mass grave if they knew they'd saved a bunch of Jewish children from a fiery death. (The villa on Bogár Street burned to the ground.)

We need to head home soon after our meal, because nowadays it gets dark around five o'clock. We meet Dr. György Orbán on Pasaréti

Road. I don't know if you remember his name, he was the director of one of the textile factories, a brilliant, talented, immensely likeable guy. He was caught distributing communist pamphlets about a year and a half ago, which really surprised me at the time. When he disappeared, I was told he'd been expelled from the country, so we'd long since given up on him. We're delighted to see each other. He says he'll try to go to Pest next week and check things out, and if I look him up later he'll tell me what he learned.

We arrive back at Pauler dead tired. It's gotten very bad for me here. Every day another relative shows up to claim someone, everyone else is being taken care of, I feel awfully lonely: the siege was pulled out from under me, and now I feel like a fish out of water. Edit Kozma's father came to collect her, the neurotic doctor was picked up by her brother-in-law, Mrs. Wald by her husband. Some relatives sent Vera a message. Everyone is getting ready to leave, they are full of plans, and I'm just sitting here like an idiot, at a loss as to what to do. In the end, I resort to what always worked for me in the past: I shed a few tears. I'm hellishly afraid of the starvation that lies ahead.

Monday, February 19

No one at the home has a watch anymore, so I can only guess at the time when I try to set out early for my parents' place. I think it's around 7:30, but it turns out it's not even 6:30 yet. The weather is nice, and the day gets light early. On the way there, I stop in at the Forbáth mansion, but the only one there is the superintendent, who is living in the cellar. The building is in rough shape, has been hit by several shells, the windows have been torn out, frames and all, everything is covered in plaster dust, crumbled masonry. The wardrobes have been broken into, their contents scattered, most of it plundered. The books from Forbáth's beautiful collection are strewn about, all torn up. The large Persian rug has been soiled (Russian folk custom!), the statues smashed, the paintings have holes punched through them — it makes you want to cry. The superintendent knows nothing of the fate of the family, yet even I knew that the parents and their younger daughter were taken away back in June because someone reported them. They were held for days at an assembly centre on Rökk Szilárd Street, after that they disappeared without a trace.

I walk on through deserted streets to my parents' place. At Széna Square, a real live person is walking toward me, and as he gets closer, I realize that it is Auer. We embrace wholeheartedly, as has become my habit. He tells me that everyone is eager for me to return to the bank, I'll get paid right away if I show up, apparently even the cafeteria is back in operation. Auer also plans to head over to the Pest side, but it's no easy matter. He is skinny, scruffy looking, in dire need of some motherly care. He recounts that in January the Arrow Cross dragged him off to one of their headquarters somewhere in Buda. To his good fortune, the building was hit by shelling that night, and he managed to escape in the ensuing chaos and hide at a friend's place. The streets hereabouts are in somewhat better shape, but the corpses still haven't been cleared away, only stacked up, the rubble has been pushed to the side so that vehicles can have room to pass in the middle of the road. No one gives a damn about pedestrians, who are forced to jump out of the way when a car approaches.

Margit Boulevard is yet another hideous sight. The building where the Regent Café was located has been levelled, and the surroundings have fared no better. There's rubble and debris everywhere. Amid the rubble, a few strange items can be seen. There are piano keys scattered in the mud, but no piano in sight. You can't imagine how sad and senseless such a lone piano key can look, with its yellowed edges. Elsewhere I spot the body of a mannequin, with the head grinning idiotically and the arm raised in an infinitely comical gesture. Even in peacetime, I couldn't bear to look at such a ludicrous pose, let alone in the mud under the wheel of an anti-aircraft gun. I know it's what they call kitsch, nonetheless I'll describe a prettily dressed but very muddy doll hanging upside down from the fender of a car that has been shot to hell.

In the meantime, the street has come to life, with Russian trucks speeding by, as well as supply wagons and horse-drawn carriages. Whenever a supply wagon stops somewhere, the Russian driver pulls out a Persian rug and covers the horse with it. Similarly, the most exquisite Persian rugs are used to cover the trucks' radiators, of course that's after they make holes in the rugs so the screws will fit. These Russkies[12] are rather sweet when they talk to their horses in a tender tone, and I'd dearly love to understand what they're saying. They make an *Rrrrrr* sound when they call to their horses, but they use a very soft R — which I try, unsuccessfully, to imitate. I like to watch how they ride their horses. I have never seen anyone ride in such a beautiful style. They seem to be one with the horse.

My parents and Juci are surprised that I turn up at such an early hour (they still have a watch hidden away somewhere). The real reason I came to see them was to bring over my share of the home's food supply. The food parcel is a big hit with everyone. And then I'm off so I can make it back to Pauler by ten o'clock, when the first transport of kids is due to leave for Hűvösvölgy. I get back in time, but I can only take a short rest because the others are ready to start the move. Yet it is very difficult to set out because we have trouble distributing the heavy load in such a way that we can carry all of it and leave nothing behind. I tie the two mattresses that Vera lent me onto my back, as I'm intending to sleep on them at Völgy Street. With the aid of the Major and using your belt and a piece of rope, I manage to bind the two gigantic mattresses on my back so securely that I don't even feel them. Of course, I also carry a chock-full string bag in each hand. (By some divine inspiration I bought these string bags right before the siege and added them to my siege gear. I don't know what I would have done without them.)

---

12 "Russki" is often used now as a derogatory reference to Russians; the use here is intended to be friendly.

On Pasaréti Road, I run into Ági Ländler from Cini's studio, but she doesn't have any news of Cini either, except that she had a Swedish protective passport. We are moving the older kids today, who can help by carrying their own belongings. Before taking off, we hold a rehearsal and beg the children not to take on a bigger load than they can easily carry, because if halfway there it turns out to be too heavy we won't be able to help them, since we're also bearing the maximum load. Naturally, the teenage boys insist that their baggage is light as a feather, they could easily carry more. Of course, not halfway but a quarter of the way there, my eleven-year-old bachelor protege lags behind, not only is his load too heavy but his suitcase keeps falling open, the handle is broken, so he has trouble carrying it. If I were to turn back with him, we would lose a lot of time, not to mention all the wasted energy, which is a real consideration these days when we have so little to eat. Finally, I decide to find the man in charge of one of the nearby buildings and ask him to let us leave part of our load there, and we'll come back for it in the evening. So, the situation is saved. We give Péter a thorough scolding and continue on our way.

When we come to the Szent János Hospital, Zsuzsi Steiner, our ten-year-old ward, bursts out crying and declares that she won't go any further. It's hard to make her tell us why not: it seems she caught sight of the corpses piled in front of the hospital entrance, although from this distance only the bare soles of their feet are visible. This child who is normally intelligent, cheerful and well balanced is wailing hysterically and demanding that we take a different route. A different route would involve either making a detour around the hill with our heavy loads, risking a "from the frying pan into the fire" type of situation in terms of corpses, or crossing Olasz Avenue, which is said to be blocked by mountains of corpses, and although I haven't seen them for myself, this rumour is validated by the smell drifting from that direction. For a few minutes, we stand around Zsuzsi without knowing what to do, one of the women tries screaming at her, which only makes her more frantic. In the end, our solution is that I give my hand luggage to one of my colleagues so that Zsuzsi can snuggle up against me and I cover her eyes tightly as we pass the hospital. The child is trembling all over. When we leave the battle zone at last, I let go of Zsuzsi so that I can retrieve my bags, and I tell the child she can now open her eyes without fear. She calms down somewhat but remains glued to my side and resumes walking with her eyes firmly fixed on the ground. She doesn't dare to look up.

We finally manage to hand the children over to Sztehlo. Relieved, we head for home, this time without parcels and children. We are bone weary and aware that tomorrow will be an even tougher day, because we'll have to transfer the younger ones, who won't be able to walk even half the distance under their own steam. We stride along beside a company of Russian soldiers, who are singing sweetly, not a march but a melancholy folk tune. This briefly gets our minds off how exhausted we are. Other interesting sights: every twenty steps or so we come across an abandoned streetcar, not merely abandoned but so riddled with bullet holes that they appear to be made of lace. They obviously must have been standing there since Christmas Eve, i.e., nearly two months now. This is dispiriting because heaven only knows when the streetcars will start moving again. I can't even picture a time when the streetcars will be back in operation on Krisztina Boulevard, where today it's impossible to take a single step because of all the debris, corpses, scrap metal and dead horses.

On Pasaréti Road, a grocery store has been shot to pieces and looted, its relatively intact shop front sign advertises ham, salami, cheese, baked goods. I almost start crying because it's so unimaginable that those items will ever be available again. En route, I stop by the apartment of the Schöpflin family, but I find out right at the entrance that they moved across to Pest, to Szentkirályi Street, before the start of the siege. By the way, the building is currently inhabited by Russian horses.

Tuesday, February 20

Yesterday they distributed our travel ration of bread made from the last remnants of flour in the home. My share was about a quarter of a kilo, which I plan to consume sparingly. It's not my turn to help with the move, so today I will tend to my own affairs, which means I'll be covering long distances all day but not eating. Mici, the maid at the Hornyánszky boarding house, who has a big linen bag filled with toasted and dried pieces of bread, takes pity on me and gives me two or three pieces. This is quite a treasure, and I tuck it away carefully.

Early in the morning, I walk to Kelenhegyi Road, where I left a lot of my belongings, but right now I'm mostly interested in my bed linen. The walk there is far from boring: the neighbourhoods of Tabán and Krisztinaváros provide a rather interesting sight. It's my first time to see the ruins of the bridges up close. Well, they did a thorough job, true German *Tüchtigkeit*.[13] On Szent János Square, the building where Béla and his family used to live has holes the size of an apartment. Two or three doors down, an airplane — more precisely the wreckage of one — is lodged in the top of the building, its nose burrowed into the roof, its wings and tail sticking up in the air. But the Danube embankment on the Buda side is something else again, the whole Promenade looks like a giant scrapyard.

The residents of the building on Kelenhegyi Road are all alive, they have ridden out the storm fairly well; moreover, they even had water the whole time. The manager immediately mobilizes everyone to look for my bed linen, which is no small challenge under these crowded conditions and in the dark. (They are living in the cellar, like almost everyone else, because here too the upstairs apartments have been completely destroyed.) I pay a visit to my Biedermeier wardrobe, it's right where I left it but by this point it has been broken into pieces. My sofa, which is also in a rather sad state but still usable, sits

---

13 German: efficiency.

in one of the windowless, totally wrecked upstairs rooms, covered with plaster dust. My pillow, my duvet and one of my flannel blankets are found. I make a giant bundle out of it all and strap it on my back. Klári gives me a kilo of bread flour as a present (which is worth about five human lives these days, although in truth its value cannot be measured in pengős, there just aren't enough pengős in the world for that!) and makes me promise to have it baked into bread to take along for my move. She says that I must GO OVER TO THE PEST SIDE, I must not stay in Buda, and especially not with the Red Cross, because in her opinion that makes no sense and has no future. According to what she heard, Pest is quite intact, life has returned there, I should go back to the bank, I should get food from the Joint.[14] Then she gives me an address; I need to go to a certain Mr. Rosta in the Discount Bank. He's the Joint representative and he'll give me free meal vouchers.

I mull this over as I stumble along the Buda Promenade with my bundle, and by the time I reach my parents' place, my mind is made up, not to move to Hűvösvölgy but to head for Pest instead. At my parents', I gobble down something that passes for lunch, then I'm on my way to Pauler. I stop every Russian soldier en route to mooch cigarettes, so that I might give them to Mici to repay her for the bread.

The Red Cross set-up on Pauler Street has thinned out considerably, only a few caregivers are left, but we still cook dinner for ourselves. I take my usual place in the wicker chair and am overcome by APATHY, everything looks terribly hopeless to me. How am I going to make it over to Pest, what am I going to do there, where should I go to sleep, who is going to give me food, etc., etc., and even if all goes well, what's going to happen to my parents? And what kind of a wimp am I that all these women around me know what to do but I

---

14 American Jewish Joint Distribution Committee.

don't? My mood is similar to the way I felt during my matriculation banquet, when everyone was overjoyed that they'd finally finished school, that they didn't need to study anymore, and I was the only one worried about what would happen next. I would have gladly stayed in school for another fifteen years (I still have dreams about attending Grade 9).[15]

Wednesday, February 21

It's my turn again to move the children's belongings to Hűvösvölgy. Before leaving the boarding house, I give the flour I received from Klári to Mici and ask her to bake me some bread for my move. On the way, a funeral procession goes by: two men are pulling a four-wheeled cart bearing a corpse laid out in a wardrobe, they used some kind of entrance hall wardrobe for the purpose, draped in a black rag. As agreed, I don't bring Vera's mattresses back to Pauler; instead, I take them over to her aunt who lives near Völgy Street. This works out well for me because she offers me some pastry. My taste buds are all messed up and can no longer appreciate such treats, I just gobble it down; it might as well be bread. Some Russian soldiers are sitting on the large balcony of one of the villas, they have several loaves of freshly baked dark bread in front of them. I walk over and with a friendly grin tell them *chleb* and *golodna*,[16] one of them is about to give me a loaf, but the other one says something to him, at which point the first one rushes inside and comes back with half a loaf and hands it to me with the words "Nem jó,"[17] pointing out that it is hard

15 The reference to Grade 9 is a joke, since at the time, high school, which started after four years of elementary school, only went up to Grade 8.

16 Russian: bread (chleb) and hungry (golodna).

17 Hungarian: not good.

and dry. But I make him understand that this doesn't bother me in the least and quickly tuck it away, thank him with a smile, and beat a hasty retreat lest they ask for it back.

On Völgy Street, I request an audience with the Reverend, who is sick: he has the flu and is in bed with a fever. But they still let me see him. He is indeed lying in bed, or rather sitting up, repairing a shoe belonging to one of the kids. I tell him that I have decided to look around on the Pest side for a job that would sustain not only me but my parents as well. He tells me that I am greatly needed here, because there are only a few caregivers and a lot of children and even more work, but he won't replace me with anyone until I get back from Pest and inform him of my final decision. Then he asks me if I need any money. I thank him and say that I don't for the time being, after all, money cannot buy you anything these days. We agree that I will let him know within a week whether I want to be a caregiver or not.

On the way home, I stop by a pharmacy in Pasarét, thinking to pick up some medicine that might come in handy at home. The pharmacy is in total ruins. The pharmacist can be found in the cellar along with what's left of the inventory, but he is not willing to give me so much as chamomile tea without a doctor's prescription.

Thursday, February 22

This day is dedicated to moving. I am the only one left from the children's home at the Hornyánszkys'. I make three runs between the Lénárds' and Pauler Street, because I don't just need to fetch the belongings I left there at Christmas but also the things that were stored at the Kramolins', which I brought over here bit by bit at the time, such as blankets, etc. On the last run, I bid a fond farewell to the owners and especially the staff, who were really good to me.

I forgot to mention that in the meantime Ernő made it home. He had been released from the hospital although his leg wound was not completely healed, which was fortunate because that saved him from being taken away for "robot."[18] At suppertime that evening, the entire Kassai-Lénárd family sits together by the light of a kerosene lamp. There is a fire in the iron stove, it's nice and warm here, and water is being heated in a pot so that I can have WARM WATER TO WASH IN. I have never been as happy and content in my whole life, and I'm anxiously awaiting tomorrow's big adventure, crossing over to the Pest side. Everyone is trying hard to talk me out of leaving, because even though the family members of my colleagues at the home were able to cross the Danube on the ice, by now you can only cross by boat, which is dangerous, as not a day goes by without a boat capsizing. You need to stand in line for days, and fights break out as people are boarding. No civilians are allowed to cross at the Újpest Bridge,[19] not even if they do half a day of "robot" in exchange. This actually happened to Mr. Schober, a cellar mate of mine on Pauler Street, who wanted to cross the river to go to his office, so he walked to the Újpest Bridge, was caught and made to carry rocks for two days without anything to eat or drink. At the end, they didn't let him cross after all, so he trudged back to Pauler Street exhausted and broken.

I go to bed early because I intend to avoid the scramble for the boat by catching the very first vessel at dawn.

---

18 The word "robot" is being used for the Russian word "rabota," from the expression "malen'kaya rabota," literally meaning "small work." People were first taken to clear debris, but for a large portion of the civilian population this manual labour often ended up with being transported to the Soviet Union to do forced labour, known by the Hungarians as *málenkiy robot*.

19 The Újpest railway bridge was blown up by the Germans around Christmas 1944, and the Soviets had built a pontoon bridge near the wreckage.

Pest

Friday, February 23

Apparently, I'm not a superstitious person since I'm willing to embark on such an adventurous undertaking on a Friday. Nünüke also gets up at dawn, of course, and bustles around. I head out in my siege dress, complete with a knapsack containing a change of underwear, a bag of dried bread and a sizable piece of bacon, which I got when they divvied up the food at Pauler Street. The "eiserne Reserve"[1] is still in the pocket of my knapsack, left over from the good old air raid days: sugar cubes, a couple of pieces of peacetime baker's chocolate, crackers, dried smoked cheese and a can of BRISLING sardines from the provisions you bought way back then! Wearing boots, a filthy raincoat over my winter coat, a Red Cross nurse's hat, carrying a pack on my back and a checkered beach bag in my hand, that's how I start off on my BIG JOURNEY. I made a deal with Nünü that I would only return right away if there was absolutely no opportunity to make a reasonable living over there. Otherwise, I would stay for at least eight to ten days or send a message, because the fare to cross is one hundred pengős each time. It is overcast with intermittent drizzle, but the

---

1 German: literally "iron reserve"; refers to an emergency ration.

important thing is that there's no wind, since I wouldn't be willing to sit in a crowded boat when it's windy. I need to walk to the shore opposite one end of Hajógyári Island, where I realize to my dismay that I am not the only wily person to arrive at 6:00 in the morning. According to my quick estimate, there are about two hundred such wily individuals and only two small boats with a capacity of eight to ten people each. Naturally, this leads to quarrelling, fighting, uproar, excitement, all happening KNEE DEEP IN MUD. Luckily my ski boots keep the mud from going the whole way up to my knees. The mud is still slightly frozen with a thin crust of ice on top, but it is evident that in an hour it will thaw and come up to our necks. This whole boat business looks hopeless anyway.

I stood in line by the boat whose owner was handing out numbers. I even waited for two round trips (they were letting people out at Dagály Street on the other side), but then I saw that the numbers were useless, the people who could fight the best were the ones getting onto the boat. Right in front of my eyes, about five steps away, a Russian officer and a fat civilian with a knapsack fell overboard. They had to be pulled out, and the civilian, in his dripping wet winter coat, started fighting again. I watched this scene for a while because it was entertaining, but then I decided to head to the Újpest pontoon bridge and try to wheedle my way across, perhaps by doing "robot" for a while then sneaking away.

I start off, but after walking for a bit I meet a group coming from the opposite direction who tell me that the Russians are not allowing a soul to cross on the pontoon bridge. For a second, the Spielberger blood surges in me, I am about to turn back and devote my life to washing diapers and wiping bums at the Red Cross home, but instead I forge on and don't even turn back when another group that went to the Újpest Bridge in vain tells me the same thing. I hear from some countrywomen behind me that at Csillaghegy you can get a boat over to Megyer or some such place for fifty pengős. This means it would be midnight by the time I get to Pest, but by now I don't care. When

I reach a point opposite the middle of Hajógyári Island (I've been walking beside the tracks of the local train), I spot a dock with two people on it. I walk over and ask if they can take me across. One of the men says that he can take me only as far as the island, but he has a buddy there who would take me on to Pest. However, it isn't worth his while to do it for just one person, I should round up a minimum of nine other people. It'll cost at least two hundred pengős per person, but he would prefer to be paid in food, for example, bread. I tell him that unfortunately I haven't got any food and try to bargain him down from two hundred, but he won't budge. I go back to the tracks and try to lure the passersby into my scheme. It's slow going because they've all found out about the possibility of a fifty-pengő crossing at Csillaghegy, and anyone who's willing to make such a long trek to save money won't sign on for a two-hundred-pengő trip. Luckily, I meet an enterprising fellow from Pest who enthusiastically gets involved in this business, and before long he has managed to recruit ten people. We embark and arrive on the island in a matter of minutes. Here our man explains that we'll have to walk to the upper end of the island, and there near the shore we'll find his buddy, who'll transport us to Újpest. We start walking on the completely deserted island, and I'm reminded of Robinson Crusoe. The thin ice keeps cracking under our feet. There's slushy snow underneath the ice. We've been tramping for a long time, and there's not a soul around. We cover the whole length of the shore, which, for the sake of variety, is muddy. There is no sign of the buddy — or anyone else, for that matter.

From the shore you can see the pontoon bridge with Russian soldiers milling around on it, beside the ruined Újpest Bridge, which has now half fallen into the river. Some of my companions are cursing quietly, but so far no one says out loud what we've all been thinking, namely that we've been duped, that they took our money and left us stranded on the island. After another half hour of running up and down along the shore, we finally say it out loud, some are even shouting it. The enterprising fellow keeps vowing that he'll swim back to the two-hundred-pengő guy and beat him to a pulp. I'm not especially scared because there are ten of us and something will eventually unfold, besides I simply can't believe that anyone would do such a thing, even if it is siege time. In any case, we exhaust ourselves sufficiently with all the running up and down that we sit on tree stumps. As for me, I eat some dried bread with bacon and follow it up with a sugar cube to ward off fatigue.

Suddenly, a boat comes into view on the Danube, rowing slowly in our direction: it's the buddy, who just finished delivering his load to the other side and is now coming to fetch us. Everyone lightens up and feels ashamed for having panicked. We board the boat happily and start off toward our intensely desired destination, the Pest shore, while I AM THINKING IN ALL CAPITAL LETTERS, words such as HISTORIC MOMENT and FATEFUL COURSE, and I'm very excited, but in a good way. I am about to find out what has happened on the other side, what has happened to the ghetto, if there is news of you, if Cini and the other friends are still alive, what's going on in the apartment on Miksa Street, what has happened to our belongings. They tie up the boat opposite the northern tip of Szúnyog Island, where we have to make a steep climb up the crumbled remains of the stone embankment, hanging on to a wire fence. As I come to the top, I nearly step on the corpse of a civilian, maybe fifty or sixty years of age, wearing a sweater, which is a welcome change from the sight of thousands of corpses in uniform. And that's my first experience in Pest.

I gallop toward Váci Road. I follow the same route I used to take when I went rowing at the Reisich boat house, but of course the street has changed quite a bit since then. Váci Road, which is almost completely intact, is a pleasant surprise. Although there is no streetcar service yet (contrary to what we'd heard on the Buda side), the rails are completely repaired. I have gotten so used to walking long distances that I'm surprised when all of a sudden I find myself at Aréna Road, which would have been an awfully long trek in former times.

It's nearing noon, I'm hungry and it would be nice to eat something hot. My first stop is to see Pista Székely's family on Visegrádi Street. Their building is in poor condition, but they have survived. Pista's father is sick in bed. They report that Pista fled his labour service company before October 15 and is now in Kolozsvár, doing well. He has already sent several letters. Of course, they don't have any news of you, my Pippancs, but they give me the address of Vajda who worked at Nova. I find Vajda at home. He also deserted in October, and as far as he knows you didn't try to escape, you stayed with the company and let yourself be captured and are now with several others in a Romanian internment camp, in Focșani. He's not sure about any of this, he's just come to that conclusion. But he regards Focșani as a favourable outcome. What Vajda says upsets me, even if I can't believe it, because you don't usually do such stupid things. It doesn't sound like you at all. He gives me Tárkányi's address, and I go to see him. Hans Kestler's wife happens to be there as well and she's bawling because according to Tárkányi her husband has been taken to Siberia. I can tell that Tárkányi is trying hard to remember what has happened to you, but he cannot say anything definite and thinks that probably you've also ended up in Focșani, but you're most likely all right because they were told that except for Dr. Singer, who was shot while escaping, everyone is okay. Later, however, Tárkányi seems to recall that you did escape along with the boys from Bácska who were heading for Yugoslavia. This version of events suits me better, and it doesn't seem improbable since you were friends with Tibi Steinitz, who I think is from Újvidék. In any case, the whole thing upsets me. I'm disappointed, because I'd hoped that I would get all kinds of good news about you.

The next stop (going in geographical order) is Gyöngyház Street, Dóri's apartment, but she is not at home. Klári Korvin is all right, the superintendent informs me, but she doesn't live on Visegrádi Street. Everywhere I go, I have to bang on the main doors for a long time, because the doors are locked day and night, just like in Buda, and there are no doorbells here either. At number 8 Kádár Street, I'm received by my aunts, and we all start bawling: everyone is okay, Cini is living at home on Hollán Street, they have already had news of Laci: someone saw him, he is well. Next, I rush over to Miksa Street; I wouldn't be surprised if a letter from you was waiting for me there.

The neighbourhood is relatively unscathed, as is the Grand Boulevard, except that all the stores have been smashed and looted, and it gives the impression of a deserted street, except that the place is bustling. On the street corners, Russian soldiers are busy making deals with Jews. Miksa Street is intact. Only our room took a hit, so half of the room has been torn away, and the remaining furniture is piled up in the other half. I go down to the cellar with the superintendent. The three trunks that were filled by Béla during the Arrow Cross heyday are still there, two of them unscathed; however, the third one, which didn't have a lock, has been completely emptied but for a few pieces at the bottom, such as my beige sandals, which makes me deliriously happy, because I didn't count on there being even this much left. The super is rather surprised at me because it seems that the other tenants would be disappointed to find so few of their belongings left. All the residents of the building are fine, including the children, who were sheltered in some Swiss protected house. I have the impression that everyone views me with a kind of hostile reserve. I don't know if it's because we fled and didn't live through the same things they did or because they know we're penniless and they're afraid we'll ask for money. I do ask the super to safeguard the chests until I can have them taken away.

I hurry over to Cini's place because it's getting dark. When I enter the small room on Hollán (which used to be an atelier and now is chock full of furniture), it's already dark. I can't see Cini's face, but as we embrace I can tell how awfully skinny she is. Four of us will be living here: Cini, me, Ágnes Schöngut and Marianne Magaziner. There's not much room, but it's very good to be all together. A small iron stove is set up by the window, its stovepipe vents to the outside through a hole cut into the board that replaces the windowpane, and a festive dinner is being prepared on the stove in my honour, consisting of *lángos* and some sort of soup. Cini already knew that I was alive and knew my whereabouts because she'd met Vera Nyilas. I'm extremely happy and content. I'm in a warm room, eating a hot meal, among friendly people, and almost everyone is accounted for, even Lilus, as Cini informs me. We haven't told each other our stories yet because there's way too much to tell. We only start the recounting later and then only bit by bit. We don't have any kind of a candle, but the moon shines into our room, and we prepare dinner by moonlight, how I always pictured Parisian student garrets. Ágnes Schöngut's father was hiding out in the hospital on Városmajor Street, and it was in this hospital that the Arrow Cross soldiers massacred everyone they suspected of being Jewish.[2] There is still a very faint hope that bácsi Schöngut managed to escape.

There are only two sofas in the room, one used for sleeping by Ágnes and Marianne, and the other by Cini and me. Of course, there is no electricity or gas here either, but THERE IS WATER COMING OUT OF THE TAP. The toilet doesn't work, but it's not because of lack of water. None of us knows what we'll eat — or if we'll eat — tomorrow, but right now no one really cares. The main thing is that today we managed to fill our bellies. The reason Cini's place is so crowded is that when the aunts were taken away, a "bombed-out" family from Sashalom moved into the vacated apartment. The family consists of a clerk from a mill, his wife and two children, an aunt, and a young man called Ödön, who sleeps in the hallway and whom we'd be wise to befriend because he knows how to fix the stove when the fire refuses to start. We often call on the poor guy's services. The

---

2 On January 14, 1945, Arrow Cross men murdered about one hundred and fifty patients and staff of the Jewish Dániel Bíró Hospital, including both Jews and non-Jews.

Tóths, for that's the name of the family, are decent, quiet people, who don't get in the way.

Saturday, February 24

I leave for the Credit Bank with a knapsack and a shopping bag (I got so used to carrying these items that I can't leave my building without them). I walk along Falk Miksa Street, where almost all the buildings are burned out. There's a terrible, stomach-turning stench everywhere, which must have come from some chemicals that caught fire. The inner city is completely deserted. You need to make a big detour around Nádor Street because of all the debris blocking the route. József Square and the Credit Bank are in a lamentable shape. The exterior of the bank is not nearly as scary looking as the interior: you need to wade through glass shards up to your waist, even though the clerks — the few who live in Pest who have shown up so far — have been tasked with clearing the place and have been at it for several weeks now. The personnel department is operational, and of course it's fully aware of its importance and is haughtier than ever. We need to stand in line in the unheated basement, with its steel-plated walls, and apply for a work assignment, food ration card, identity papers and armbands with Cyrillic lettering.

I find out that many of my colleagues have spent the whole siege here in the shelter of the Credit Bank, which was quite well equipped for the purpose. Each day the bank provides these resident employees with one plateful of food, for which they charge one pengő per person. I also learn that all the clerks who show up for work are entitled to a plate, but you need a lot of pull to get it. I immediately launch my campaign, but without any success. The director's office is located where in peacetime the bank's medical office used to be (that's what the sign still says), but now it's the great Perényi who holds office there. The sign on the room right beside it reads "Light Treatment," where I once had a quartz lamp treatment, but now houses the personnel department. Jews everywhere you look.

The foreign exchange department was converted into a procurement group, and that's where they distribute food to those clerks who can prove, based on their employee card, that they worked that week. According to this system, I would only be eligible for food rations at the end of next week. On the other hand, they give out the money right away. The first payment is about twenty-five hundred pengős. This comes in handy because I only brought a couple of thousand pengős with me, the proceeds from selling Nünüke's diamond earrings, but I want to get hold of all kinds of food ASAP so that I can take it over to my parents. The bank itself has been completely plundered, the vaults and the safety deposit boxes were all emptied out, as were the clerks' lockers, I'm told. I would like to ascertain right away whether any of your things I stashed with my colleague Károly Kiss are still there. But sadly that's not possible because you need all sorts of permissions and an escort. The entrance collapsed, you can only get into the area by climbing up a ladder from the courtyard. You also need a candle because it's pitch dark inside. Long and complex preparations are required. In addition, I need to find the key for the lock that my colleague Nusi Dobrovolny has hidden somewhere. I also have to get hold of Károly Kiss, because the locker is under his name, and if the things are still there, he's the only one who can remove them. Suffice it to say, nothing can be done about this matter today. They don't give me any work to do today. Instead, I will have to show up Monday morning in the teller's hall, where I will be assigned work.

I walk away disappointed. As I leave, someone mentions that there is a COFFEE HOUSE OPEN on Párizsi Street. I must have a look at it. I go there: you can buy an ersatz coffee without sugar for one pengő, and for two and a half pengős you even get saccharin in it. I happily guzzle down two large glassfuls, the hot liquid feels really good. Nothing else is available in the coffee house, but I am beside myself with joy, it feels so great to be in a clean — although cold — hall with tables and chairs, ashtrays on the tables. At one of the tables a man and woman are so wrapped up in one another it's as if the siege had never happened.

I slowly make my way toward Kőváry's place because I think you might have sent a letter there. But no such luck. The Kővárys are happy that I'm okay. Their apartment is in shambles, the windows are missing. They are living in the kitchen of a ground-floor apartment, but they have already started repairing a room overlooking the courtyard in their upstairs apartment. Both the Arrow Cross and the Russian soldiers looted the building, but according to Judit there are still quite a few of my things left. She tells me to come back tomorrow, Sunday, and we will gather what's left. As an aside, she invites me to have a meal with them when I come. The word *meal* is intoxicating. I've been worrying about what would happen to me, where and what I would eat. Cini has her meal at her aunt's, who has hardly any food and cannot invite guests. Ágnes and Marianne usually manage to get invited to a midday meal elsewhere, and as for supper, we just prepare something for ourselves at home.

It's getting dark by the time I get back to Cini's place from the Kővárys'. Everyone is already at home and in a good mood, making plans, arguing, and I feel so alone. Cini is an enthusiastic communist, which means she's completely foreign to me. I don't even feel like arguing with her. I'm tired and very, very depressed. The way I see it, there won't be a life worth living here, even fifty years from now. I'm also burdened by the looming prospect of starvation. I see no future in a career as a bank clerk. The typewriters have all been confiscated by the Russians, the furniture has been smashed to pieces, no business is being conducted, I don't know what use the bank would have for clerks. Cini and her friends are saying that it's time to start the collective art studio she's been planning for ages. Guszti Seiden is in charge of organizing it and has sent me a message that he is counting on me as a photographer. When discussing the studio, nobody mentions money, food or making a living, but unfortunately I'm not an idealist, especially not when I'm hungry. Back when I was in the bomb shelter, I kept thinking that it was time to change my vocation: I should either devote myself to photography or to taking care of children. However, I decide that for the time being I'll keep going to the bank to clear the rubble until something better comes along.

Sunday, February 25

I pick up my belongings at the Kővárys': my black toiletry bag, Dénes's trench coat, a bunch of towels, your neckties, your small alarm clock and a few of my dresses. The items that have gone missing are a pair of shoes and all my tea towels (brand new). Judit manages to get me some food from the Russians, flour for one hundred and eighty pengős, dried beans for fifty pengős, and I add them to my package. They give me a really good dinner: bean soup with vegetables and little dumplings and a noodle and potato dish. Judit and her family are leaving for Szeged. Her husband was offered a contract with the theatre there, which he readily accepted, since all the news coming from Szeged is good: they have plenty of food, you can buy everything and at bargain basement prices, and as much as you want. It makes me dizzy to hear her say that at the Szeged market you can buy a cheese Danish and potato scones.

At home on Hollán Street, we concoct a good supper. Everyone is bragging about what they ate for the noon meal. We can usually talk about food for hours and we're not the only ones to indulge in that pastime. Ágnes Schöngut is the winner of the dinner story prize, since she usually eats at their old cook's place and gets paprika chicken with *nokedli*[3] and cheesecake, etc. Sometimes she brings us leftovers.

---

3 Traditional Hungarian egg and flour dumplings.

Monday, February 26

I show up for work at the bank. They give me a bucket and a shovel: I have to scoop up the broken glass on the third floor and carry it down to the garbage heap in the courtyard. Despite all the weight I've lost, I find it relatively easy to climb the stairs. Unlike many others, I don't feel weak. The procurement group is distributing BREAD AND BACON today, but regrettably, I don't get any. The only people who qualify are those who worked the previous week and can show proof.

Luckily, I run into my colleague Károly Kiss, who lets me have his whole bread portion and half of his bacon, so I don't have to worry about starving to death this week. I get a lovely one-kilo white loaf, which I would dearly like to devour right away but will have to make last for a whole week. In addition, Károly Kiss offers me half of his morning snack: meatloaf and some fine homemade bread. I gobble it up immediately. I wrap my bread supply in a thin napkin and carry it in my knapsack all week long.

In the afternoon, I go to see Gizella. I find her in the Swedish hospital, the same place where I saw her at Christmastime. She bursts into tears of joy at the sight of me. Her roommates tell me how often she has spoken of me, how worried she'd been when she heard that the castle was under fire. The place is without heat, the quality of "nursing" is deplorable, yet even now they get served hot food THREE TIMES A DAY and BREAD EVERY DAY, which is a big deal. Otherwise, she is fine, except that she'd had a bit of frostbite on her feet. Pippancs, she has long since given up on you, was sure you were no longer alive, that you'd been hanged, shot, quartered, starved to death. This makes me extremely angry, but I don't get into an argument with her; however, I know that I will seek her out as little as possible even though the poor thing is desperate for company. That doesn't matter, I simply can't stand her negativity.

Tuesday, February 27

In the morning, I looked up Dr. Geiringer, who was recommended to me by the Becskis. Because I don't like drinking boiled water, I have decided to get a shot against typhoid fever. I pay fifty pengős for the first shot. Afterwards, I go to the bank to clear away glass, but by now I have figured out how to take it easy and to make as few trips up and down the stairs as possible. I skip out at the first opportunity and on Gizella's advice go to see a high official in the central bank to find out what happened to your typewriter that was in his keeping. As it turns out, the gentleman hasn't looked into the matter yet. He had put it in a safe but he's not too optimistic that it's still there since his bank was looted just as badly as ours. He tells me to come back in a couple days. Both the institution and Szabadság Square where it is located are looking all crumbled. On the way home, I drop in at the Hercegs'. They are okay, although their apartment has suffered a lot of damage. There is no news about Laci yet.

By now I am going to the Credit Bank on a regular basis to clear the rubble. The days unfold in a monotonous fashion, I am becoming more and more depressed and more and more alienated from the others. I have rounded up quite a bit of food for my parents, such as flour, lard, cooking oil, legumes, pasta, eggs, but for the time being there is no way of getting over to the other side of the river because boat traffic has been halted. Many people try to cross at Budafok, but that's a very long distance and I wouldn't be able to carry such a heavy load all that way. It's not worth it to make the trip with a lighter load, because I wouldn't be going for sentimental reasons but to supply my parents with food for a couple of weeks. I am going through a rough patch again because I cannot imagine what they might be eating. After all, Juci's family doesn't have any food either. Although Cini keeps repeating that I shouldn't worry about my parents, my mother must surely have come up with some solution that never even occurred to me, my mother is not the type to sit around twiddling her thumbs waiting for starvation or for a lucky break.

I'm starting to run out of things to wear because I only brought one change of clothes with me, and they are also dirty now. I was only able to wash them in cold or at most lukewarm water in the cellar, if there was ever any water for this purpose. Several times, Gizella shows up at Cini's early in the morning, when I am about to get up, each time with a different request. First off, she wants me to smooth things over with your brother Laci, who got his nose out of joint when she wouldn't lend him your typewriter (we haven't even brought it home from the bank yet, we only know that it's intact), and I should ask Laci to accept it. Next, she wants me to accompany her on a visit to the super at Szalay Street and threaten to report the woman to the Communist Party if she doesn't return the missing sheets. Her third request is that I go with her to the cellar on Szalay Street to retrieve some antique embroidered bellpulls before the Russians plunder the place. And so on. I never argue with her. I promise everything she asks and then I sabotage it. She forgets the whole thing by the next day and never mentions it again.

Sunday, March 4

A red-letter day: I HAD A BATH IN HOT WATER UP TO MY CHIN at Lilus's place, I ALSO WASHED MY HAIR while I was at it. For the first time in three months. If I add that I thoroughly washed all my dirty laundry in hot water, you will understand how this improved my well-being and my whole outlook on life, and I couldn't get too upset that it was a Sunday and everyone else was invited for lunch except me. Everyone I could have counted on to offer me a meal was living on the Buda side. Cooking is a difficult problem these days. Few households have a proper stove, most people cook over a drum stove, sometimes substituting tin boxes for pots, the smoke making their eyes water, and others put their pans on embers inside the tiled stove, some use kerosene heaters, and none of these solutions is ideal.

Tuesday, March 6

Another red-letter day: when I return to Hollán Street, Cini rushes up to tell me "GREGI IS ALIVE" and shows me a page torn out of Pista Havas's notebook that has your handwriting on it, which says, I AM FINE, I AM HEALTHY, IN BUCHAREST FOR THE TIME BEING. The note also contains Havas's address and a message that he can only be found at home early in the morning. Early the next day, I gallop over to Népszínház Street. The guy can't exactly recall your face, but he relays the message that you will be home very soon. He tries to talk me out of writing to you since you most likely won't be there by the time the letter arrives, because he, Havas, will only be travelling back to Bucharest at the end of the week. Fortunately, I've become the persevering sort, so I write you a short message nevertheless and take it over to him. Then I feverishly start looking for an apartment or a furnished room for the Tolnais. At this point, it's my idea that the four of us, including my parents, can live together, but finding an apartment is no easy task even at this early juncture.

In the meantime, I keep trying to sniff out where and when I might get over to Buda. People keep telling me that the wooden bridge at Sziget Street is finished already, "It will be open for traffic tomorrow." I've been hearing this for weeks, but it's just not happening. They are still working on the new bridge, and every once in a while troops march over it from Pest to Buda, but civilians are not even allowed to get close to the bridge.

One afternoon when I was in the vicinity of Sziget Street (I had some business nearby, I don't remember exactly what, all I told Cini was that I'd pop out for a minute and be back soon), I noticed that the bridge was decked out with flags. So, I head over that way to check out what the flags mean: a new Russian victory or perhaps that they're opening it up for traffic after all? But before I can even get close, Russian soldiers start herding me, along with many others, in the direction of the bridge. That's the first time I hear the words: "Davay, davay!"[4] and they're driving us toward the bridge. As luck would have it, there's a snowstorm, just like in bad movies, but today of all days, I don't have my dirty siege trench coat on, only my cherished black winter coat, which I'd worked long and hard to rid of siege dirt. They take us over to the island, where I'm handed a paintbrush and a crappy wash basin filled to the brim with bluish grey oil paint (a sample of the colour can still be seen on the aforementioned winter coat), and then they herd us to the Buda side of the bridge, where I SPEND THE WHOLE AFTERNOON PAINTING THE BRIDGE BLUISH GREY, in a snowstorm, with the wind in our faces, just a stone's throw away from my parents' place, opposite the Lukács Baths. And to this day, you can tell that the bridge was painted by yours truly, although I have to say, for a first bridge it's not too bad.

In the meantime, I find the whole thing amusing. The Russian supervisor doesn't like my painting technique. He grabs the brush from my hand and shows me the right way to do the job. After that, I start a conversation with a woman wearing pants; the poor thing was picked up on the street that morning and brought over here. She's been forced to paint the bridge ever since, but from the exterior of the bridge, standing on some sort of scaffolding, clinging to it with one hand and painting with the other. She complains to me that for hours now she has needed to pee, and each time she crawls onto the bridge and tries to make the Russian guard understand gesturing with her arms and legs why she needs to go to the bushes, the Russian chases her back. Obviously, he doesn't understand her, or maybe he worries that she'll try to skip out, but another possibility is that he doesn't understand why she couldn't pee right then and there. They make

4 Russian: Come on, come on!

us work until it gets dark (until about half past five), and that's when they tell us in Russian that we may go home, be it to Buda or to Pest. I'm so angry I could scream, because I could easily go see my parents now, but there's no point in arriving empty-handed and being a burden to them. Besides, maybe Cini's family would think that I got shot if I disappeared without even leaving a note. I head back to the Pest side in a huff. It's pitch dark by the time I get home, it's not a good time to be out on the streets. Cini's family is anxiously waiting for me and can't imagine what might have happened to me. When I recount where I've been and what I've been doing, they think I'm joking.

Thursday, March 8

What makes this day notable is that it's the first time I do community service. Everyone in every building is required to show up one day a week for community work, such as clearing rubble or hauling away trash or whatever else is needed. The powers that be take this seriously, although I don't remember what the punishment for non-compliance is. It's an awfully cold day with a bone-chilling wind. We need to appear at half past six in front of the office (on Tátra Street), from where we march to the administration building of District v. But first we spend a whole hour waiting around on the street. We wait around some more in front of the administration building, and then they take us over to the rubble on Klotild Street to haul away debris (before retreating, the Germans blew up an ammunition depot in a school without first alerting the neighbourhood, so half of Klotild Street was blown sky-high, and to this day your uncle Pali hasn't been dug out from under the rubble of one of the buildings).

We have just started the work when Russian soldiers arrive to take us God knows where. After a long march, we come to a sudden stop and find ourselves beside the Danube, past the Horthy Miklós Bridge, where they make us wait around for another half hour. Then they give each of us a damned heavy shovel and send us back. It turns out the only reason they made us march here was to pick up the shovels. When we reach Margit Bridge, I'm already fuming, so you can imagine my state when we get to Újpest Bridge, our destination. A few people try to slip away, but the Russian soldiers run after them and bring them back, laughing derisively. On the way to the site, they let us stop to rest once, and everyone had to pee right then and there, because the Russians didn't want anyone to go off anywhere more private, since in the past people had managed to sneak off that way. So, somewhere near the Újpest Bridge, just a few steps from the water, they made us dig a two-metre-deep, eighty-centimetre-wide ditch, using the shovels (*bien entendu*,[5] not spades). The ground was completely frozen; however, there were only three pickaxes and there were a hundred of us. Those three pickaxes kept changing hands, we fought over them. In the afternoon, a cartload of pickaxes arrived (to this day, I don't understand why they didn't make us march back to Horthy Bridge for the pickaxes!), but unfortunately they were three-person pickaxes, the kind that three men could barely lift. Nonetheless, I kept pickaxing away. The only problem was that the wind was blowing right through me, my nose kept dripping non-stop (another siege symptom), and I ended up with little icicles hanging from it. But then I got mollified, because loaves of bread were brought from Hajógyári Island and distributed to us. Each person got about three hundred to four hundred grams of bread, and it was nice and white, except unsalted like Russian breads usually are.

We worked until six in the evening, I must confess, and by the end my back was really sore, my hands were blistered from the pickaxe, but on the plus side I got a suntan, as if I'd been skiing at Turracher Höhe. Then we made our way slowly back. I should have gone to the administration building for my work ticket, but I simply wasn't willing to do it. It wasn't the work itself that made me mad but all

---

5 French: of course.

the unnecessary waiting around and the stupid marching back and forth. I decided that from now on, if at all possible, I would duck out of community service.

Meanwhile, I got my second typhoid shot. Normally, I tolerate shots well, hardly have any fever, feel okay overall. This time, however, the second shot gave me diarrhea, which was unpleasant because I wasn't well nourished, to say the least, and the diarrhea made me extremely weak, and of course there was no possibility of being careful about what I was eating. One ate whatever was available. I won't even mention the appalling state of the toilets in the Credit Bank. During this period, food for my parents keeps accumulating in my cupboard, and it's very distressing that I have no way of getting it over to them. Recently at the Credit Bank, we got some soy flour, salt, etc., all sorts of treasures that you can't even buy for money on the Buda side. On the Grand Boulevard, one can buy whatever one wishes. Although the stores are not yet open, there are vendors all up and down the street selling their wares from baskets, often asking a different price for the same item. The only thing that seems to have a standard price is matches: twelve pengős a box, but within days the price drops to six pengős, and I buy a big batch of them for the folks in Buda. I quickly buy up all kinds of things: thumbtacks, shoelaces, mother-of-pearl buttons and most of all NEWSPAPERS. The ability to shop sends me into an absolute frenzy.

I continue going to the bank to clear away rubble. The procurement group receives a new shipment of bread and bacon, which is supposed to be distributed among those who didn't receive any last time even though they were entitled to it. I am not entitled, only hungry, which prompts me to burst in on the head of the procurement group and keep pestering him until — after he'd kicked me out five times and I'd gone back for the sixth — he issues me some bread (for one hundred twenty pengős per kilo). It wasn't my turn, but I left him no choice. If the poor Spielberger ancestors knew that one of their descendants had deviated so much from tradition, they'd be turning in their family crypt. And that's how I HAVE BREAD for a few days.

One fine day while clearing rubble, I have the misfortune of running into Auer, who tells me that he has already started getting the Marketing Department on the first floor up and running again. They don't have typewriters yet, but I should come upstairs and work for him anyway. I foolishly agree to this, and from that day on I have to sit in an unheated, dusty and dirty office from nine to about half past three. I'm so frozen that my arms and legs turn shades of blue and green and purple. It's so cold that not even my siege dress can keep me warm. From time to time, I sneak out to drink a bit of ersatz coffee in the coffee house on Párizsi Street, in the hope it'll warm me up. By the way, these days I also drop by the Szabadság coffee house every morning, where in the dark and drafty room, behind broken shutters full of holes, they serve ersatz coffee with sweetener for two and a half pengős, and you can open your knapsack at a table, take out your bread and bacon, and eat some using your pocketknife. Several times, complete strangers asked me for a bite of bread or bacon. Some would even offer money for the bread (but I DIDN'T GIVE THEM ANY! You won't believe how greedy and selfish one becomes when hungry). One time when I was waiting in line at the tellers' hall of the Credit Bank, I took out my bread, and an unfamiliar colleague sidled up to me and asked for some. Of course, I obliged, but I found it strange that she'd ask since she'd been given the same amount as I, in fact, she must have had an easier time acquiring hers, because she didn't have to fight for it the way I had. Lately, I'm often aware of how selfish I've become. This realization saddens me and makes me feel even more disconnected from people. On another occasion, a well-dressed old man stops me on the street saying that there must be some food in that bulging knapsack of mine and could I give him any. I take pity on him, although at the time all I have are carrots. The old man tells me in a disappointed tone that he's not able to chew them.

In those days, word got out that at the Újpest market you could buy carrots and other vegetables, but you'd need to go there on foot, and the market was only open two days a week. Then I learn of an address on Király Street where you can buy vegetables in the backyard. Next, I discover a vegetable shop across from the stock market on Nádor Street, but all they have is celeriac for twenty-eight pengős a kilo. I purchase some and have raw celeriac for lunch several days in a row. Now I can't even look at it anymore. Carrots are my mainstay, they're what I take to the bank for lunch whenever they're readily available. At Cini's apartment, we usually eat pearl barley, sometimes prepared sweet, and once we made it with a paprika and onion sauce. It's a special event when we manage to get hold of some potatoes (they're eighty pengős a kilo, if ever there are any to be had!). By the evening, I am ravenous, having had only celeriac or carrots for lunch. I attack dinner and devour it. If I'm able to eat my fill, a half hour later I'm sure to have an awful stomach ache and end up losing all I've eaten. This is distressing because I'm convinced that I have developed gastroptosis.

Procuring firewood is a daily chore. You try to dig usable pieces of wood from the rubble, from the debris, and take them home to be burned. It's a common sight: well-dressed ladies and gentlemen dragging huge beams behind them with the aid of a piece of rope or wire. We usually go to the banks of the Danube to hunt for wood. On one occasion, I bring home not just wood but also some cotton batten that I found in an overturned crate, which we can use as kindling. That crate and numerous similar broken ones nearby contain thousands of empty glass vials, many of them smashed to smithereens despite the careful packaging. Among the ruins of the warehouse buildings, there's a lot of merchandise strewn about, some of it completely soaked, the rest shattered. One time as I am rummaging for usable wood and lift a long weather-beaten plank, I spot the corpse of a woman with dyed canary-yellow hair, lying face down, but by now the sight doesn't faze me a bit.

I'm really bored with the office, especially since I'm constantly freezing, but I show up for work anyway because I often meet people there who are travelling to Romania, and I slip letters for you, addressed to Liechtmann, into their pockets. All this time I keep sniffing around for a way to get over to Buda. I also go to see Old Nádas, because I heard at Miksa Street that he'd been there looking for us after the siege and left his address. He lives with his younger brother and his wife on the top floor of the building at 41 Katona József Street. He is incredibly old and ugly. His hands and legs shake, and he just sits there the whole day wearing an offended expression, his mouth turned down at the corners, detesting the world. Nothing interests him. All he does is complain and lament, how everything he owned is lost and gone. He was taken to the ghetto from a building under papal protection (such things really did exist), and during the bombing he stayed upstairs in an apartment because there was no room left in the shelter. Both he and Uncle Gyula listen with sour looks on their faces as I tell them how splendidly Béla managed all the way through the siege and how well he supported himself. They are miffed because the two of them had been predicting for years that Béla would end up on the gallows and that he couldn't take a step without their help and that he would pay a high price for not heeding his not just wiser but indeed infallible elders.

They hadn't received any news of Béla from Christmas until my visit (in early March). They didn't know if he was dead or alive, and what's more, according to what they heard from Buda, it was more likely that he was no longer alive. Yet I couldn't discern any signs of joy or contentment now that I'd brought them such good news of Béla. Instead, they seemed disappointed that their dire predictions had not come true. I was used to the Nádas way, but in this instance I found their behaviour appalling, considering that these days most of us are overjoyed to run into people we hardly knew and to see that they've come out of this whole circus alive. Nonetheless, from then on Old Nádas is a frequent visitor at Hollán Street. He keeps grilling us about what Béla has been up to, in the hope of learning something incriminating. Of course, I'm very careful to make sure he won't find out anything of the kind. I stay mum about Irén and about the fact that Béla has been living with her all this time, it's enough that he finds this out when he goes to her place for a visit. Let him have a stroke there, not here. How would we women manage to carry him down from the fourth floor? Old Nádas usually visits us in the evening, while Gizella prefers to come in the early morning, so my roommates start dropping hints about my moving out, they feel our small room can't accommodate so much visitor traffic. Or they propose the solution that Old Nádas and Gizella move in together. Joking aside, the fact remains that this is all very depressing, especially since I'm not in the best of moods anyway these days. I feel I fit in here less and less. I'm starting to heartily detest everyone, and I'm constantly worried that my parents are starving over on the other side of the river.

In the meantime, I follow up on my idea of getting training as a child care worker under the new regime. I get in touch with Kati Schöpflin, the head of a daycare centre in District IV, and tell her about my aspirations. Mrs. Anna (Neuwirth) Vértes (the sister-in-law of Kató Vértes), a well-respected educator, is at the centre when I visit. They try to convince me to start working there right away because I'm badly needed. They cannot pay me "for the time being," but I can get one meal a day, the same that's issued to the children by National Assistance. Well, the offer doesn't suit me. It would not be sufficient to support me, let alone my parents. But I keep mulling it over for a long time, because I would dearly like to work with children.

Auer is planning to leave for Debrecen and tells me he might go on to Bucharest from there, and he's dreaming about never coming back. His appearance is rather neglected, and it's clear that he's starving. Actually, all the directors of the Credit Bank walk around looking like vagabonds. Beards have come into fashion — God knows why — everybody is sporting one. Each time I look at Director Wertheimstein, I have to laugh: with a pointed goatee and wearing a threadbare winter coat, a dirty Basque beret, and with a bag hanging from his shoulder, he looks exactly like Doré's illustration of Don Quixote de la Mancha. One day we get word that you can buy a plate of food for one pengő — no coupon required — at the soup kitchen operating in the building (if it can even be called a building) of the former Erzsébet Square dairy shop. On hearing this news, the whole bank empties out. I dash over with my stunningly beautiful colleague Alexa Herresbacher, but by the time we get there a long line has formed. We recognize the illustrious directors of the Credit Bank, such as Auer, Eberwein, Kövy and Richard Frank, etc., in their shabby clothes, standing in line with mess tins in hand, hoping to get a portion of watery bean soup. Of course, we aren't given any utensils. Alexa hasn't brought anything along, so the two of us share my mess tin and spoon, and later Auer borrows my spoon as well. From that day on, I sneak out every noon hour to go there, but I'm not always lucky because whenever they serve some better fare there is none left for those of us without a coupon (coupons are only handed out at city hall to individuals who can prove they are entitled). On Sunday, I also walked over there from Hollán Street, but without success, because that day they served savoy cabbage, and people snapped it up fast.

Gizella is creating a big problem for me because the Swedish hospital is supposed to close and she has no place to go. A few boarding houses have reopened, and I check them out one by one, but none of them is willing to admit an old woman. They lack the staff, they explain, which means the guests are obliged to do their own cleaning and even fetch water for themselves from downstairs. The most they might provide in the way of meals is breakfast — tea without sugar — and there's no heating either. Rooms that are rented by the month are also scarce for old women, because the owners would rather rent to people who can help with the household chores. Laci Tolnai has resurfaced, but it seems that one cannot count on him. Gizella asks me several times if she could stay at Cini's, and I have to explain to her each time that at present Cini only has one small room that is shared by the four of us (as she could have seen with her own eyes during her morning visits), with two people sleeping in each bed. But I can tell that she is not listening and takes it badly that I don't offer her a space in Cini's apartment.

I'm in a bad mood because every morning I go over to Hollán with the hope that you're already there, and every time I end up disappointed and angry. To make matters worse, I've been having diarrhea for days, most likely from the typhoid shot. All the running to the toilet at night tires me out so much that instead of going to the office in the morning, I lie in bed, and when I feel a bit better I get up and tidy the cupboard. Out of the blue, néni Ilus (who'd been bombed out) contacts me to say that she's seen civilians walking around on the bridge. At this news, I hastily pack up the food, putting lard, oil, eggs, flour, semolina, beans, into a knapsack, bags and baskets. On the fly, I even purchase some outrageously expensive pastry flour from a woman in the building, and I dash down to Sziget Street. But she had it all wrong, there are no civilians on the bridge, only women carrying rocks to build the embankment as their community service. I hang around feeling dejected and don't dare move closer lest I get pressed into service like the last time. I'm almost overcome by the Spielberg-Oettingen impulse, and I want to turn back, but I happen to strike up a conversation with an interesting middle-aged woman who occasionally talks to the soldiers in Russian. I lament that I'm not able to take the food over to my starving relatives, and she says that she's in the same boat. She has been trying to go across for days without success. Now there's a faint hope of getting to the other side, since one of the Russian soldiers seems approachable, and she will try to make a deal with him: we would help to carry rocks in exchange for being allowed to cross the bridge in the evening. She is in negotiations with a rather funny-looking Russian, who has a big moustache and a pockmarked face. He assigns her the job of supervisor and explains that if we work diligently until the evening, we can then cross over to Buda. At this, I put my belongings down by the railing, in a place where I can keep an eye on them, and start carrying the rocks, which is no small feat in my weakened state. The guard lets us take rests quite often, and in the meantime quite a few volunteers, all wanting to reach the Buda side, have joined in the work. Time drags on, but we'll soon find out if we'll be allowed to cross or if the pockmarked guy was only having us on. At last, six o'clock arrives, they make us line up, and we set out. In moments, I AM ON THE BRIDGE, but I still don't dare to believe it because they might send us back from the island, or even from the opposite shore. When finally I AM IN BUDA, I start running to avoid being sent back.

It's getting dark, and the front door is locked, of course. I have to bang on it a long time before someone lets me in and grills me about whom I'm visiting and why. At Juci's, they greet me with loud cheers. They'd heard that not a soul could cross the Danube, but knowing how "shrewd" I am they couldn't imagine that in all this time I'd be unable to find a way to get over to the Buda side. I unpack the food onto the table, and they stand there gazing at it with awe. Buda is so dead, they say, there's not even any bartering going on because people don't dare leave their houses. The Russians are plundering relentlessly and swept through Juci's building several times but DIDN'T ENTER HER APARTMENT. Cini had it right: You really don't need to worry about Nünüke. When their food supply ran out, she simply set out for Filatorigát, where she jumped on a local train and travelled to Pomáz. There she exchanged her wedding band for eight kilos of bread flour, potatoes, cornmeal and beans, and left for home lugging a fifteen-kilo parcel. Fortunately, when she got off at Filatorigát, she met bácsi Gólya, who helped her carry the heavy bag home. For her part, Juci goes to villages along the Danube, such as Tahi, but money doesn't buy you anything, so she exchanges children's clothes for food. This is all terribly exhausting, because as I mentioned, the local train stops at Filatorigát and you need to schlep everything on foot from there. Now they'll have provisions for a couple of weeks at least. But if I don't manage to get back to Pest, they'll be stuck with one more mouth to feed. Juci, however, is happy about this possibility and encourages me not to return to Pest, that way the two of us could go bartering together. But I still haven't given up hope that one fine day YOU will show up.

The next day I visit Béla and Irén, who are fine. Béla has a job, and Irén's belly is nice and round by now. They have everything they need and even give me some of their firewood. On the third day, I walk over to see the Reverend in Hűvösvölgy to tell him not to count on me. On this occasion, I find walking difficult. I am distressed, because I worry that my weakened state is due to malnutrition and that from now on I will keep tottering about. Later I realize that it has to do with the diarrhea and springtime lethargy. Sztehlo receives me with open arms, wants to know what's going on in Pest and offers me money again. This time I accept it: I get a lump sum payment of one thousand pengős as a reward for having allowed them to shelter me and feed me. I call on Piroska, and the two of us go to visit Jancsi Máté, who is sick in bed at his father-in-law's apartment. This time I go to look at the burned-out buildings, a depressing sight. I catch a glimpse of Kecske Street from a distance, and it's in the same wonderful shape.

In the meantime, Nünüke went to the District III administration building and received a piece of paper entitling her to move back to her old apartment. But what condition is that apartment in? They gave us a requisition for sugar beets, but we only pick them up once, because they're so bad it's not worth wasting shoe leather on them. I also look up the Szántó family, who used to live on Kecske Street and hid some of my belongings. They now live in a nice apartment on Ürömi Street. My books, photography equipment and even my English teapot are intact. They serve me a bean dish, which I really appreciate because I'm very hungry. These days it's rare that anyone offers you food, but it seems I'm so skinny that they take pity on me. Another time I drop in on Boci on Uszály Street, where she's living with her mother. They too offer me something to eat, a memorable experience: A HUGE SLICE OF BREAD WITH CHEESE SPREAD AND BEET SALAD. Of course, it's imitation cheese spread, made from riced potatoes, mustard, chopped onions and oil. I ask for the recipe right away, because it's tasty and filling. Unlike the traditional beet salad, this one is made with raw beets. I really like it, and I've been preparing it that way ever since.

Every evening, I walk down to the bridge to see if they'll let me go across or to look for the pock-faced guy who could arrange for me to go over the next day. But to no avail. Russian secret police officers wearing green caps control the head of the bridge, and they are very strict. I watch as a large group of people comes from the direction of Pest, carrying hefty bundles, and an officer chases them back to Pest. There's a man who's been skulking around, trying to make a deal with the officers, and I see him craftily manage to slip into the group from Pest and let himself be chased to the Pest side with them. For now, crossing over at Sziget Street seems hopeless, and I am considering an acquaintance's idea, namely walking to Filatorigát, taking the local train to Szentendre, then walking to Monostor, crossing the island on foot to Horány, proceeding by boat to Dunakeszi-Alag, and finally from there to Pest by train. This scheme seems a bit too adventurous for me, so I'd rather wait, since sooner or later they must open the bridge. In the meantime, they have repaired the Ferenc József Bridge, which has suffered the least damage, for although the middle part is missing, the two pillars at either end are intact, but they don't let me pass there either. However, there have been precedents for people finally being let through after having hung around for a long time. Therefore, one fine day I set out in the direction of Ferenc József Bridge, just on spec, but when I reach Fő Street, I hear that the Ferenc József Bridge is now open.

And so, after a very long trek, I arrive at the Credit Bank and learn that Auer has left without my being able to give him a letter for you. Pest has changed a lot in the few days I've been away: a bunch of food stores have opened, IT IS POSSIBLE TO SHOP, albeit at exorbitant prices. My place in the bank is gone, because after Auer's departure, the Oversight Committee moved into his office. But at the last minute, Rapoch shows up. I run into him in the big hall of the accounting department, and we embrace each other warmly, to the great delight of our colleagues. Immediately, HE INVITES ME FOR THE NOON MEAL at his mother-in-law's place, on Wekerle Sándor Street. I get a really good meal, and I'm proud that at long last I'm the one who's been invited somewhere, not just Marianne and Ágnes. Afterwards, I shoulder my bag and head for home. I am sweltering, the bag is heavy and the morning trek tired me out.

I can hardly wait to get home. I'm almost there and am at the corner of Hollán Street and Lipót Boulevard when I notice a big crowd in front of Glasner Bakery. Although it's not my habit, I walk over there to find out what's going on, and I see an old woman lying on a bench with people surrounding her. When I get closer, I realize that the old woman is none other than GIZELLA. Her eyes are open, she's muttering something, but when I talk to her, she doesn't respond. I ask the bystanders to keep an eye on her so she doesn't fall off the bench. I rush to the apartment to fetch Cini, and the two of us run back to the bench. By that time, a woman we know is trying to give her some water, but Gizella won't drink it. The woman recounts that G. had been complaining of diarrhea. They were having lunch together only half an hour ago at the Joint, and that's when G. suddenly took sick. I ask her to remain by G.'s side. Cini and I hurry over to the Swedish hospital, which is about to be shut down. We are given the runaround while looking for a doctor or nurse, finally we find a stretcher in the courtyard, which we grab and race back to the Glasner corner.

Gizella is still not back to normal. Her eyes are open and she's talking but not making any sense. We put her on the stretcher and carry her to the Swedish hospital, where we're forced to halt in the entryway because we can't carry her up the stairs. After a lengthy wait, we find a nurse to help us take the stretcher upstairs. It's impossible to get hold of a doctor or anyone in charge because everything is topsy-turvy in the hospital since it is about to close. Later that day, I return to see Gizella: she's asleep and breathing evenly. There appears to be only one other patient in the ward, an old woman who has no relatives and keeps weeping all day, wondering aloud what will become of her when the hospital closes. Then, from one of the dark corners the death rattle of a filthy, ugly old woman can be heard. There's a huge puddle under her bed because no one has been cleaning up for days. The weeping woman tells me that Gizella has found a room to let by the month and plans to move there tomorrow. I'm convinced that Gizella won't last until morning given the way she looked when I first came upon her on the street.

I dig up Laci Tolnai's address and rush over there, but nobody's home. I leave a note asking him to come and get me at Hollán, if not tonight then first thing tomorrow so that we can visit Gizella together. In the evening, I drop in to see her one more time. Your mother is still asleep. Next morning, I wait for Laci but he doesn't show, so I leave a message asking him to follow later and I head to the hospital. Gizella comes to meet me. She's in fine form, full of beans, has been up since six o'clock and has washed her lingerie. She has no memory of the previous day's incident and can't believe that we carried her here on a stretcher all by ourselves. She intends to move into the room she's renting with the Brichta family on Szent István Boulevard. Her new hosts will have someone fetch her belongings.

It seems that the Ferenc József Bridge will be in operation from now on, but considering how long the walk is, I only go to visit my parents once a week, on the weekend. Each time I go, I carry a big bundle, because it's still difficult to get food on the Buda side. The next Sunday, March 25, Nünüke and I make our way up Gellért Hill to the villa on Bérc Street to see if any of our belongings are still there. Indeed, we do manage to salvage a few items from what's strewn about, I even find one of my pillows, albeit full of shards of glass. Nonetheless, I'd like to take it home as it's quite the treasure since we have hardly any bed linen. The superintendent warns us that we'd better disinfect it first because the villa had been occupied by lice-ridden Russians. For the time being, I leave it there in the cellar. We cram everything into the only piece of hand luggage that survived, although it's badly battered. And pushing a sturdy stick through the handle, Nünü and I each grab an end and tote the bag home. On the way, I point out Pauler Street to Nünüke. The sight of it makes her sick, even though by this time the street has been fully cleared.

At the bank, they are cleaning the rooms where my department used to be located, and gradually the whole staff has returned, except for poor Mr. Fränkel, who was so very optimistic about our survival. He was taken to Teleki Square last November, and there has been no trace of him since. A bad omen. By now I even have a typewriter, although it's only a decrepit Underwood, but at least I no longer need to line up to beg for the use of a typewriter to transcribe dictations. As I mentioned before, I spend my weekends in Buda.

Saturday, March 31

I cross to the Buda side once again. Juci receives me with the news that my cousin Béla had a small accident, a grenade detonated while they were clearing rubble and his whole body was peppered with shrapnel. He is currently staying home in his apartment. I go over there, but by that time he has been transported to the Siesta Sanatorium, because it turns out his injuries were not as minor as initially thought. By the next day, he develops such a high fever and is in such terrible pain that he can't even move. If he wants to turn over, he has to hoist himself up by means of a long leather strap secured at the end of the bed. Blood keeps seeping through his dressings, and his bed is soaked in it. By the third day of his fever, he is delirious. Old Nádas, his father, stands at the foot of his bed all day watching over him. In his feverish state, Béla beckons me over and quietly asks me to summon a neurologist because he worries that he's going mad, and all I can make out from his mumbling is that he fears he might kill someone. I reassure him that Dr. Hajdú is on his way. He repeats several times, "Get rid of my father!" (This is not a bad idea — it's a shame no one thought of it ten to twenty years earlier!) Irén is in her sixth month and behaves admirably, stays calm and doesn't lose her head. Only later did we learn that she was unaware of the great danger Béla was facing.

This week I go to check on him every other day. It seems likely that the young man will die of his injuries. The doctors appear to concur on this opinion, and they must have shared it with Béla's father because Old Nádas starts pestering me to tell him exactly where in the garden Auntie Böske buried the family jewels. I lie and say that I don't know, at which point he tries to talk me into coaxing it out of Béla. There's no way I will tell him the location, because if, God forbid, Béla should die, when the old guy learns that his son and Irén aren't married he won't leave a crumb for Irén or their coming child. Later Béla gets somewhat better, but he still has a high fever, and his wounds are worsening rather than improving. He asks me to look up his former boss, Mr. Gara, as well as Dr. Hajdú in Pest. I oblige him. Gara sheds tears of joy upon learning that Béla is still alive, they thought he'd perished during the siege. Hajdú, whom I'd met once before at the district administration building, has the same frosty demeanour as ever but is looking leaner. Nevertheless, he receives me quite amicably. He promises to visit Béla as soon as he can.

Friday, April 13

Cini and I are summoned for community service again. We have to clear the debris from the cellar of a building on Légrády Károly Street, it's dirty, hard and unpleasant work. We keep at it until three in the afternoon and then skip out. By this time, lunch is no longer an issue because I can get a meal in the bank for one pengő, I just need to supply my own spoon. The food is lousy, of course, but it provides a convenient solution to the problem of the noon meal. Bread is available everywhere now, except it's awfully expensive: fifty to sixty pengős. All along, I keep writing you letters and trying to send them with anyone who even might be heading your way.

Saturday, April 14

Béla's leg took a turn for the worse and it needed to be amputated. His left leg had to be cut off above the knee. His fever went down immediately afterwards. I am extremely upset. Old Nádas is fit to be tied because he thinks the amputation was too hasty, he would have liked to get a second opinion, but of course that's what happens when no one seeks his advice or approval. In any case, it looks like Béla has been saved.

On one occasion I visit Dr. Anna Szívós. Their garden has been all tidied up, we sit on lawn chairs on the sunny terrace and eat fritters. I would be enjoying myself immensely if Anna weren't giving me a psychological exam. She tries out the new Hermann test[6] on me, which involves answering a lot of questions such as: Have I become a misanthrope since the siege, what my weight was before and after the siege, if there were changes in my behaviour, in my love life, in my bodily functions, how hard it was to endure starvation, etc., etc.

I spend Sunday afternoon with Béla at the sanatorium, his fever has returned. He is aware that this is a bad sign; it most likely means that the amputation was performed too late. He has been waiting for me impatiently: he asks me to arrange for him to marry Irén on the spot. To make this happen, I don't return to the bank in Pest the next day, rushing instead from office to office. They send out a medical officer to certify whether Béla's condition is grave enough to justify such a wedding and thus waive the need to apply for a special dispensation. Sadly, the medical officer determines that Béla's condition is indeed so critical that he issues a written permit for a "Deathbed Wedding." This document opens doors everywhere. I immediately take it to the justice of the peace, and he and an assistant show up

---

6 Imre Hermann (1889–1984), Hungarian psychoanalyst, created a test to look at the effects of wartime deprivation.

at the sanatorium that very afternoon. As they are about to start the ceremony, they find out that Irén is still a minor and they cannot obtain her parents' permission because her father is somewhere in Somogy County. Fortunately, the justice of the peace is an extremely decent and intelligent man. He whispers to me that he will come back tomorrow, by which time there should be a parental permission available, it's no business of his where we get it or who signs it. Consequently, the wedding takes place the following day, but I am not present, because I have to go back to the office. One of the witnesses is Lívia, the other is a young doctor from the sanatorium. Béla's condition doesn't improve, so the doctors try giving him a blood transfusion. They obtain the blood from Jóska, the young railway guy who Béla had dragged out from under the rubble.

The day after that, I call on Gara, Hajdú and Grünberger, begging each of them to go see Béla, who has been feeling miserable since the operation. It would really cheer him up to have good friends visit. The only one to oblige is Gara, who in spite of being old and sick walks to the sanatorium to visit Béla and tries to reassure him about his prospects. So far, neither of the two physicians has paid him a visit, although they both promised they would.

Thursday, April 19

It's a great day because your FIRST LETTER PACKED WITH DETAILS arrived, long and written in pencil. It's cause for jubilation, although I'm unpleasantly surprised to learn that you're in hospital, a possibility that never even crossed my mind. I'm really worried about what exactly is happening with you. I would like to go there to be by your side, and I'm really upset that because of all sorts of complications I don't dare to go.

The next day I have community service: transporting waste to a dumpsite by the Danube. The garbage has been accumulating for the past half year from the same Swedish hospital that gave shelter to your mother during the siege. I never would have fathomed that there could be so much difference between kinds of garbage. A more disgusting sight is unimaginable, even to someone who has trained herself to handle such sights. You can find everything here, from filthy cotton balls to rotting mattress remnants, and to top it all, we have to push our carts against the wind, which blows all of the filth back into our faces. The whole scene reminds me of a novel by Louis-Ferdinand Céline. I can't skip out this time and need to keep working until 3:30. All the while, I am trying to figure out a way I could still travel to Bucharest to see you.

My friends complain that I've become very sour and bitter, and truth be told, I feel that I don't fit in with them anymore. On one occasion, Cini bought me a ticket to an Imre Ungár[7] concert. Considered objectively, it was a beautiful concert, but it couldn't hold my attention for one second, all I could think of was that we still didn't have a place to live or any idea what our future holds.

On a Sunday in April, God knows why, I decide to go to the Farkasrét Cemetery to try to find Auntie Böske's grave because no one has gone to visit it since the funeral. Right away, Irén volunteers to accompany me. We saunter over there along a beautiful route. The cemetery office can't tell me the grave's location, since all the records have been burned to ashes. We search for it for hours based on our recollections but without success, so eventually we give up. By the next Sunday, however, I find out the grave's number from Old Nádas and I go there again, this time by myself. The grave is in a terrible state, wheel tracks running over it, the cross is broken, indeed the whole cemetery is busted and shattered, with shards and shrapnel everywhere. But it is still frequented by a lot of people, which you can tell from the many flowers left at the graves, and THE BIRDS ARE

7 Imre Ungár (1909–1972), a famous Jewish Hungarian classical pianist who survived the war in hiding.

SINGING AGAIN just like last year. (Forgive me, my Pipus, for the literary allusion.)

It is around this time that my bleakest period begins: everything turns out badly, whatever I attempt, my efforts are in vain, and I keep bawling my eyes out in despair. I try to look up Levente Thury, but he is not at home. (I invested half a day in this mission, going on foot all the way to Németvölgy Road.) I write you a long letter and take it to the man who brought me yours, but he'd left suddenly, a day earlier than planned. This irked me, but I got over it. Then I decide to entrust it to Mr. Polgár, so I go over to his place, but Mr. Polgár had left that morning suddenly as well, as he'd had an unexpected opportunity to go by car. I'm on the verge of marching down Nádor Street in the middle of the day, crying, and I don't mean just whimpering but bawling at the top of my lungs, like this: BOO HOO HOO, boo hoo hoo! As to apartments, everyone is giving me the brush off. Old Nádas is no help, says he can't walk any distance.

Then comes the big hullabaloo for May 1. I walk to Szabadság Square with Cini and Lívia. When we get there, those two go up to the balcony to take pictures, while I stay down on the street in the crowd and keep on crying and crying, and I hate the whole damn thing. I'm also cold. I meet Miki Gimes and Zebi, so I have to stop my crying but fortunately only for a short time. On Children's Day, Cini and I head to the zoo to take pictures, but it is overcast. I'm tired and hungry, and this doesn't hold my attention either. Dead tired, we make our way home. Cini is lucky because she can get excited about things. The next morning, we are still in bed when there's a knock on the door. When it opens, who should walk in but Laci. We scream like maniacs, everyone is in tears, including Laci. This is the end of our "girls residence." Marianne and Ágnes move out, and all of a sudden I'm homeless too, although Cini and Laci urge me to stay. Fortunately, their neighbour Olgi Hermann, who hasn't heard from her husband yet, kindly invites me to move in with her. I'm comfortable at Olgi's, and we get along very well, but from then on, I cry even more, as it seems I can't bear it that other women's husbands have already come home.

My Pippancs, I will end my diary here, because from this point on you basically know everything from my letters.

The siege diary was hard to write, but I feel good that I did it and managed to get a lot of stuff out of my system that was weighing me down. Try to read between the lines. Goodbye, Kispipi, I will stop now!

Mrs. Margit Tolnai (née Kassai)
Budapest, May 10, 1945

Afterword

I knew Kas (the nickname used by Margit Tolnai, née Kassai) over the last eighteen years of her life. Much of the information here about Kas's life after her diary ends was provided by her daughter, Frances Tolnai, as well as a few close friends of Frances who shared some of their memories of Kas. Frances, Kas's only child, has the original of her mother's manuscript about the siege of Budapest and about the events during the eight to nine months preceding the siege during World War II. This manuscript, which her mother used to refer to as the "siege diary," was probably typed by Kas herself in 1945.

When Kas's husband, György Tolnai, returned from labour service after the war, he resumed his pre-war position with the Massey-Harris Company, who transferred him to France in 1946, and the couple moved to Lille. In 1946–47, Kas was employed as a multilingual secretary at the Paris Peace Conference. At the end of 1947, her husband was transferred again to the Massey-Harris head office in Toronto, Ontario, Canada. In November 1947, just before their departure date, Frances was born prematurely in Paris. This delayed Kas's departure from France, but she joined her husband in Toronto when Frances was four months old. Frances was named after Kas's maternal grandmother, Franciska Goldschmidt. The family lived in Toronto until György, who by then had taken a position with the World Health Organization (WHO) of the United Nations, was transferred to Alexandria, Egypt, to the WHO Eastern Mediterranean Regional Office (EMRO). For two years, Kas and Frances lived in Alexandria, where Kas learned to speak Arabic. In 1959, Kas and her daughter returned to Toronto, from which time Kas and György were separated. According to Canadian law, they did not divorce, although according to Hungarian law the marriage had dissolved. György Tolnai continued to work for the WHO and was eventually relocated to Switzerland. From 1962 to 1966, Frances lived with her father in Geneva and attended the International School of Geneva. György Tolnai continued to live in Switzerland until his death in 1990.

As far back as Frances can remember, at least in her own lifetime, her parents did not consider themselves Jewish. According to her birth certificate, Frances is Protestant. She was in her teens when she first heard about being Jewish, and it was not from her parents. Kas and György took their daughter to various churches, although never to a synagogue. Many immigrant parents did not tell their children about their Jewish ancestry to protect them from antisemitism. Kas did share some stories with Frances about her life during the war. Sometimes Kas talked to her daughter about how she had gone into hiding after the Arrow Cross Party took control of Hungary. She told her how, quite by accident, she obtained work at the Red Cross and how it was through the Red Cross, with many other volunteers, that Kas cared for orphaned Jewish children in different children's homes, which were being run by the Lutheran pastor Gábor Sztehlo. Kas also told Frances about how, during the siege of Budapest, day after day, she fetched water and food for the residents and the staff of the children's homes. She also described to Frances the challenges of travelling between Buda and Pest when there were no longer bridges connecting the two parts of the city, to deliver food to her parents, who were in hiding.

One of Kas's favourite adages was "we must keep rowing." To this day, Frances thinks of her mother's maxim, which means: we must try, we must strive to do what we can. According to her own description, Kas was rather timid in her youth; later in life, she learned to overcome her fears and became strong-minded and unswerving. She raised her daughter to be brave and to learn to dispel fear and sadness. Kas considered it infinitely more important that Frances become a good person than that she achieve awards or excel in her academic pursuits. In Frances's view, her mother was a woman of great wisdom; she was imaginative, resourceful, clever, quick-witted and down to earth. Frances would describe her father as having intellectual wisdom and her mother as having life wisdom; she clearly saw life wisdom as the greater wisdom. As becomes abundantly clear from her memoir, Kas was able to solve all manner of problems she encountered.

This is not to say that Kas did not also have her share of intellectual wisdom, evident in her facility with language. In her resumé from 1974, Kas notes that during her years in secondary school, she studied classical Greek and Latin, as well as modern languages. Kas enrolled in university courses to study various modern languages and literature. Along with Hungarian, she spoke and read English, French and German. For decades, Kas worked at the Department of Political Economy at the University of Toronto. She was first hired as a secretary; later on, she became the department's business officer, and then for several years, she was the administrative assistant to the chair of the department. She enjoyed working in the academic atmosphere of the university.

Frances's close friends who had the opportunity to become acquainted with Kas described her as somewhat reserved, kind and open-minded. When I first met Kas, she was already in her early seventies. I had the pleasure of being introduced to a simply but tastefully dressed woman with nicely coiffured short white hair. She was pleasant, relaxed and seemed interested in meeting me. Her face would light up when she smiled.

Kas loved to read. Among other things, she read contemporary literature in German and French; she did not want to lose her language skills while she was living in a predominantly English-speaking milieu. She was an ardent Scrabble player, played at Scrabble clubs and took part in Scrabble competitions. She also enjoyed playing the piano. When she came to visit us and saw our piano, she sat down and started to play. She played for a long time and with obvious enjoyment, first from the sheet music she saw on the piano, then by heart. She played both Hungarian folk songs and classical pieces. She adored Hungarian poetry. Several times she telephoned me to say that all evening she kept recalling a line or a stanza from a poem but could not remember the poem's title or author. Would I know from the line, the title or author of the poem?

She enjoyed good food, as is apparent in her memoir. To celebrate Kas's seventy-fifth birthday, Frances and I and our respective partners organized a weekend at a resort where we treated Kas to the food, poems and music we knew she most enjoyed. When we celebrated my PhD defence, Kas immediately joined the impromptu Hungarian "girls' choir" and sang enthusiastically with us. She was in her late seventies by then. She always seemed to have a good time in the company of people many decades her junior.

Kas had a lifelong love of photography. We learn from her memoir that during the autumn of 1944 she was a photographer's apprentice. A few of the pictures she took during and just after the siege have survived. Kas won awards for her photographs and several of them were published in magazines. Her specialty was portrait photography. Numerous albums are filled with black-and-white photos of her daughter. She was also a film buff. If we wanted to know what was being shown in the movie theatres, what was worth seeing, we asked Kas. A friend noted that Kas seemed particularly interested in films set in the period toward the end of World War II, when it was abundantly clear that the Germans had already lost the war.

With her "siege diary," Kas was not attempting to offer a historical account of the events to her husband who was far away. She believed that the historical, political, and strategic aspects of the events could be illuminated much better by other people. This is how she put it: "I only want to report what happened to ME, what the whole thing was like for ME." The "whole thing" to which she refers is that "some things have happened to me, to Budapest, to the Jews, to Hungary, etc., that can't be called either trivial or insignificant."

Kas's diary-memoir is not merely a personal account of how she experienced that terrible period from March 1944 until May 1945; it is also a lesson in history. For me, as a child of a mother who survived Auschwitz and of a father who survived Mauthausen, it is also about what could have happened to my grandparents, parents and all our relatives if, in 1944–45, they had lived in Budapest rather than in the countryside. As a psychologist, I am trying to understand what personal characteristics and factors that, in addition to luck, may have contributed to not only Kas surviving the hideous trauma inflicted by the Holocaust but also helped to inspire her child to live a good and substantial life. I believe that in Kas's "siege diary" we can all find many good questions, provided we are open to asking.

Dr. Éva Anikó Székely

Although I grew up speaking what we called "family" or "kitchen" Hungarian, I do not read or write Hungarian. Therefore, I am delighted that my mother's "siege diary," as she always called it, is getting published in English so that I can finally read it.

When I was a child, my mother often told me stories about her experiences in the cellar and stories about the children she looked after during the siege of Budapest. When I was older, she gave me a copy of her diary, and I know she hoped I would someday learn to read Hungarian so I could read it. But that never happened.

I gave my close friend Éva Székely a copy of the diary knowing she would be able to read it and was possibly going to try to translate it. Éva decided early on that she didn't feel she had the facility in English to capture my mother's literary style. However, the publication of my mother's diary in English would not have happened without Éva's extremely enthusiastic pursuit of this project. I am so grateful to Éva for this, and I know my mother would be as well. Through Éva's contacts in Hungary, we learned of the Hungarian publisher Magvető's interest in my mother's diary and of Gergely Kunt's role in bringing the diary, which my mother had donated to a Hungarian library on one of her visits to Hungary, to Magvető's attention.

I want to also thank my friend Father Paul Findlay, who lives here in Nova Scotia, for his labour in photographing each page of the diary — the pages were too old, fragile and dark to be photocopied/scanned directly. Father Paul provided me with digital photo files, which I then sent on to interested parties.

I don't remember how we first contacted the scholar and translator Ladislaus (Laci) Löb, but Éva and I were thrilled at the prospect of having him translate the diary into English. Sadly, Löb passed away in early October 2021 having translated about two-thirds of the manuscript. With the help of the Azrieli Foundation and the translation team of Marietta Morry and Lynda Muir, the translation was finished, and I am glad that not only do I get to finally read it but so many others do as well.

Frances Tolnai

Letter Regarding Diary Publication, 1945

Near the end of producing this book, the editors discovered a letter written by Margit's husband, György Tolnai, to a person called Jóska, likely an acquaintance of György's. This letter, along with a copy of forty pages of Margit's siege diary, were in the possession of the family of George Gerbner, an assimilated Hungarian Jew who left Budapest in 1939 and returned in 1945. George Gerbner had worked in journalism, which might be why Margit's writing and the letter from György ended up in his possession.

This letter, translated on the next page and followed by a photograph of the original, sheds light on Margit's interest in having her writing published and György's enthusiasm for the project. György clearly sees value in both the diary's description of important events as well as the connection readers will find with his wife. Although dated March 1945, the letter refers to events after this time, and Margit was still writing her diary during the next two months and had not yet reunited with her husband.

Dr. György Tolnai
Budapest V, 18 Klotild Street V. em. 4

March 31, 1945

Dear Jóska,
In her last letter to you, Kiskas wrote that she has certain plans, or rather dreams, about the siege diary she had written for me. With this letter, I am enclosing a sizable excerpt that I believe will interest you more than the general reader, because you will learn more about Kas than about the siege.

The reason I am only sending an excerpt is that even though the siege diary is 120 pages long, only 40 of those pages were typed in duplicate. We are sending you the last 40 pages, as well as the introductory page that was written afterward, which was also typed in duplicate. When you read it, you must keep in mind that when the curtain rises, we are already in the third act.

To be exact, the time is a couple days before January 18, 1945, when the Szálasi regime has already been in power for 3 months, the siege of Budapest has been going on for 3 weeks, and Pest is about to fall within a few days. Kas on the other hand is holed up in Buda where she will only be liberated the day before the siege ends. By this time, Kas has been in hiding for 3 months: she fled to avoid being deported from the ghetto, for a while she survived by using fake papers, then eventually with the help of a Lutheran pastor, she managed to get work in several children's homes run by the Red Cross, and at the beginning of her text she has been living in the bomb shelter of the building at 13 Pauler Street for a couple of weeks, where shrapnel hit one of the old residents in the head when he heedlessly went outside to the courtyard. She is surrounded by stench, darkness, numerous adults, and a lot of children. From here on you should read it for yourself.

The whole diary talks more about children than about the siege, I have suggested "Bombs And Babies" [György writes the title in English] as an appropriate title. However, it does indeed let you get to know Kas well.

You will find several names that are familiar to me but not to you — but this shouldn't bother you. I didn't go to the trouble of creating a footnote for every name. Here are just a few: Gizella = Mrs. Tolnai [György's mother]. Nünüke = Mrs. Kassai [Margit's mother]. Cini = Erzsébet L. Zinner, a photographer, and also Kas's best friend, it was in her studio that Langer took your photograph. Béla = Kas's young cousin, who initially manages to save her and her family, but ultimately comes to a bad end. The rest are not worth explaining.

Yet there is something else: the siege diary starts a few days after the Germans marched into Hungary — on March 19, 1944 — when our forced labour battalion, which had been working in Pest for a short while at that point, was taken to Transylvania again. It should be noted that after this time we were able to correspond only rarely, and after July not at all. The diary finishes when Kas hears news about me, that I had spent the intervening time in captivity then in a hospital in Bucharest, and the correspondence resumes to some extent at the beginning of May 1945. This means that this excerpt describes the last weeks of the siege and the ensuing weeks under Russian rule. Of course, even Kas does not consider either this excerpt or the whole diary in its original form as addressed to me to be of interest to the public, she only asks you to evaluate whether it's possible to make something out of such material, and how.

[Handwritten across the bottom]
At the very end you will find copies of our previous letters.

[Signed] G. [György]

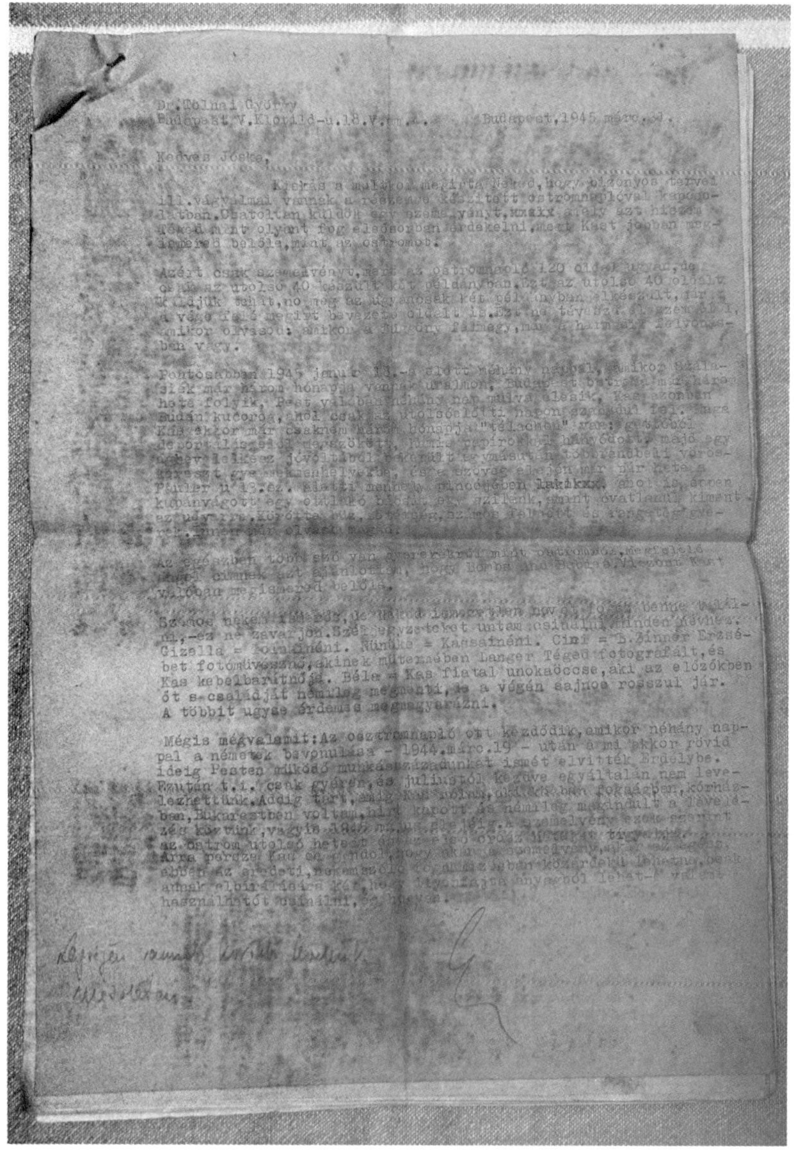

Letter to Jóska from György Tolnai. Gerbner Family Archive, photograph by Katharine Gerbner.

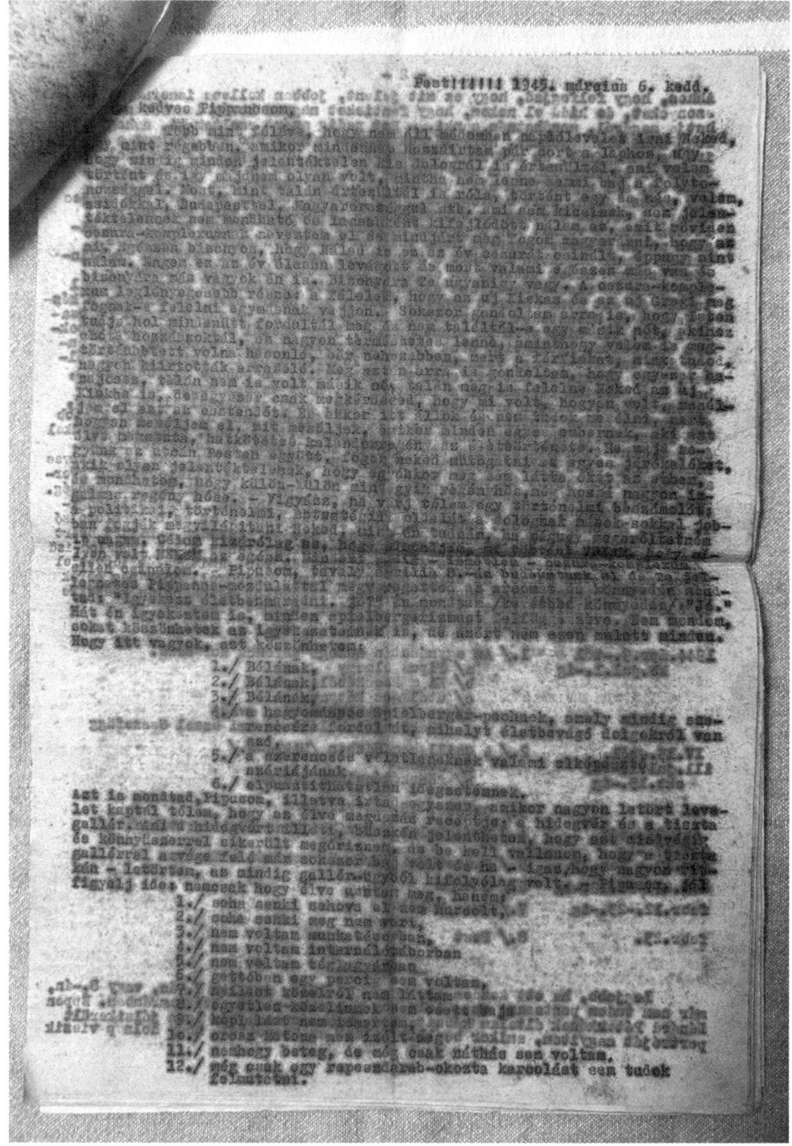

Page from Margit's siege diary. Gerbner Family Archive, photograph by Katharine Gerbner.

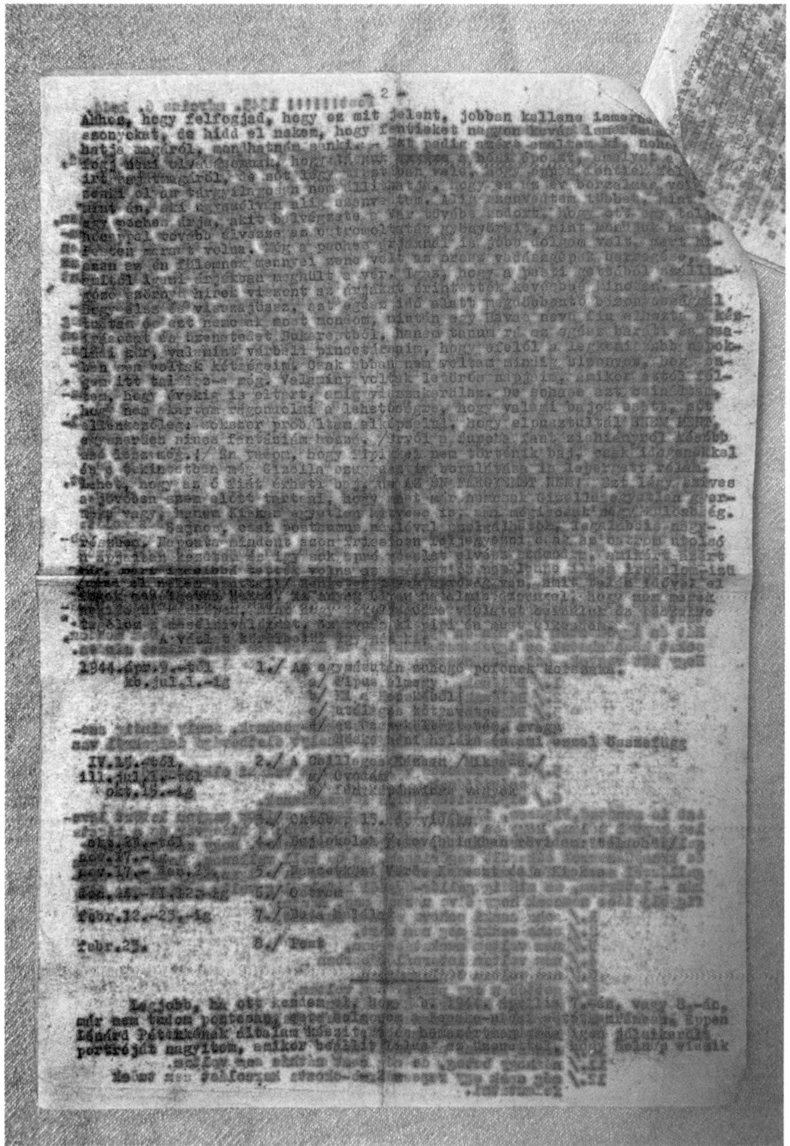

Page from Margit's siege diary. Gerbner Family Archive, photograph by Katharine Gerbner.

Photographs

Portrait of Margit Kassai. Budapest, 1931.

Margit's mother, Janka Beck (Nünü). Toronto, circa 1950s.

Margit's father, József Kassai (Püpüke). Budapest, circa 1946.

Portraits of Margit in Budapest. Top row: 1937 and 1939; bottom row: 1941 and 1944.

Budapest in ruins. Photograph by Margit Kassai. 1945.

Budapest in ruins. Photograph by Margit Kassai. 1945.

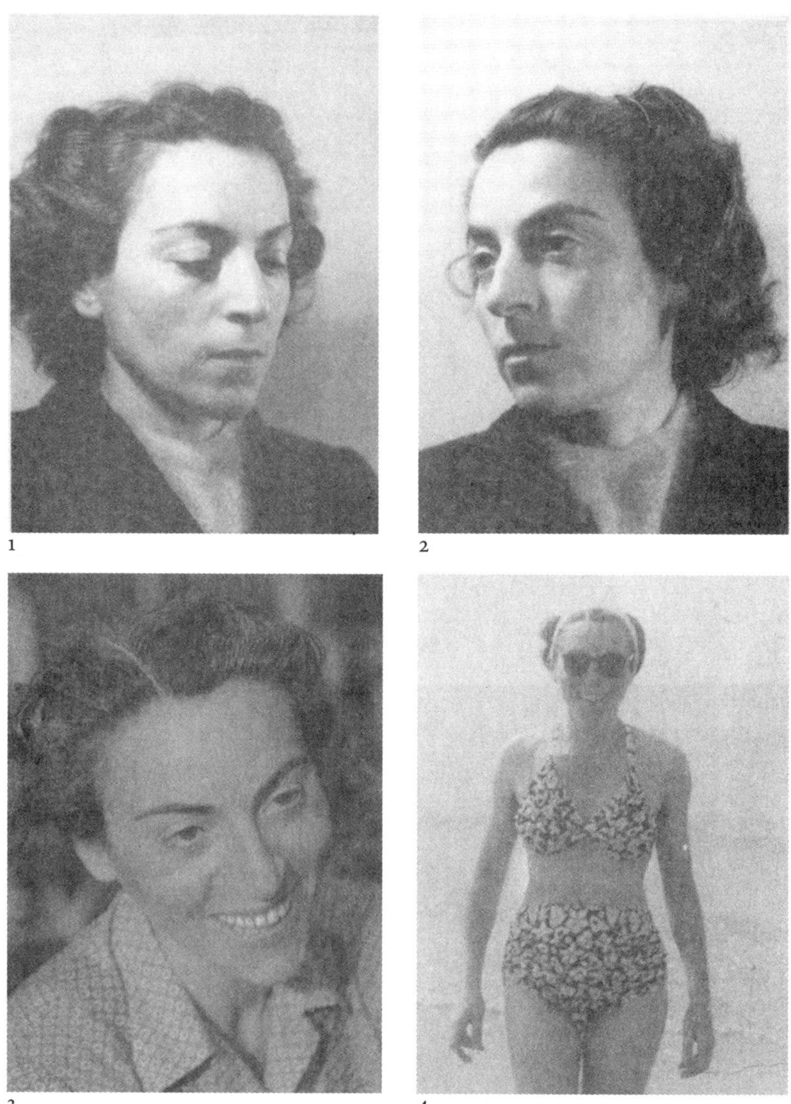

1 & 2 Margit in Paris. 1946.

3 Margit. Lille, France, 1947.

4 Margit. France, 1947.

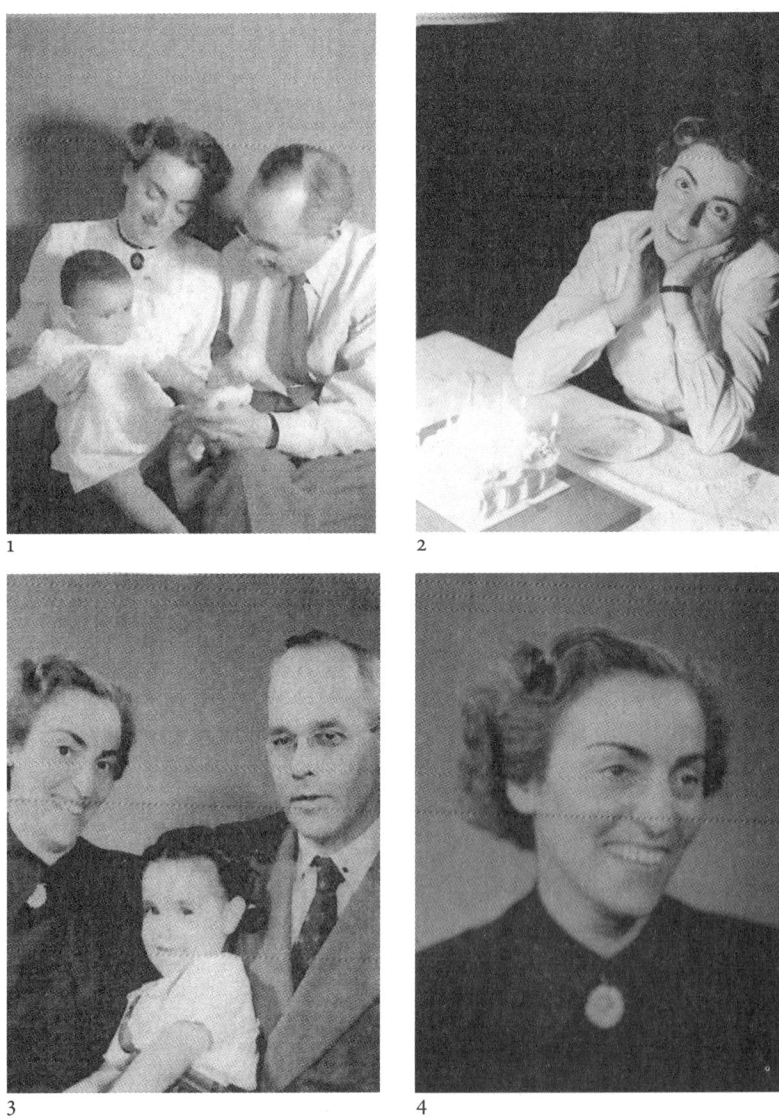

1 Margit, her husband, György Tolnai, and their daughter, Frances, on Frances's first birthday. Toronto, November 23, 1948.

2 Margit celebrating her fortieth birthday in Toronto. January 25, 1949.

3 Margit with her husband and daughter. Toronto, June 1951.

4 Margit. Toronto, 1951.

1

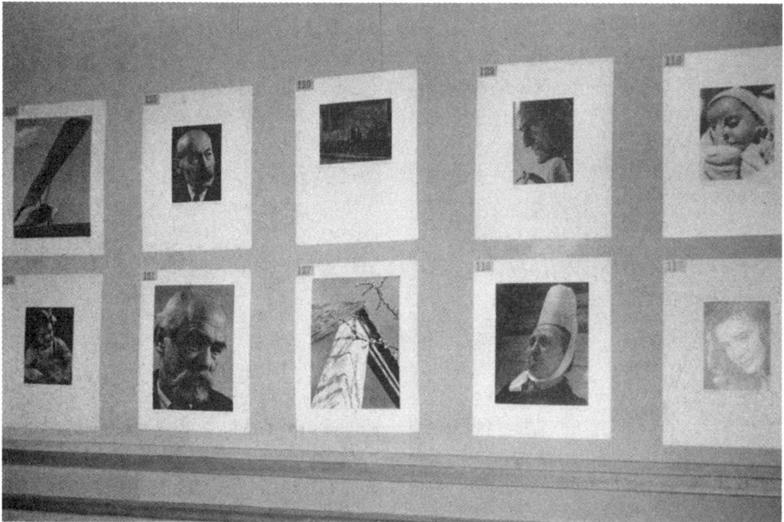

2

Margit at an exhibit of her photography, with her daughter, Frances, at around eleven years old. Alexandria, Egypt, circa 1958.

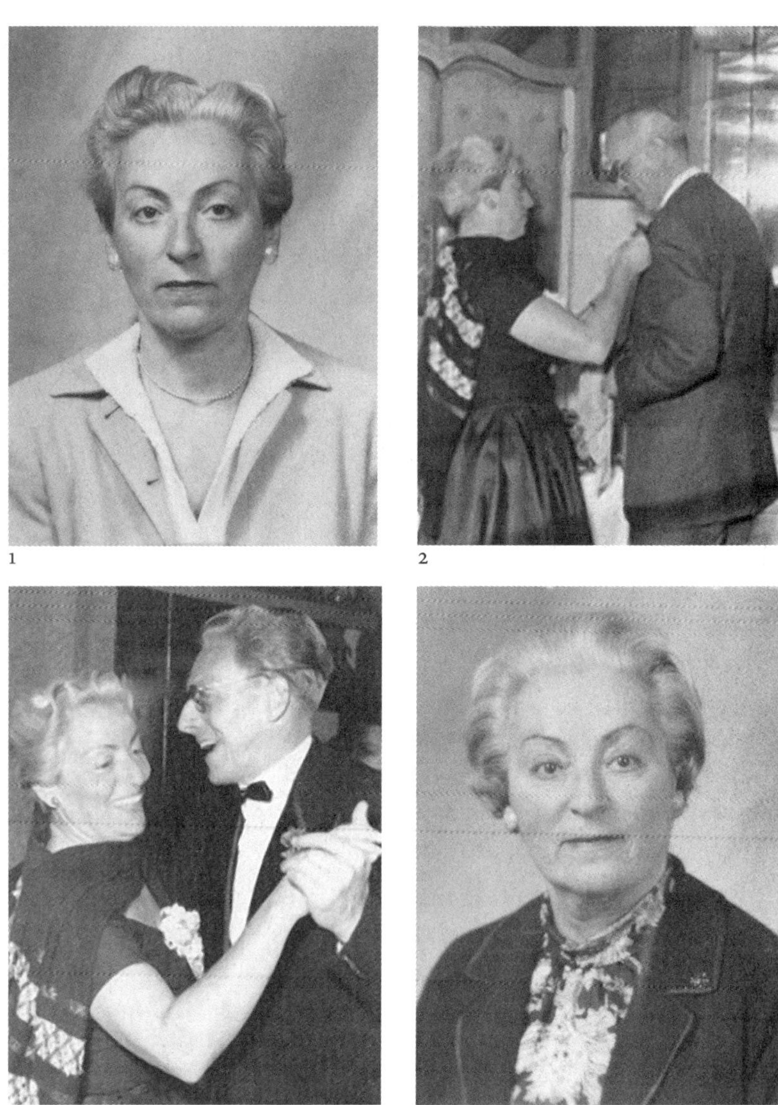

1 Margit's passport photo. 1957.

2 Margit and her husband at a formal event while living in Egypt. Alexandria, 1959.

3 Margit dancing with a friend. Alexandria, 1959.

4 Margit. Toronto, 1968.

1

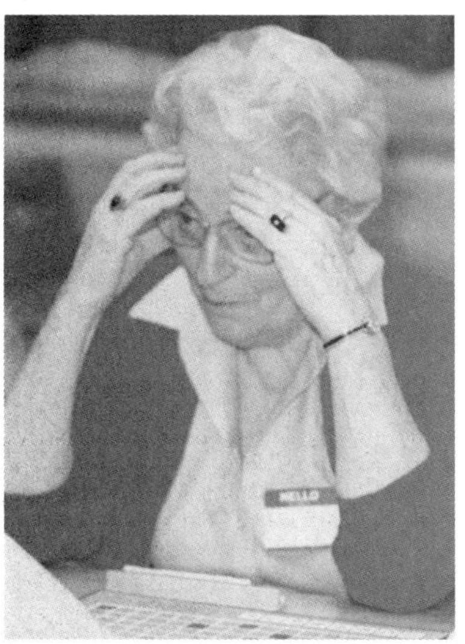

2

3

1 Margit at her retirement dinner at the University of Toronto. 1974.

2 Margit at a Scrabble tournament. Hamilton, 1989. (Originally published in the *Hamilton Spectator*.)

3 Margit (right) with friend Éva Anikó Székely. Toronto, 1996.

1

2

1 Margit, left, with her daughter, Frances, at a summer retreat in Kalamazoo, Michigan. 1985.

2 Margit and her daughter, Frances, with a member of the ship's staff while on a cruise together in the Caribbean. Circa early 1990s.

Acknowledgements

After the publication in 2020 of the original Hungarian version of Margit Kassai's diary-memoir edited by scholar Gergely Kunt, two Hungarian Holocaust survivors played a key role in taking the first steps toward the possibility of an English version. Paul Marer, retired professor at the then Budapest-based Central European University (since forced to move to Vienna), put Kunt in touch with Ladislaus Löb, professor emeritus of German at the University of Sussex in England. Löb had translated into English several works in German and Hungarian on topics related to the Holocaust, making them accessible to English readers. Löb greatly admired Margit's memoir and was enthusiastic about translating it. Sadly, he passed away before completing the work. This edition is dedicated to his memory.

We are extremely grateful to the translators Marietta Morry and Lynda Muir for completing the translation and for their ability to recreate the unique and inimitable style of Margit's text. They not only expertly translated Kassai's narrative but tirelessly answered the editors' translation and research queries, contributing extensively to the publication.

Our deepest appreciation also goes to Anna Elődi, who reviewed the translation to ensure a seamless narrative, and to Judith Szapor and Marlene Kadar for their contributions to the footnotes.

Glossary

American Jewish Joint Distribution Committee (JDC) Colloquially known as the Joint, the JDC was a charitable organization founded in 1914 to provide humanitarian assistance and relief to Jews all over the world in times of crisis. In late 1938, due to rising antisemitism, the JDC began relief operations in Hungary, providing funds to help Hungarian Jews and Jewish refugees and emigrants. The JDC established the Hungarian Jewish Relief Committee in Budapest in 1939, which organized twenty soup kitchens, thirteen children's homes and other programs to help Jews experiencing extreme poverty during the war.

Arrow Cross Party (in Hungarian, Nyilaskeresztes Párt — Hungarista Mozgalom; abbreviation: Nyilas) A Hungarian right-wing extremist and antisemitic party founded by Ferenc Szálasi in 1935 as the Party of National Will. The newly renamed Arrow Cross Party ran in Hungary's 1939 election and won 15 per cent of the vote. The party was fought and largely suppressed by the regime in the coming years, but re-emerged as a major force in March 1944, when Germany occupied Hungary; in August 1944, the party was temporarily banned. Under Nazi approval, the party, led by Szálasi, assumed control of Hungary from October 15, 1944, to March 28, 1945. Starting on November 6, with the last group leaving on December 11, 1944, Arrow Cross authorities rounded up approximately 70,000 Jews and sent them on death marches toward Greater Germany. Tens of thousands died or were murdered along the way, and some 50,000 survivors were handed over to the Germans. Between October 1944 and January 1945, the Arrow Cross murdered thousands of Jews in Budapest. *See also* Szálasi, Ferenc.

Aryan A nineteenth-century anthropological term originally used to refer to the Indo-European family of languages and, by extension, the peoples who spoke them. It became a synonym for people of Nordic or Germanic descent in the theories that inspired Nazi racial ideology. "Aryan" was an official classification in Nazi racial laws to denote someone of pure Germanic blood, as opposed to "non-Aryans," such as Slavs, Jews, part-Jews, Roma and others of supposedly inferior racial stock. The term was used in a similar way in countries like Hungary that were allied with or occupied by Nazi Germany.

Association of the Christian Jews of Hungary (in Hungarian, A Magyarországi Keresztény Zsidók Szövetsége) A council established by leaders of Protestant churches in Budapest on July 14, 1944, to defend the interests of Jewish converts to Christianity, church officials from Jewish backgrounds and those in mixed marriages. This included campaigning to the authorities for better treatment, such as exemptions from deportations and other anti-Jewish decrees. These efforts caused many Jews to convert or seek conversion during the Nazi occupation.

Born, Friedrich (1903–1963) The Swiss chief delegate to the Red Cross in Hungary from May 1944 to January 1945 who is credited with saving the lives of between 11,000 and 15,000 Jews. During his time as delegate to the Red Cross, Born issued up to 15,000 Red Cross letters of protection, designated several buildings as Red Cross-protected homes and concealed up to 6,000 Jewish children. The Soviet army ordered him to leave Hungary after the war. In 1987, Yad Vashem honoured Born with the title of Righteous Among the Nations for his role in saving Jews during the Holocaust. *See also* Red Cross.

Budapest ghetto The area of Budapest in which Jews were confined, established by Hungary's Arrow Cross government on November 29, 1944. On December 10, the ghetto was sealed off from the rest of the city. Jews under the protection of neutral states were first moved into a separate, smaller ghetto known as the international ghetto, but most of them were soon transferred into the main, larger one. By early January 1945, the population of the overcrowded ghetto reached close to 70,000, and people lacked sufficient food, water and sanitation. Supplies dwindled and conditions worsened during the Soviet siege of Budapest, which began in late December 1944. Thousands died of starvation and disease. The ghetto was also vulnerable to Arrow Cross raids, and thousands of Jews were taken from the ghetto and murdered on the banks of the Danube. Soviet forces liberated the short-lived ghetto between January 16 and 18, 1945. *See also* yellow-star houses.

Children's Day A day for celebrating the rights and happiness of children, observed in Hungary since 1931 and occurring annually on the last Sunday in May. Children's Day is recognized globally and dates back as far as 1857.

forced labour service (also referred to as Auxiliary Labour Service or forced labour battalions) Units of Hungary's military-related labour service system (in Hungarian, Munkaszolgálat), which was first established in 1919 for those considered too "politically unreliable" for regular military service. After the labour service was made compulsory in 1939, Jewish men of military age were recruited to serve; however, having been deemed "unfit" to bear arms, they were equipped with tools and employed in mining, road and rail construction and maintenance work. Though the men were treated relatively well at first, the system became increasingly punitive. By 1941, Jews in forced labour service were required to wear an armband and civilian clothes; they had no formal rank and were unarmed; they were often mistreated by extremely antisemitic supervisors; and the work they had to do, such as clearing minefields, was often fatal. By 1942, 100,000 Jewish men had been drafted into labour service, and by the time the Germans occupied Hungary in March 1944, between 25,000 and 40,000 Hungarian Jewish men had died during their forced labour service.

Gestapo (German; abbreviation of Geheime Staatspolizei, the Secret State Police) The Nazi regime's brutal political police that operated without legal constraints to deal with its perceived enemies. During the Holocaust, the Gestapo set up offices in Nazi-occupied countries and was responsible for rounding up Jews and sending them to concentration and death camps. They also arrested, tortured and deported those who resisted Nazi policies.

Good Shepherd Committee (in full, Subcommittee of the Hungarian Reformed Church's Universal Convent of the Good Shepherd Mission) An organization established on October 20, 1942, by Pastor Gyula Muraközy and the Universal Convent of the Reformed Church of Hungary. It became the main Hungarian association of Jews who had converted to Protestantism, with Pastor József Éliás, who had a Jewish background, as its head. Before the German invasion of Hungary in 1944, the association helped both Jews and non-Jews interned in camps. After the German invasion and especially after the rise to power of the Arrow Cross in October 1944, the association and Pastor Gábor Sztehlo, who joined the Good Shepherd Committee as a representative of the Lutheran Church, began rescuing Jewish children. *See also* Sztehlo, Gábor.

gymnasium A word used throughout Central and Eastern Europe to mean high school or secondary school.

Horthy, Miklós (1868–1957) The regent of Hungary during the interwar period and for much of World War II. Horthy presided over numerous governments that were aligned with the Axis powers, pursued antisemitic politics and was responsible for killing thousands of Jews. After the German army occupied Hungary in March 1944, Horthy served primarily as a figurehead to the pro-Nazi government led by Döme Sztójay; in this role he met with Hitler in spring 1944 and agreed to deport Hungarian Jews to Nazi death camps, even though Axis defeat seemed inevitable by this time. Credited with suspending the mass deportation of Hungarian Jews in July 1944, Horthy quickly changed his mind in August and agreed to resume deportations, which was only prevented by deteriorating conditions at the front. Horthy planned to withdraw Hungary from the war on October 15, 1944, but the Nazis supported an Arrow Cross coup that same day and forced Horthy to abdicate.

Hospital in the Rock (in Hungarian, *Sziklakórház*) Opened in February 1944, the hospital was built in a network of medieval cellars and stretched for several kilometres under the Buda Castle. Both civilians and soldiers were treated here during the siege of Budapest.

Jewish Council (in German, Judenrat) A group of Jewish leaders appointed by the German occupiers to administer the ghettos and carry out Nazi orders. The councils tried to provide social services to the Jewish population to alleviate the harsh conditions of the ghettos and maintain a sense of community. Although the councils appeared to be self-governing entities, they were under complete Nazi control. The councils faced difficult and complex moral decisions under brutal conditions — they had to decide whether to cooperate with or resist Nazi demands, when refusal likely meant death, and they had to determine which actions might save some of the population and which might worsen their fates. The Jewish Councils were under extreme pressure, and they remain a contentious subject.

Red Cross (International Committee of the Red Cross, ICRC) A humanitarian organization founded in 1863 to protect the victims of war. During World War II, the Red Cross provided assistance to prisoners of war by distributing food parcels and monitoring the situation in prisoner-of-war (POW) camps and also provided medical attention to wounded soldiers and civilians. After the German invasion, the Red Cross played a significant role in saving Jews in Budapest, encouraging Hungarian organizations such as the Good Shepherd Committee to shift from charitable goals to the task of saving lives. Today, in addition to the international body, the ICRC, there are national Red Cross and Red Crescent societies in almost every country in the world. *See also* Born, Friedrich; Red Cross children's homes; Sztehlo, Gábor.

Red Cross children's homes Protected homes set up in Budapest in the fall of 1944. Under the leadership of Friedrich Born, the International Red Cross created two departments to deal specifically with child protection: Section A, headed by Ottó Komoly, to help Jewish children, and Section B, headed by Gábor Sztehlo, to help children of Jews who had converted to Christianity but who were still designated as Jewish under Hungarian and Nazi decrees. A system of homes (twenty-eight sites by February 1945) and warehouses for the storage and distribution of food and fuel was created. About 2,000 people, most of them children but also some mothers, caregivers and nurses, were living in these houses during the siege of Budapest. *See also* Born, Friedrich; Red Cross; Sztehlo, Gábor.

Schutzbrief (German; pl. *Schutzbriefe*; letter of protection) A document provided by neutral embassies in Budapest during the Nazi occupation stating that the holder was under their protection. However, these letters of protection had no international legal meaning and therefore provided less protection than a *Schutzpass*. The Swiss Red Cross delegate Friedrich Born issued up to 15,000 Red Cross letters of protection. See also *Schutzpass*; Born, Friedrich.

Schutzpass (German; pl. *Schutzpässe*; protective pass) A document that identified the holder as a Swedish subject. Swedish diplomat

Raoul Wallenberg issued these passes to at least 15,000 Hungarian Jews, thereby saving them from deportation. See also *Schutzbrief*.

Shabbos (Yiddish; Sabbath) The weekly day of rest beginning Friday at sunset and ending Saturday at nightfall, ushered in by the lighting of candles on Friday evening and the recitation of blessings over wine and challah (egg bread). A day of celebration as well as prayer, it is customary to eat three festive meals, attend synagogue services and refrain from doing any work or travelling.

SS (abbreviation of Schutzstaffel; Defence Corps) The elite police force of the Nazi regime that was responsible for security and for the enforcement of Nazi racial policies, including the implementation of the "Final Solution" — a euphemistic term referring to the Nazis' plan to systematically murder Europe's Jewish population. The SS ran the concentration and death camps and also established the Waffen-SS, its own military division that was independent of the German army.

starred buildings *See* yellow-star houses.

Szálasi, Ferenc (1897–1946) The founder and leader of the Hungarian right-wing extremist Arrow Cross Party, which actively collaborated with the Nazis in Hungary, notably in the persecution and deportation of Jews. Following the Nazi-orchestrated coup in Hungary on October 15, 1944, Szálasi was the leader of Hungary until March 1945 and continued Hungary's war on the side of the Axis. Szálasi had fled Budapest by the time the Soviet and Romanian forces had surrounded the city in late December 1944, and he continued to rule over a shrinking territory in western Hungary. He was convicted of war crimes and executed in 1946 in Budapest. *See also* Arrow Cross Party.

Sztehlo, Gábor (1909–1974) Lutheran pastor known for his role in saving children during the Nazi occupation and Arrow Cross rule of Hungary. In May 1944, he was appointed the representative of the Good Shepherd Committee in charge of providing food and clothes to Jewish converts to Christianity and to their dependents when they were called up for labour service. Sztehlo worked with the Red Cross and the Good Shepherd Committee to find homes for Jewish children and to provide them with papers stating they had converted to Christianity, to help them avoid anti-Jewish persecution. After the war, he also founded Gaudiopolis, a children's republic. In 1972, Yad Vashem honoured Sztehlo with the title of Righteous Among the Nations for his role in saving Jews during the Holocaust. He is credited through his acts of resistance with saving the lives of about 1,600 Jewish children and 400 Jewish adults. *See also* Good Shepherd Committee. Red Cross.

yellow-star houses (in Hungarian, *csillagos házak*; also known as Jewish houses). Designated buildings marked with a yellow Star of David that Jews in Budapest were forced to move into three months after Germany occupied Hungary. These yellow-star houses functioned much like ghettos, serving to segregate Jews and plunder their homes. More than 200,000 Jews were assigned to fewer than 2,000 apartment buildings. They were allowed to leave the buildings for two hours in the afternoon, but only if they wore an identifying yellow Star of David on their clothing. *See also* Budapest ghetto.

Index

The Azrieli Foundation was established in 1989 to realize and extend the philanthropic vision of David J. Azrieli, C.M., C.Q., M.Arch. The Foundation's mission is to support a wide spectrum of initiatives in education and research. The Azrieli Foundation is an active supporter of programs in the fields of education, the education of architects, scientific and medical research, and the arts. The Azrieli Foundation's many initiatives include: the Holocaust Survivor Memoirs Program, which collects, preserves, publishes and distributes the written memoirs of survivors in Canada; the Azrieli Institute for Educational Empowerment, an innovative program successfully working to keep at-risk youth in school; the Azrieli Fellows Program, which promotes academic excellence and leadership on the graduate level at Israeli universities; the Azrieli Music Project, which celebrates and fosters the creation of high-quality new Jewish orchestral music; and the Azrieli Neurodevelopmental Research Program, which supports advanced research on neurodevelopmental disorders, particularly Fragile X and Autism Spectrum Disorders.

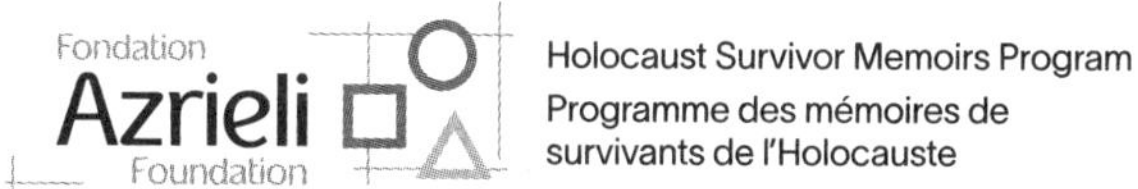

The staff members dedicated to the Holocaust Survivor Memoirs Program are: Jody Spiegel, Arielle Berger, Catherine Person, Marc-Olivier Cloutier, Carson Phillips, Catherine Aubé, Matt Carrington, Devora Levin, Michelle Sadowski, Elizabeth Banks, Monika Kolanka, Candace Alper, Susanne Bachert and Emily Standfield.